FROM THE DIARY OF FRANCIS T. CARROLL
43RD PRESIDENT OF THE UNITED STATES

JANUARY 1, 2009

Writing this on a helicopter, somewhere over the Nevada desert.
I can see out for miles from up here, and everything I can see
looks brown, dry, dead. Seems appropriate, really. It's all coming
down to the wire, and honestly, none of it's happening the way it
was supposed to.

I thought we'd have a chance to **fight**, you know? That's why I made
all those plans… built up our military, funneled all that money
into researching laser guns and so on. I didn't think it would
happen like this, just wiped out without so much as a…

Well, it's not over yet. Yes, the *Clarke* hasn't sent a signal in
ages, so who knows what they're all up to, or even if they're
still alive up there. Can't depend on them anymore, although I'm
sure they did their best. Say what you want, but those folks are
heroes, all of them.

Dr. Portek tells me the aliens, through their proxy Major Gabriel
Drum, asked for six hundred and sixty-six people to be chosen to
somehow survive what's coming. He wasn't clear on the details—I'm
not sure there are many details—but that's what they wanted. So
that's something, I suppose.

Of course, Drum's also the son of a bitch who blew up my
mountain—burned up a bunch of good people. **My** people. Would've
been nice to start something new with all of them, but hey… I
roll with the punches. It's politics. You have to.

So… this is it, I guess. We don't know how, we don't know when,
but it really seems like it's the end of the world. What else is
there to say?

Oh… I know.

Happy New Year.

LETTER 44 VOLUME VI: THE END

WRITTEN BY
CHARLES SOULE

ILLUSTRATED BY
ALBERTO JIMÉNEZ ALBURQUERQUE

COLORED BY
DAN JACKSON (CHAPTERS 1, 2, 4-6)
AND SARAH STERN (CHAPTER 3)

LETTERED BY
CRANK!

BOOK DESIGNED BY
JASON STOREY WITH KATE Z. STONE

COVER DESIGNED BY
KATE Z. STONE

EDITED BY
ROBIN HERRERA

LETTER 44

SOULE ★ ALBURQUERQUE ★ JACKSON ★ STERN

VOLUME VI: THE END

06

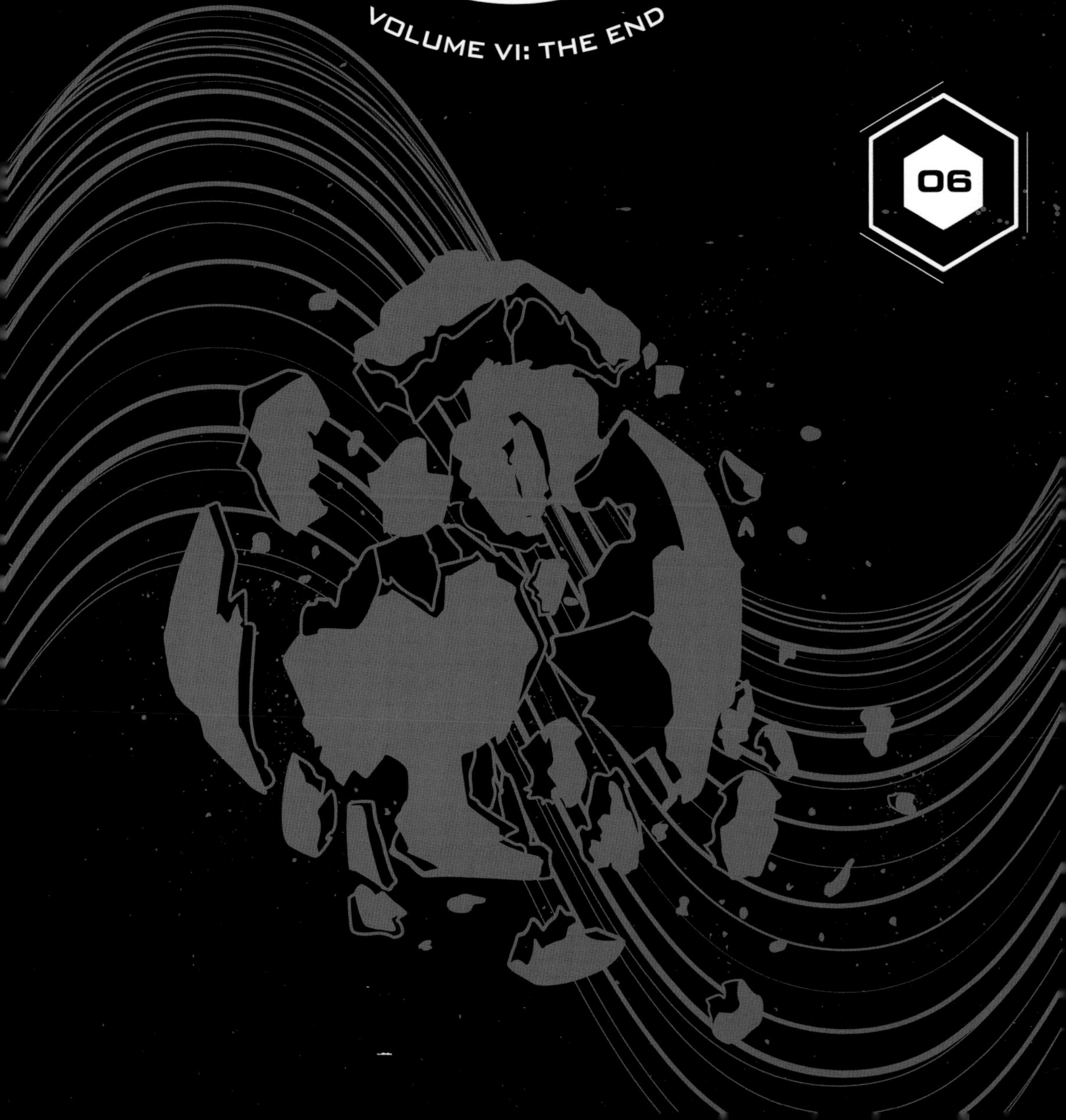

LETTER 44

THIS VOLUME COLLECTS ISSUES 29-31 and 33-35
OF THE ONI PRESS SERIES *LETTER 44*

Oni Press, Inc.

Founder & Chief Financial Officer /// **Joe Nozemack**
Publisher /// **James Lucas Jones**
V.P. of Creative & Business Development /// **Charlie Chu**
Director of Operations /// **Brad Rooks**
Marketing Manager /// **Rachel Reed**
Publicity Manager /// **Melissa Meszaros MacFadyen**
Director of Design and Production /// **Troy Look**
Graphic Designer /// **Hilary Thompson**
Junior Graphic Designer /// **Kate Z. Stone**
Digital Prepress Lead /// **Angie Knowles**
Executive Editor /// **Ari Yarwood**
Senior Editor /// **Robin Herrera**
Associate Editor /// **Desiree Wilson**
Administrative Assistant /// **Alissa Sallah**
Logistics Associate /// **Jung Lee**

1319 SE Martin Luther King Jr. Blvd. Suite 240
Portland, OR 97214

onipress.com
facebook.com/onipress | twitter.com/onipress | onipress.tumblr.com

charlessoule.com | @charlessoule
ajaalbertojimenezalburquerque.blogspot.com

FIRST EDITION: January 2018

Letter 44, Volume 6. January 2018. Published by Oni Press, Inc. 1319 SE
Martin Luther King, Jr. Blvd., Suite 240, Portland, OR 97214. Letter 44 is ™
& © 2018 Charles Soule. All rights reserved. Oni Press logo and icon ™ & ©
2018 Oni Press, Inc. Oni Press logo and icon artwork created by Keith A. Wood.
The events, institutions, and characters presented in this book are fictional.
Any resemblance to actual persons, living or dead, is purely coincidental.
No portion of this publication may be reproduced, by any means, without the
express written permission of the copyright holders.

ISBN: 978-1-62010-468-2 | eISBN: 978-1-62010-469-9

Library of Congress Control Number: 2014931101

10 8 6 4 2 1 3 5 7 9

Printed in China

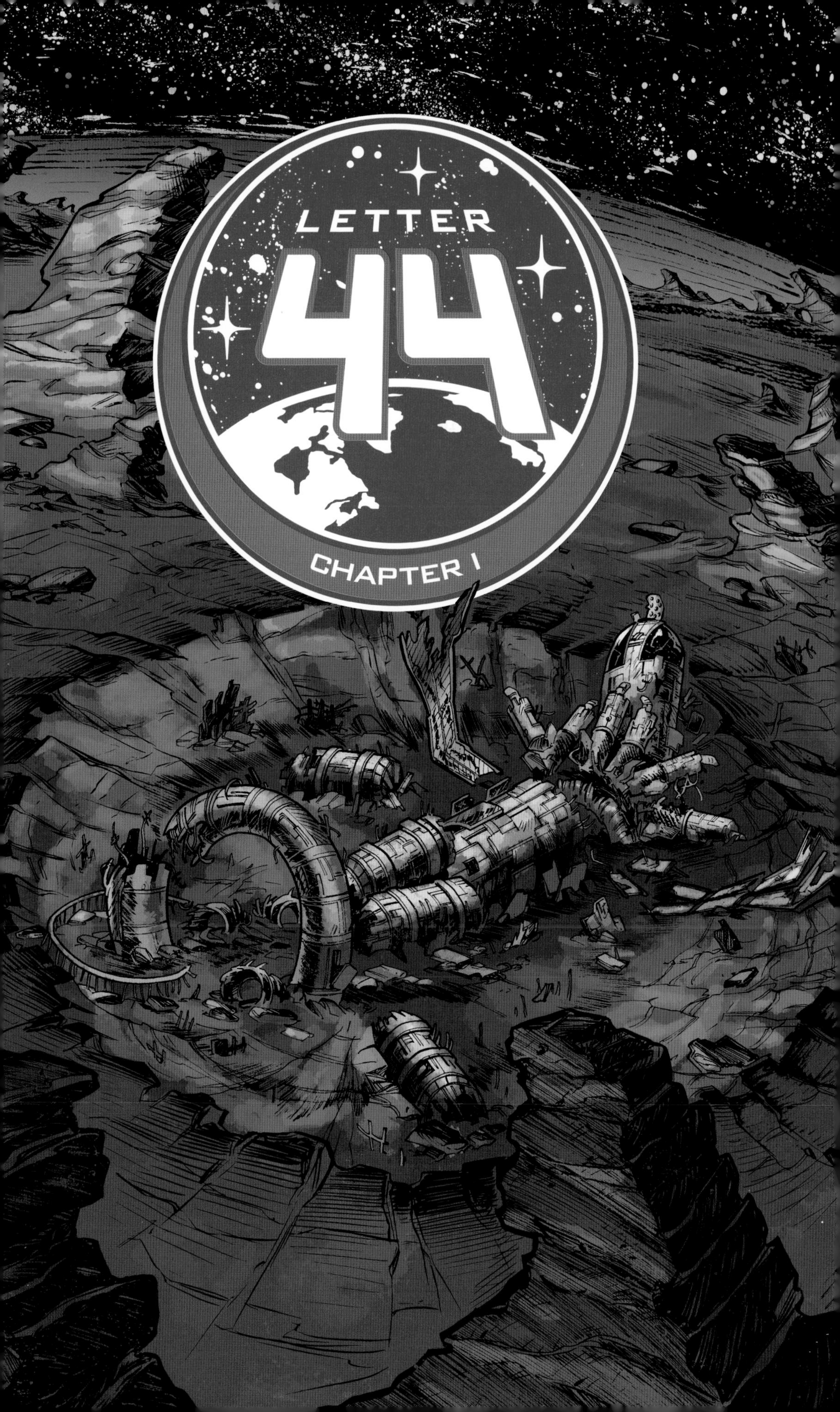
LETTER
44
CHAPTER I

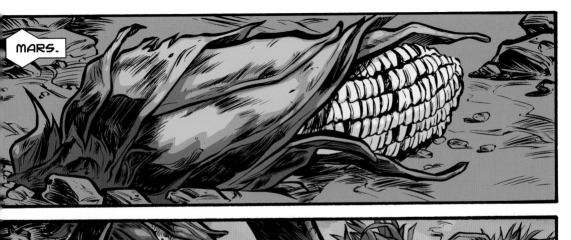

MARS.

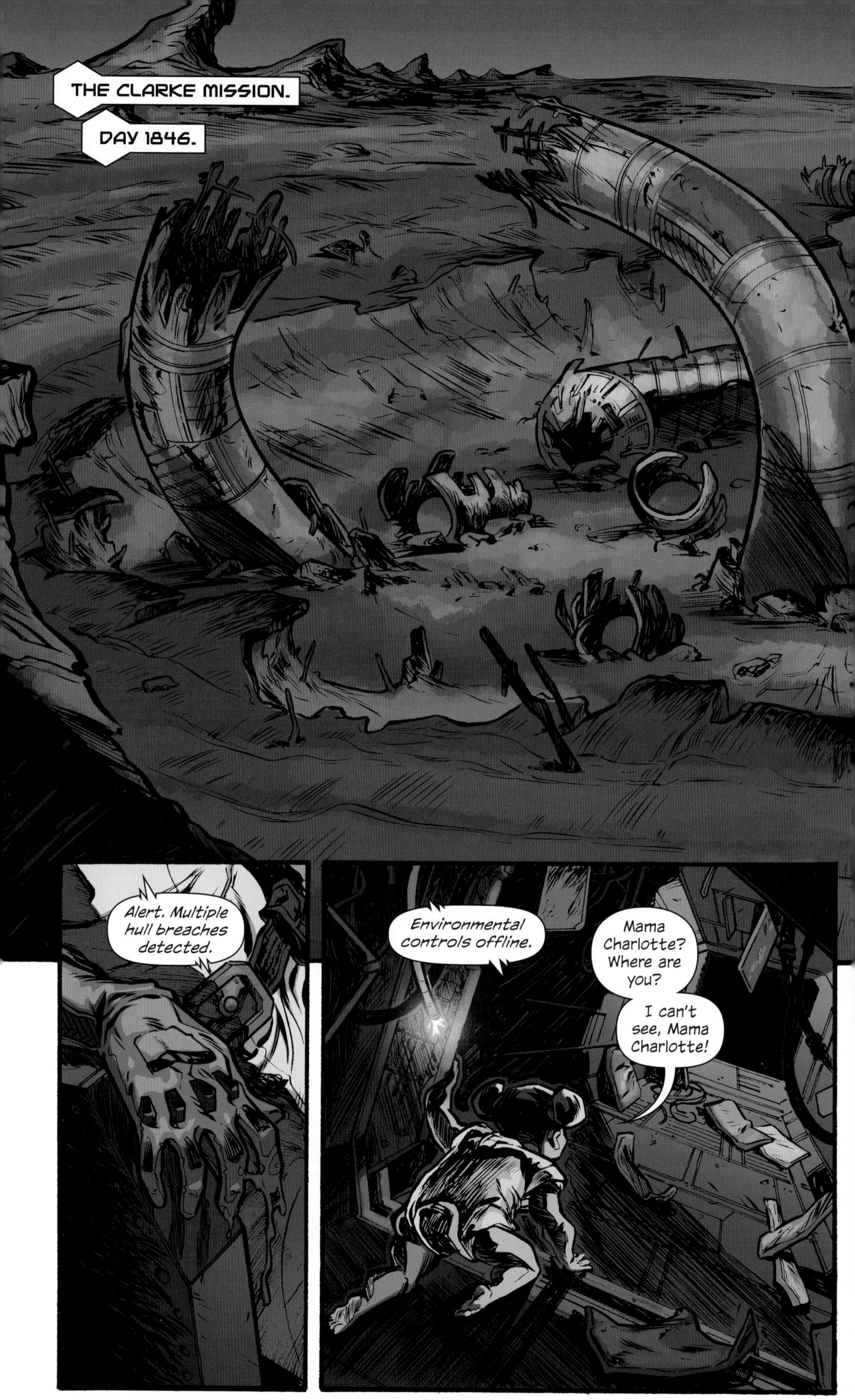

THE CLARKE MISSION.
DAY 1846.
Alert. Multiple hull breaches detected.
Environmental controls offline.
Mama Charlotte? Where are you?
I can't see, Mama Charlotte!

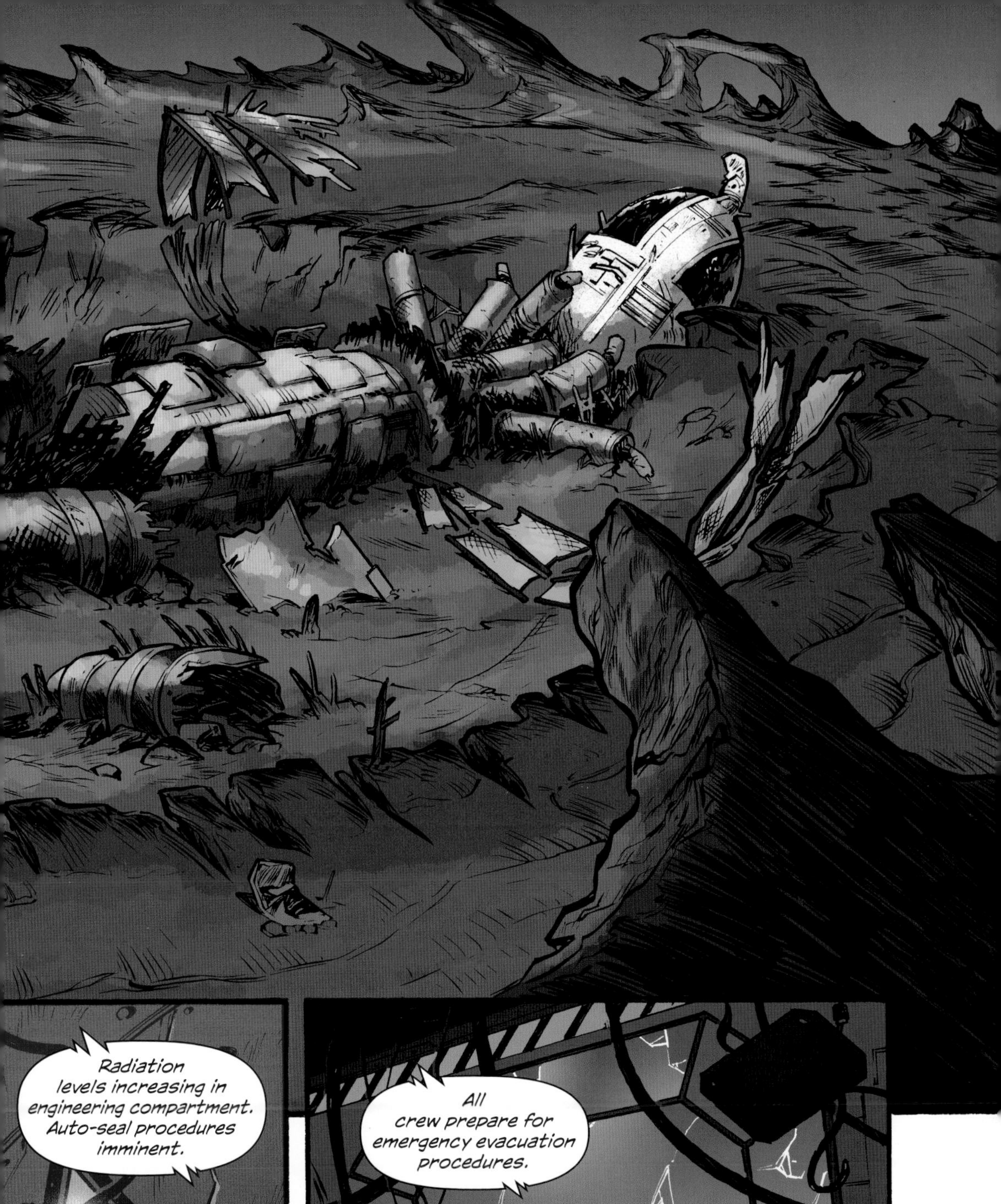
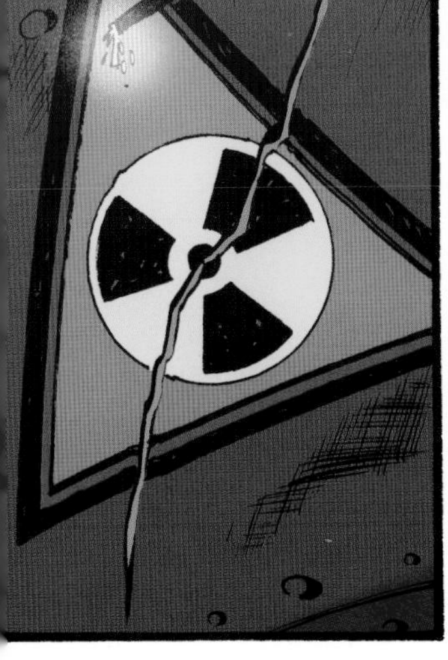
Radiation levels increasing in engineering compartment. Auto-seal procedures imminent.
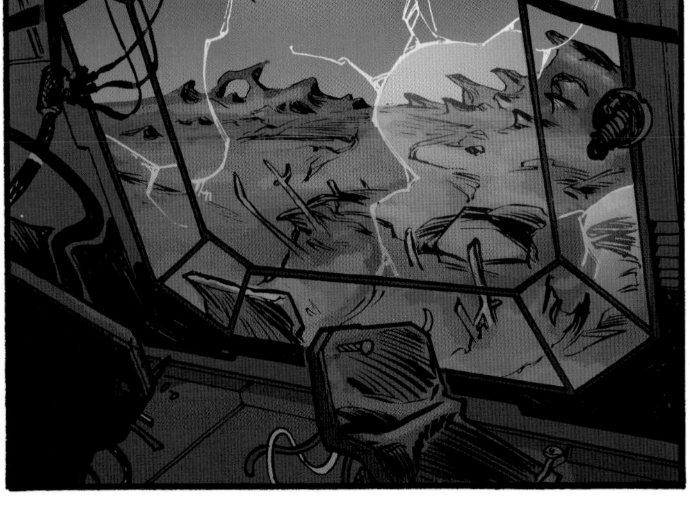
All crew prepare for emergency evacuation procedures.

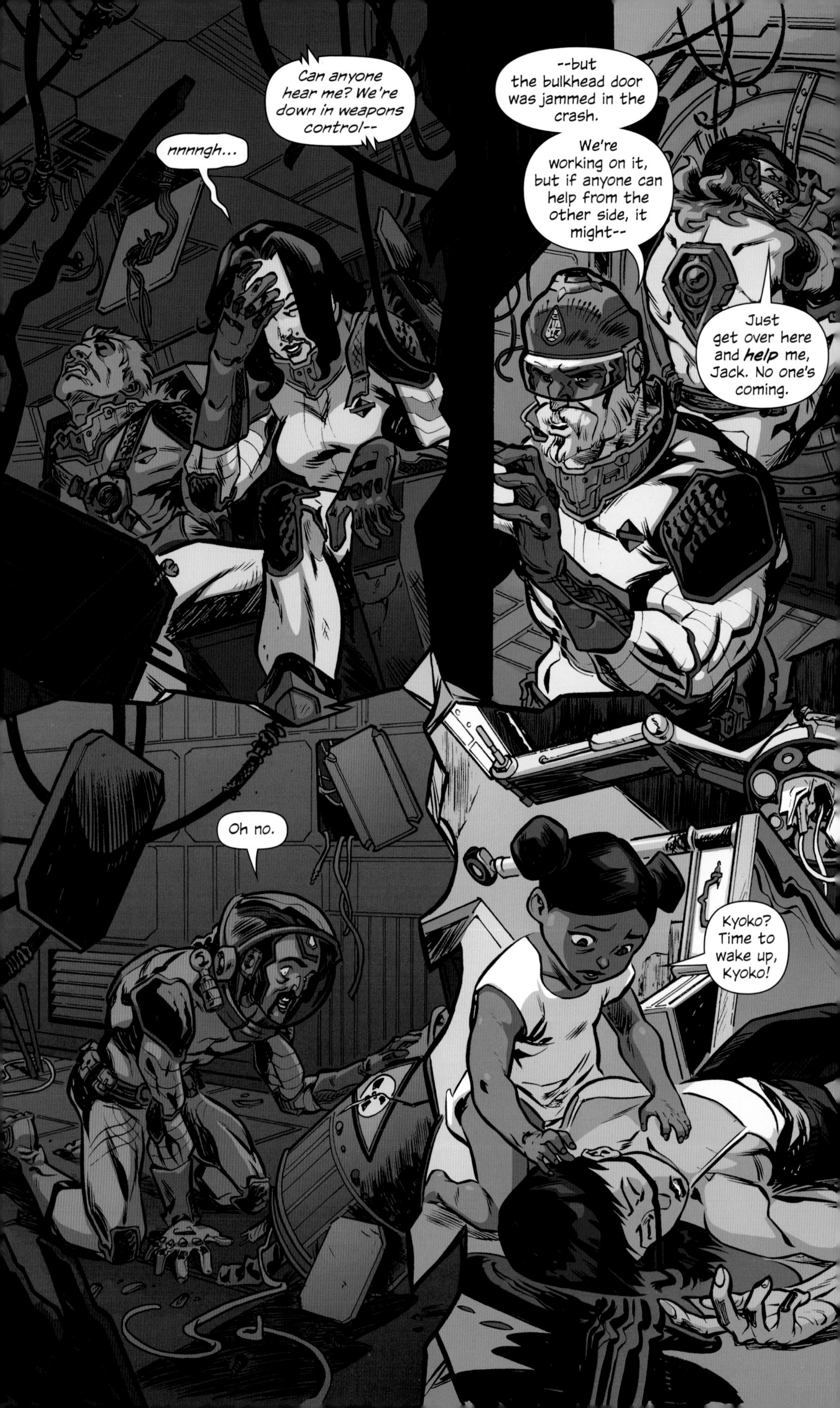

nnnngh...
Can anyone hear me? We're down in weapons control--
--but the bulkhead door was jammed in the crash.
We're working on it, but if anyone can help from the other side, it might--
Just get over here and ***help*** me, Jack. No one's coming.
Oh no.
Kyoko? Time to wake up, Kyoko!

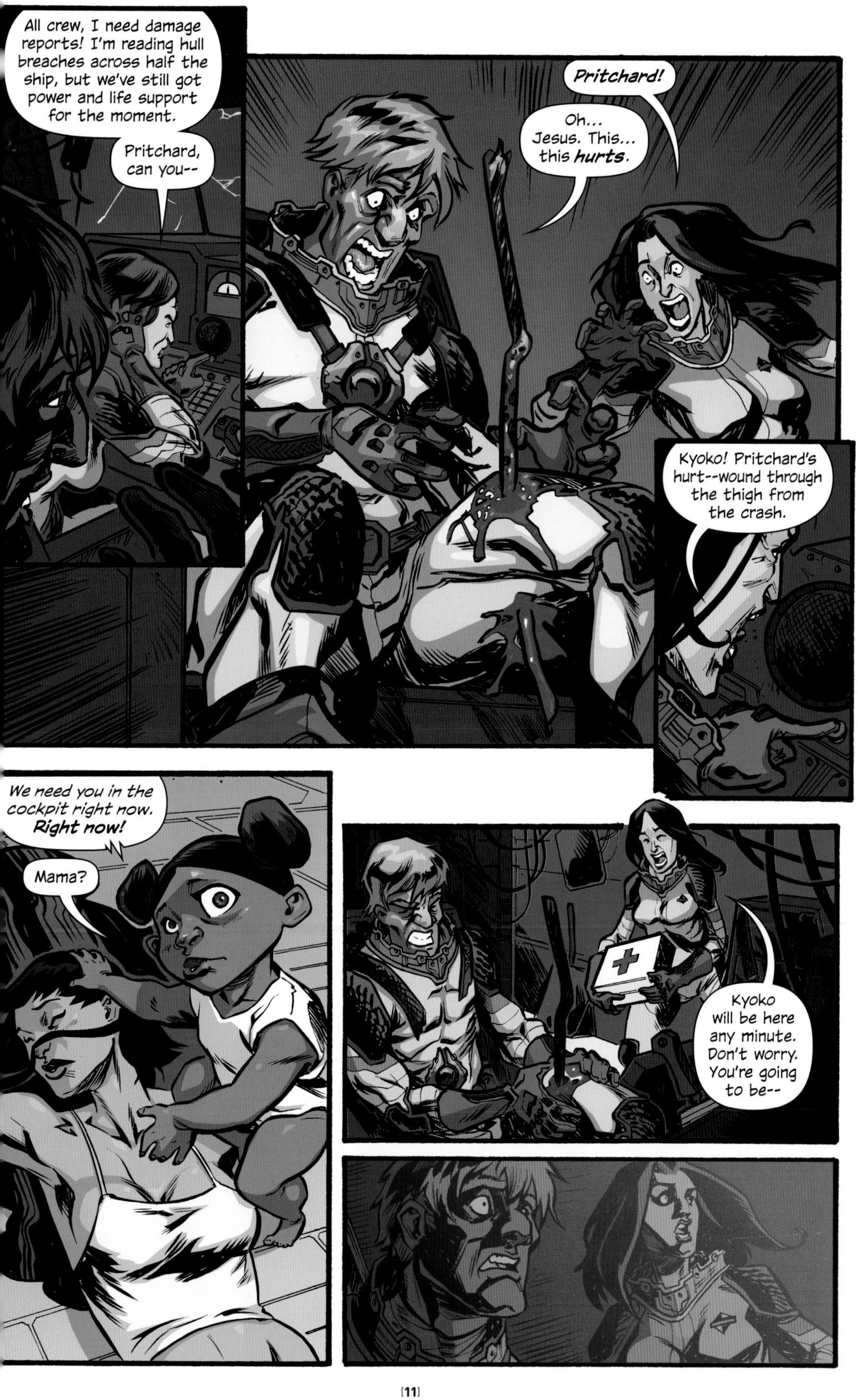
All crew, I need damage reports! I'm reading hull breaches across half the ship, but we've still got power and life support for the moment.
Pritchard, can you--
Pritchard!
Oh... Jesus. This... this *hurts*.
Kyoko! Pritchard's hurt--wound through the thigh from the crash.
We need you in the cockpit right now. ***Right now!***
Mama?
Kyoko will be here any minute. Don't worry. You're going to be--

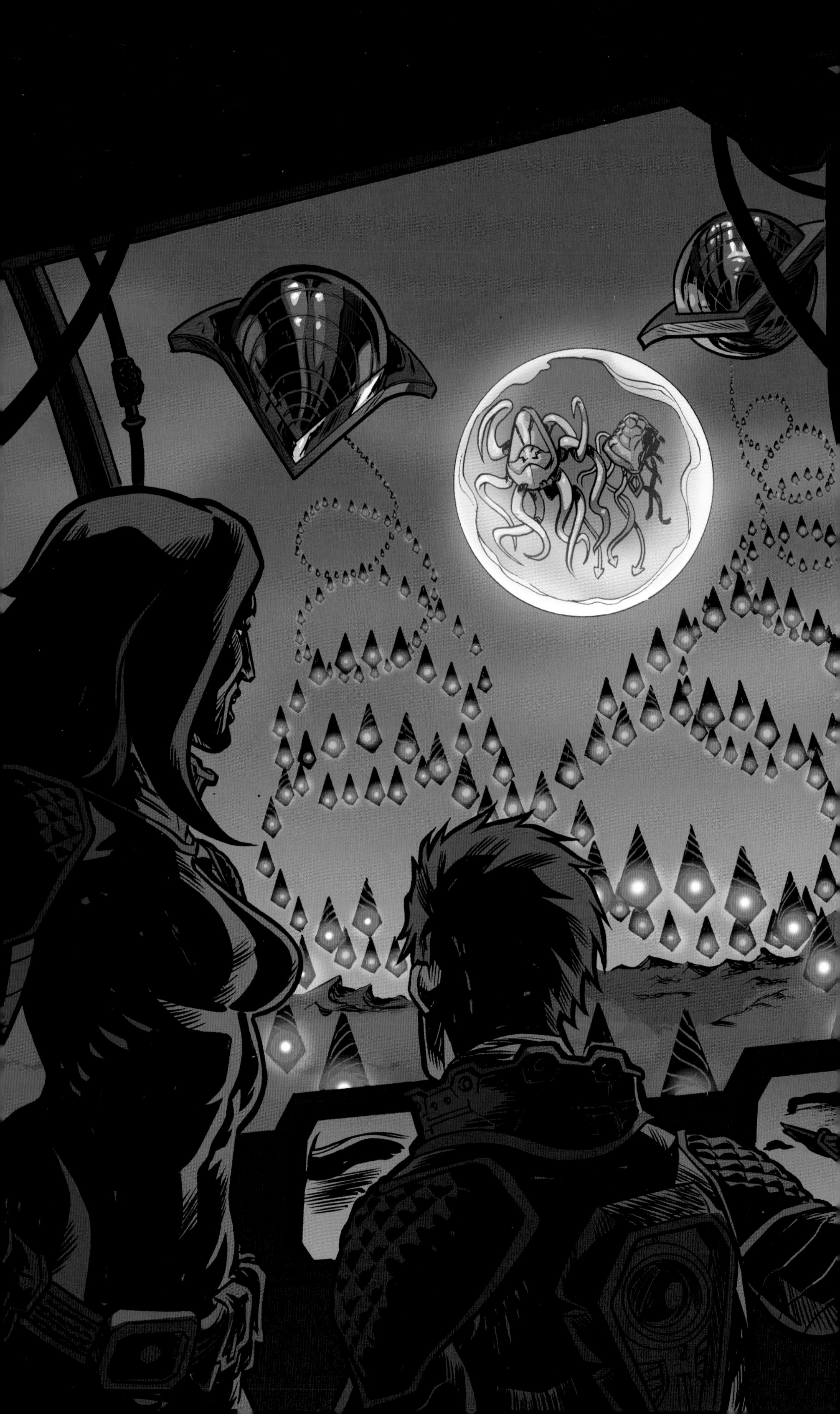

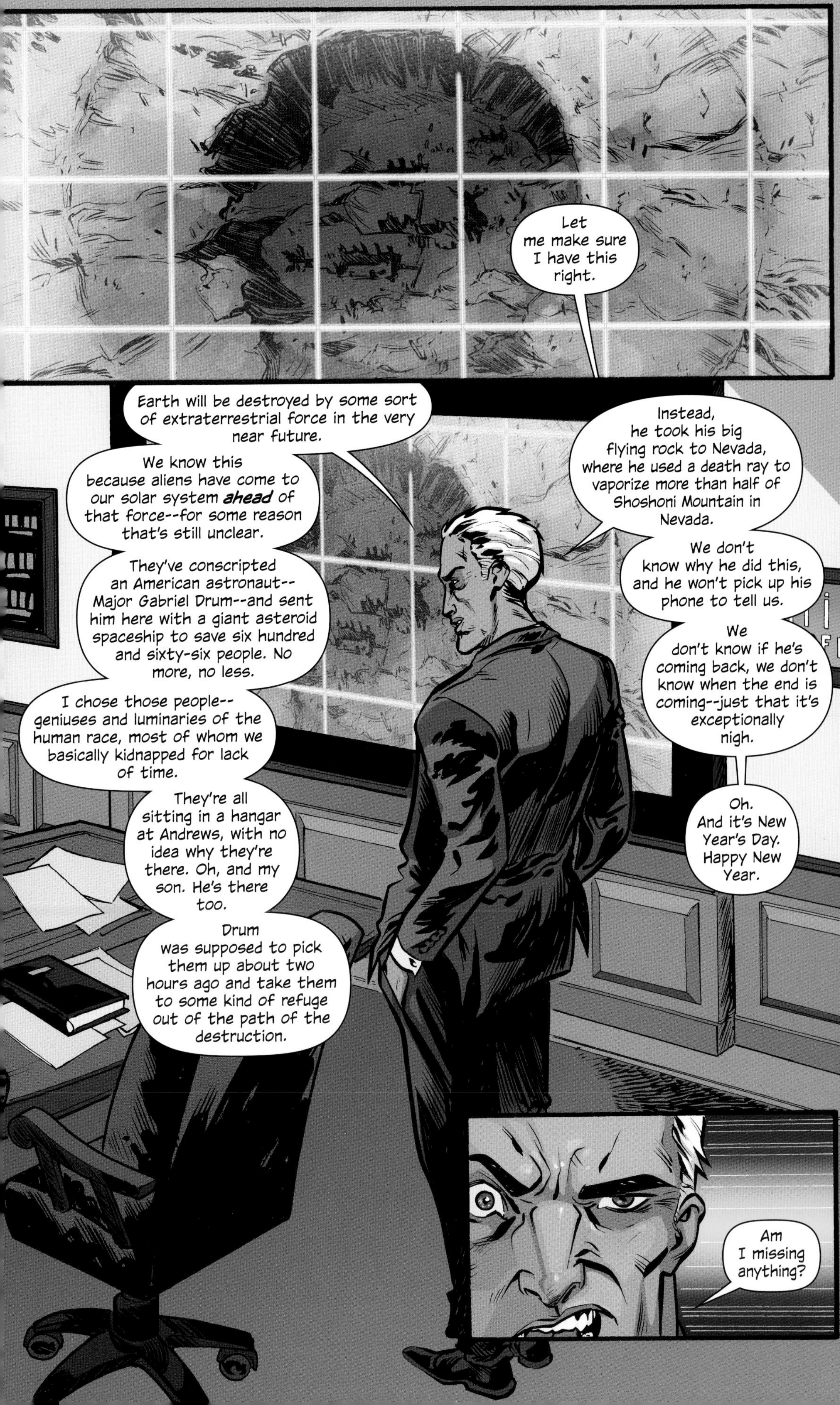
Let me make sure I have this right.
Earth will be destroyed by some sort of extraterrestrial force in the very near future.
We know this because aliens have come to our solar system ***ahead*** of that force--for some reason that's still unclear.
They've conscripted an American astronaut--Major Gabriel Drum--and sent him here with a giant asteroid spaceship to save six hundred and sixty-six people. No more, no less.
I chose those people--geniuses and luminaries of the human race, most of whom we basically kidnapped for lack of time.
They're all sitting in a hangar at Andrews, with no idea why they're there. Oh, and my son. He's there too.
Drum was supposed to pick them up about two hours ago and take them to some kind of refuge out of the path of the destruction.
Instead, he took his big flying rock to Nevada, where he used a death ray to vaporize more than half of Shoshoni Mountain in Nevada.
We don't know why he did this, and he won't pick up his phone to tell us.
We don't know if he's coming back, we don't know when the end is coming--just that it's exceptionally nigh.
Oh. And it's New Year's Day. Happy New Year.
Am I missing anything?

The mountain's contents, Mr. President. Shoshoni Mountain was the site of a decommissioned continuance of government bunker.

A refuge where US leadership could ride out a nuclear war.

Huh. Zoom in for me, AJ.

Decommissioned.

Then who the hell are *they*?

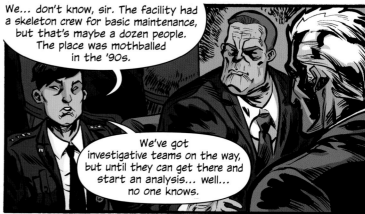

We... don't know, sir. The facility had a skeleton crew for basic maintenance, but that's maybe a dozen people. The place was mothballed in the '90s.

We've got investigative teams on the way, but until they can get there and start an analysis... well... no one knows.

Does it seem likely that Major Drum blew up a mountain at random--

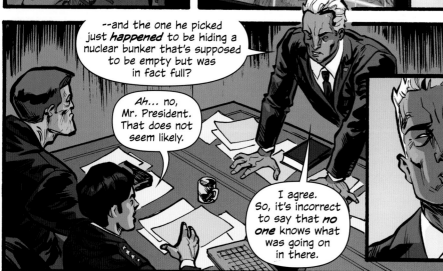

--and the one he picked just *happened* to be hiding a nuclear bunker that's supposed to be empty but was in fact full?

Ah... no, Mr. President. That does not seem likely.

I agree. So, it's incorrect to say that *no one* knows what was going on in there.

Drum knows.

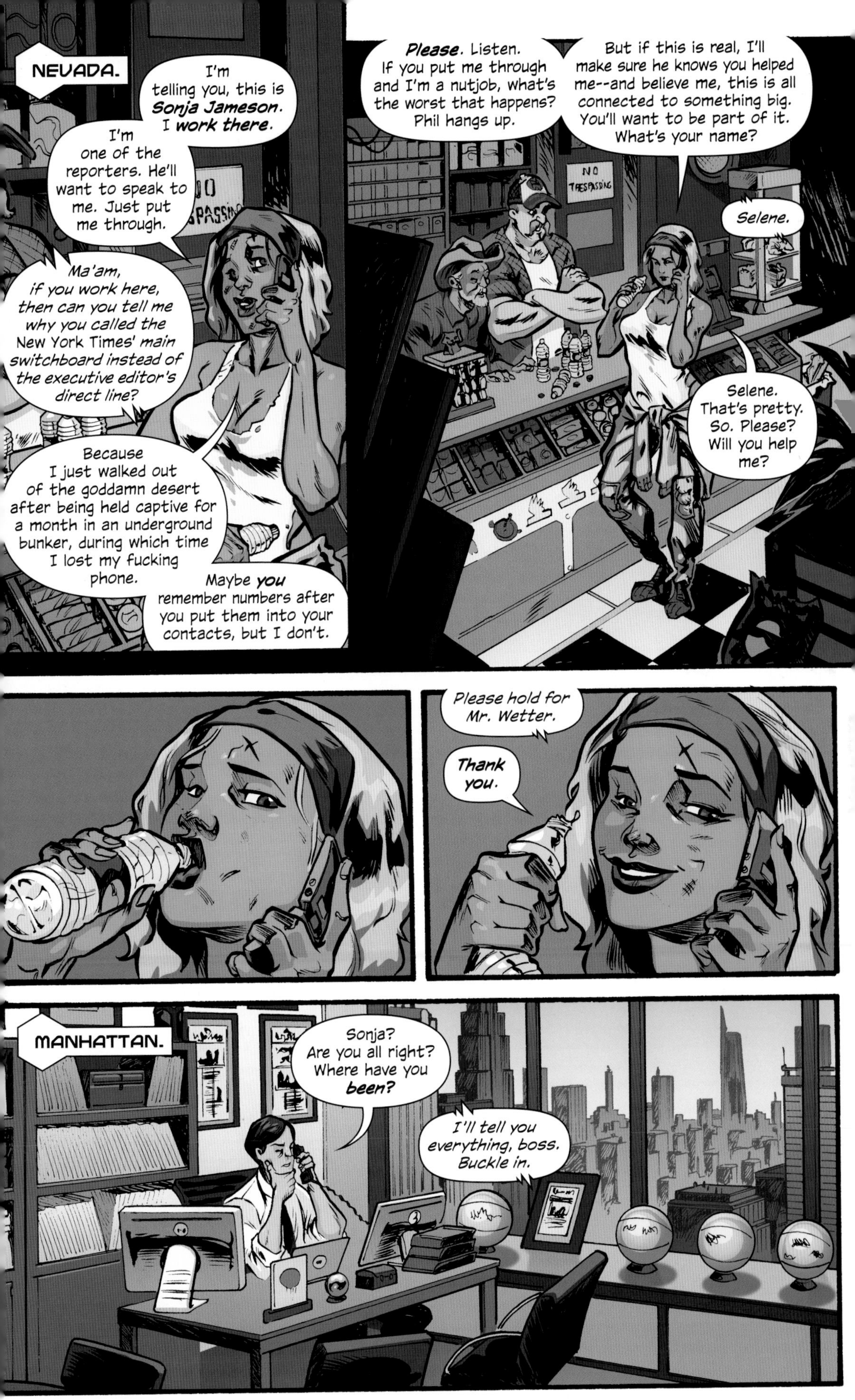
NEVADA.
I'm telling you, this is Sonja Jameson. I work there.
I'm one of the reporters. He'll want to speak to me. Just put me through.
NO TRESPASSING
Ma'am, if you work here, then can you tell me why you called the New York Times' main switchboard instead of the executive editor's direct line?
Because I just walked out of the goddamn desert after being held captive for a month in an underground bunker, during which time I lost my fucking phone.
Maybe you remember numbers after you put them into your contacts, but I don't.
Please. Listen. If you put me through and I'm a nutjob, what's the worst that happens? Phil hangs up.
But if this is real, I'll make sure he knows you helped me--and believe me, this is all connected to something big. You'll want to be part of it. What's your name?
Selene.
Selene. That's pretty. So. Please? Will you help me?
Please hold for Mr. Wetter.
Thank you.
MANHATTAN.
Sonja? Are you all right? Where have you been?
I'll tell you everything, boss. Buckle in.

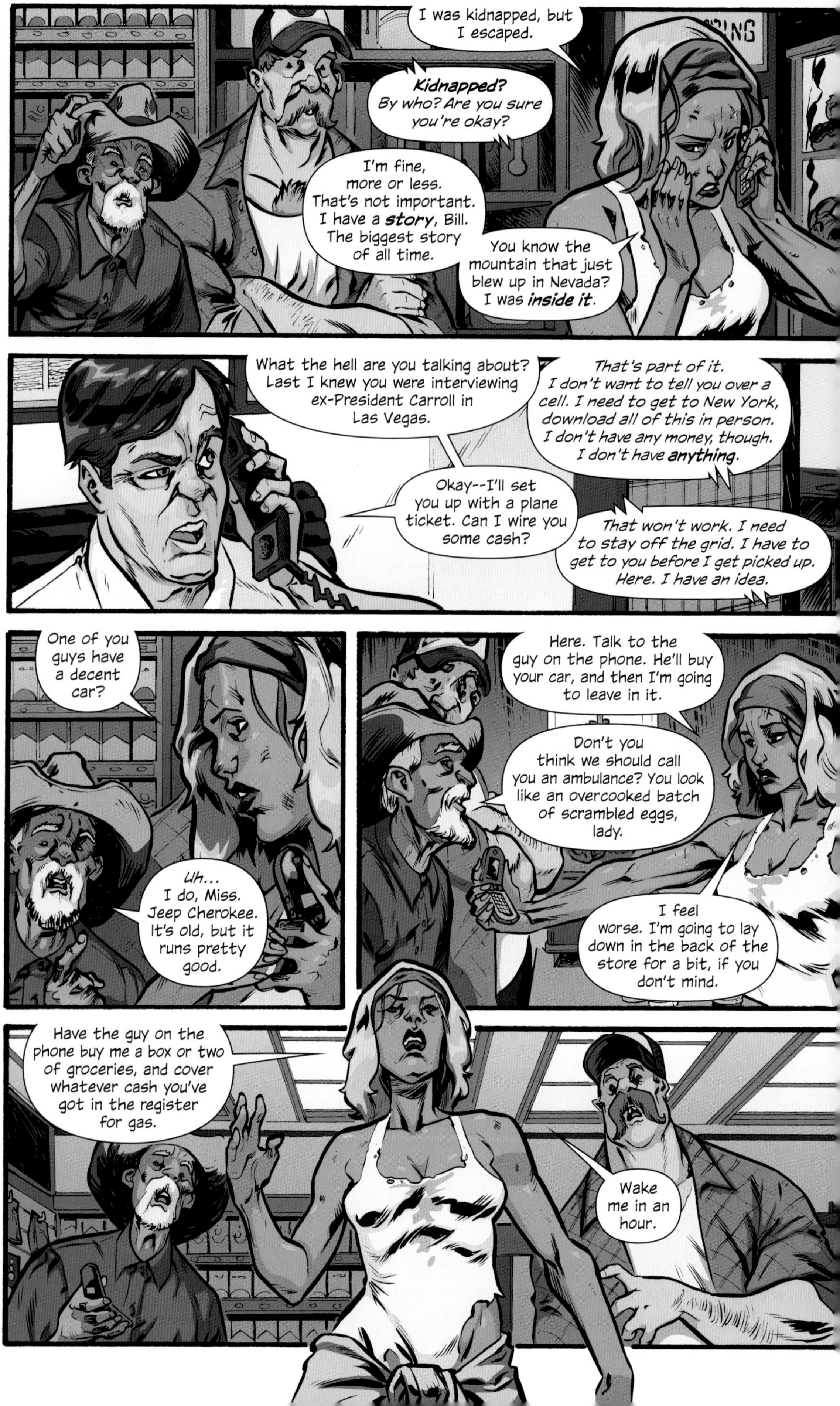
I was kidnapped, but I escaped.
Kidnapped? By who? Are you sure you're okay?
I'm fine, more or less. That's not important. I have a ***story***, Bill. The biggest story of all time.
You know the mountain that just blew up in Nevada? I was ***inside it***.
What the hell are you talking about? Last I knew you were interviewing ex-President Carroll in Las Vegas.
*That's part of it. I don't want to tell you over a cell. I need to get to New York, download all of this in person. I don't have any money, though. I don't have **anything**.*
Okay--I'll set you up with a plane ticket. Can I wire you some cash?
That won't work. I need to stay off the grid. I have to get to you before I get picked up. Here. I have an idea.
One of you guys have a decent car?
Uh... I do, Miss. Jeep Cherokee. It's old, but it runs pretty good.
Here. Talk to the guy on the phone. He'll buy your car, and then I'm going to leave in it.
Don't you think we should call you an ambulance? You look like an overcooked batch of scrambled eggs, lady.
I feel worse. I'm going to lay down in the back of the store for a bit, if you don't mind.
Have the guy on the phone buy me a box or two of groceries, and cover whatever cash you've got in the register for gas.
Wake me in an hour.

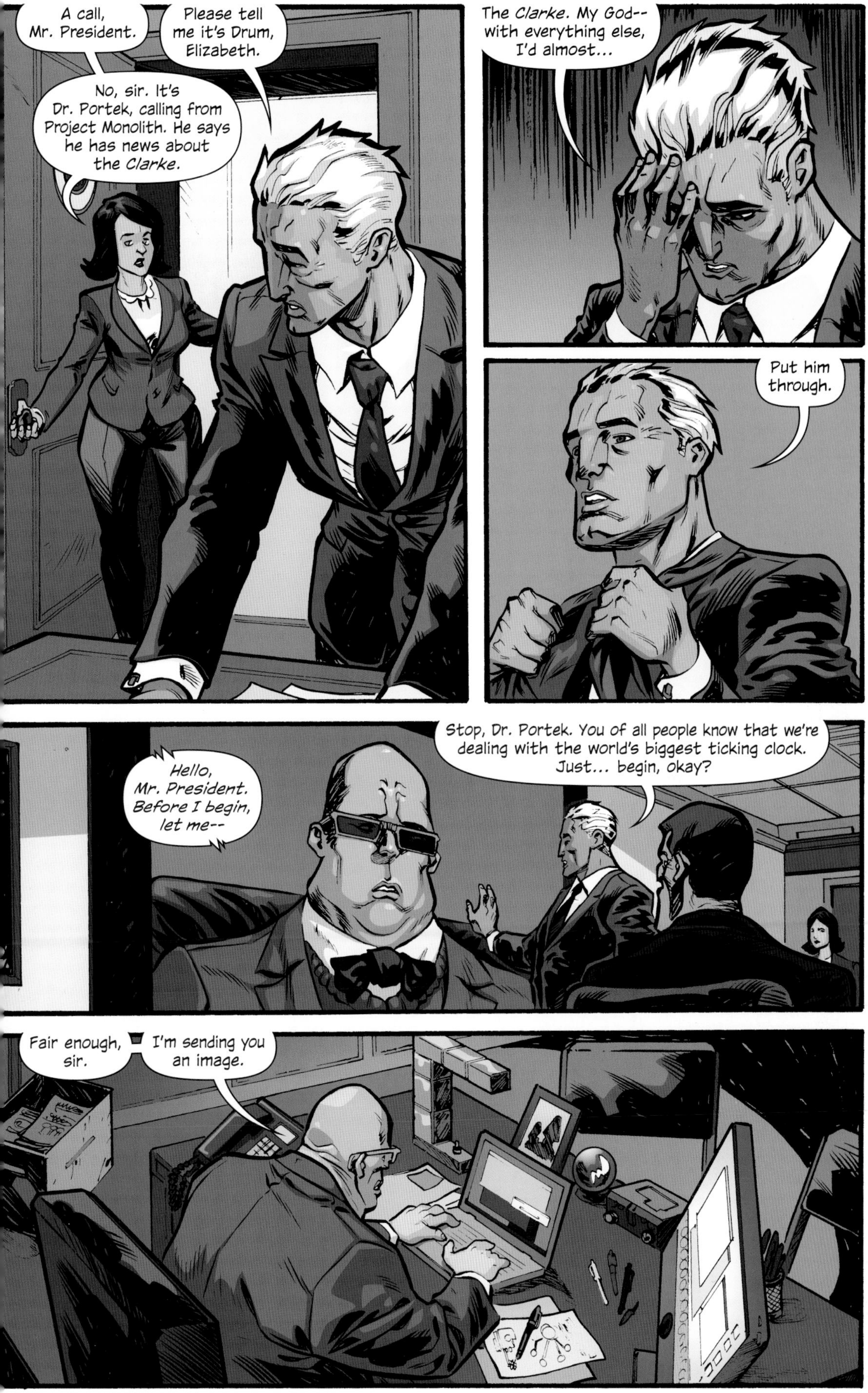
A call, Mr. President.
Please tell me it's Drum, Elizabeth.
No, sir. It's Dr. Portek, calling from Project Monolith. He says he has news about the *Clarke*.
The *Clarke*. My God--with everything else, I'd almost...
Put him through.
Hello, Mr. President. Before I begin, let me--
Stop, Dr. Portek. You of all people know that we're dealing with the world's biggest ticking clock. Just... begin, okay?
Fair enough, sir.
I'm sending you an image.

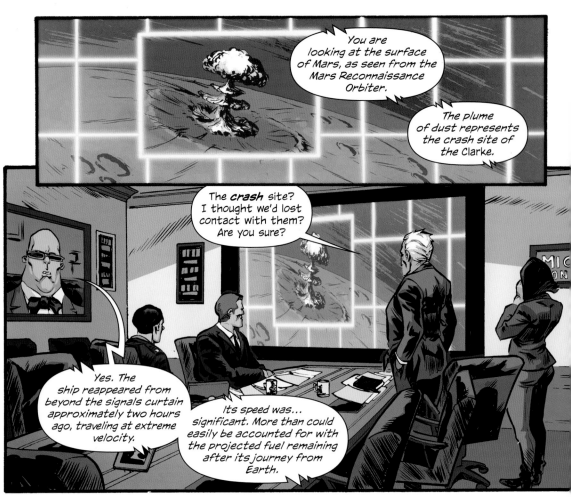

You are looking at the surface of Mars, as seen from the Mars Reconnaissance Orbiter.

The plume of dust represents the crash site of the Clarke.

The **crash** site? I thought we'd lost contact with them? Are you sure?

Yes. The ship reappeared from beyond the signals curtain approximately two hours ago, traveling at extreme velocity.

Its speed was... significant. More than could easily be accounted for with the projected fuel remaining after its journey from Earth.

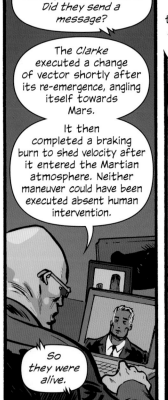

Was anyone alive aboard? Did they send a message?

The Clarke executed a change of vector shortly after its re-emergence, angling itself towards Mars.

It then completed a braking burn to shed velocity after it entered the Martian atmosphere. Neither maneuver could have been executed absent human intervention.

So they were alive.

Were is the operative word, sir. They impacted the surface at high speed. And even if they survived, they aren't equipped for a long-term stay on the planet.

If they aren't dead now... it's just a matter of time. I'm sorry.

And do we know **why**? Do we know **anything**?

Little more than I've told you, sir. We'll keep watching the crash site for activity.

I know we were hoping the Clarke crew could somehow work with the aliens to save this planet, or at least learn more about what's coming.

As that hope now seems... ah, **slim**... I thought you should be informed.

Yes, of course. Thank you for telling me. Please let me know if you learn anything else.

This, whatever happened at tha bunker... it's all connected.

I'm sure of it.

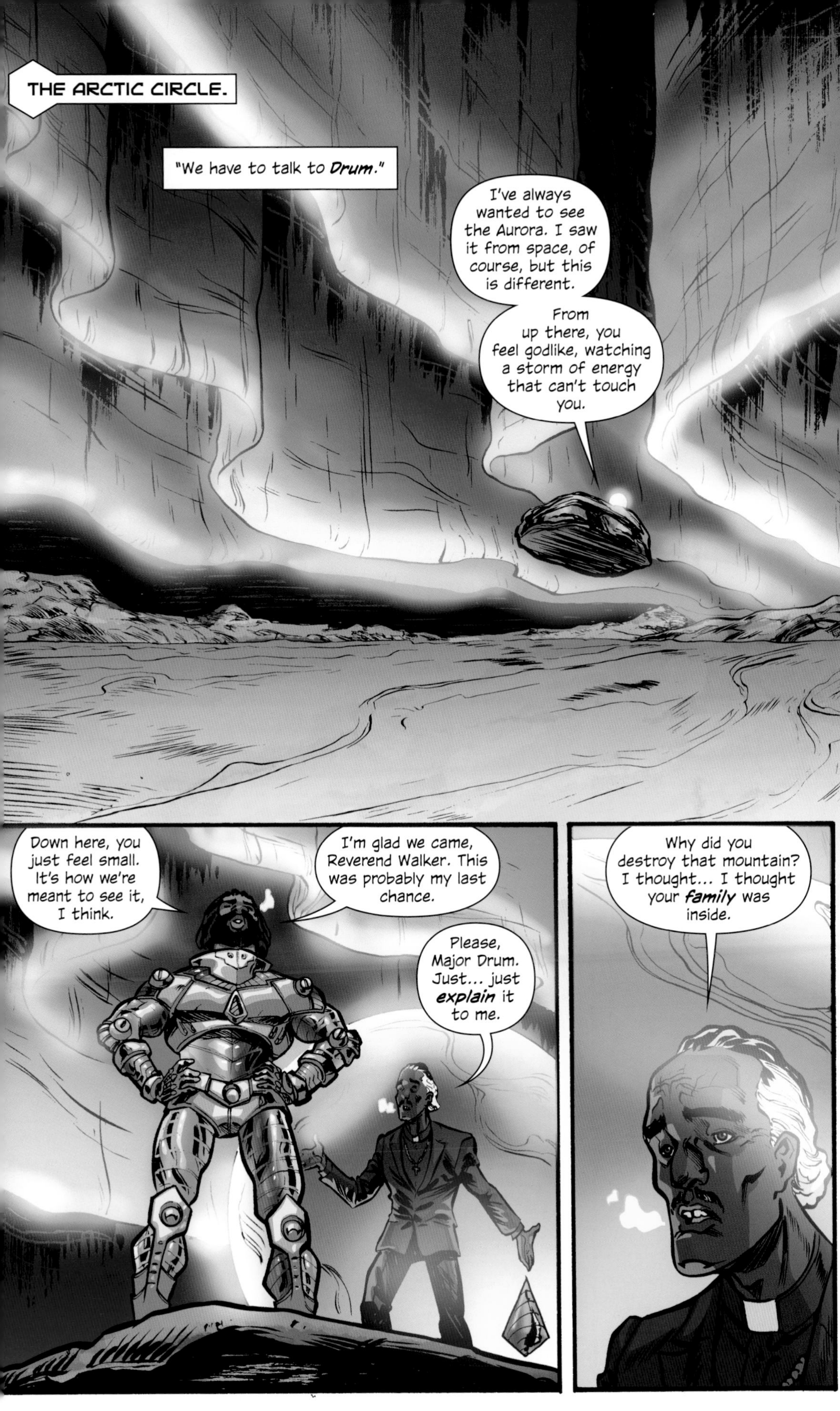
THE ARCTIC CIRCLE.
"We have to talk to *Drum*."
I've always wanted to see the Aurora. I saw it from space, of course, but this is different.
From up there, you feel godlike, watching a storm of energy that can't touch you.
Down here, you just feel small. It's how we're meant to see it, I think.
I'm glad we came, Reverend Walker. This was probably my last chance.
Please, Major Drum. Just... just *explain* it to me.
Why did you destroy that mountain? I thought... I thought your *family* was inside.

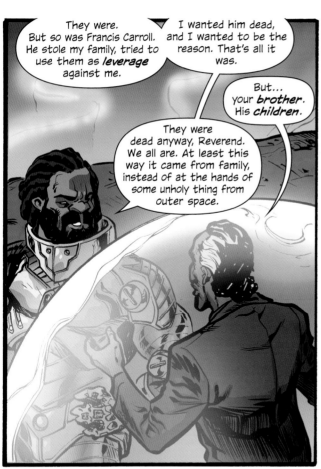

They were. But so was Francis Carroll. He stole my family, tried to use them as *leverage* against me.

I wanted him dead, and I wanted to be the reason. That's all it was.

But... your *brother*. His *children*.

They were dead anyway, Reverend. We all are. At least this way it came from family, instead of at the hands of some unholy thing from outer space.

I think I've seen enough here.

Is there anywhere you'd like to go in the world? Something you'd like to see?

None of it will be around for very long.

TWEE TWEE

The satellite phone the President gave me... it's him. It has to be.

Don't you think you should tell him the truth? Doesn't he deserve to know?

Doesn't *everyone* deserve to know?

I... suppose you're right.

Mr. President, I--

Thank God I finally got you, Major Drum. I have news about your colleagues on the Clarke.

[20]

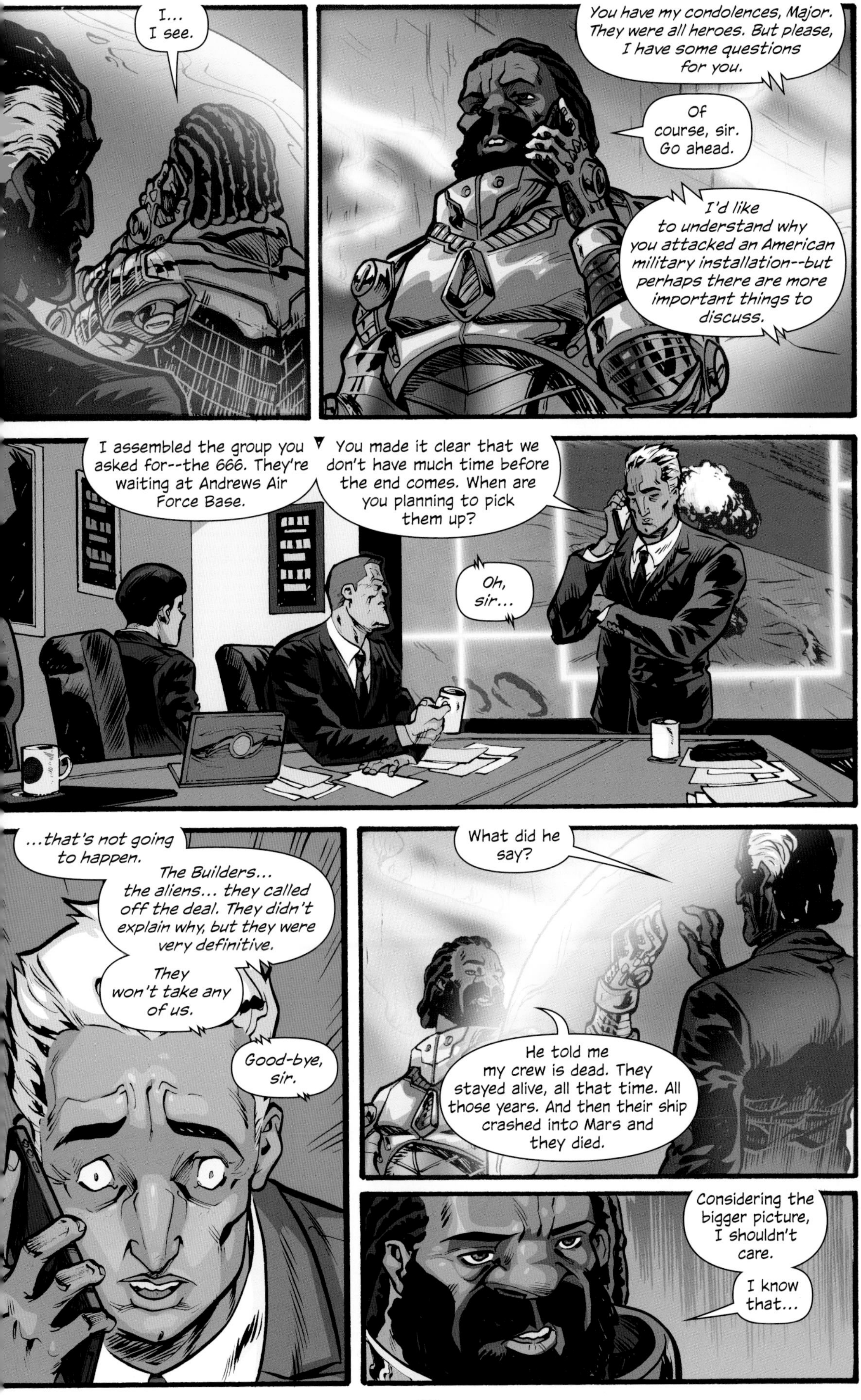
I... I see.
You have my condolences, Major. They were all heroes. But please, I have some questions for you.
Of course, sir. Go ahead.
I'd like to understand why you attacked an American military installation--but perhaps there are more important things to discuss.
I assembled the group you asked for--the 666. They're waiting at Andrews Air Force Base.
You made it clear that we don't have much time before the end comes. When are you planning to pick them up?
Oh, sir...
...that's not going to happen.
The Builders... the aliens... they called off the deal. They didn't explain why, but they were very definitive.
They won't take any of us.
Good-bye, sir.
What did he say?
He told me my crew is dead. They stayed alive, all that time. All those years. And then their ship crashed into Mars and they died.
Considering the bigger picture, I shouldn't care.
I know that...

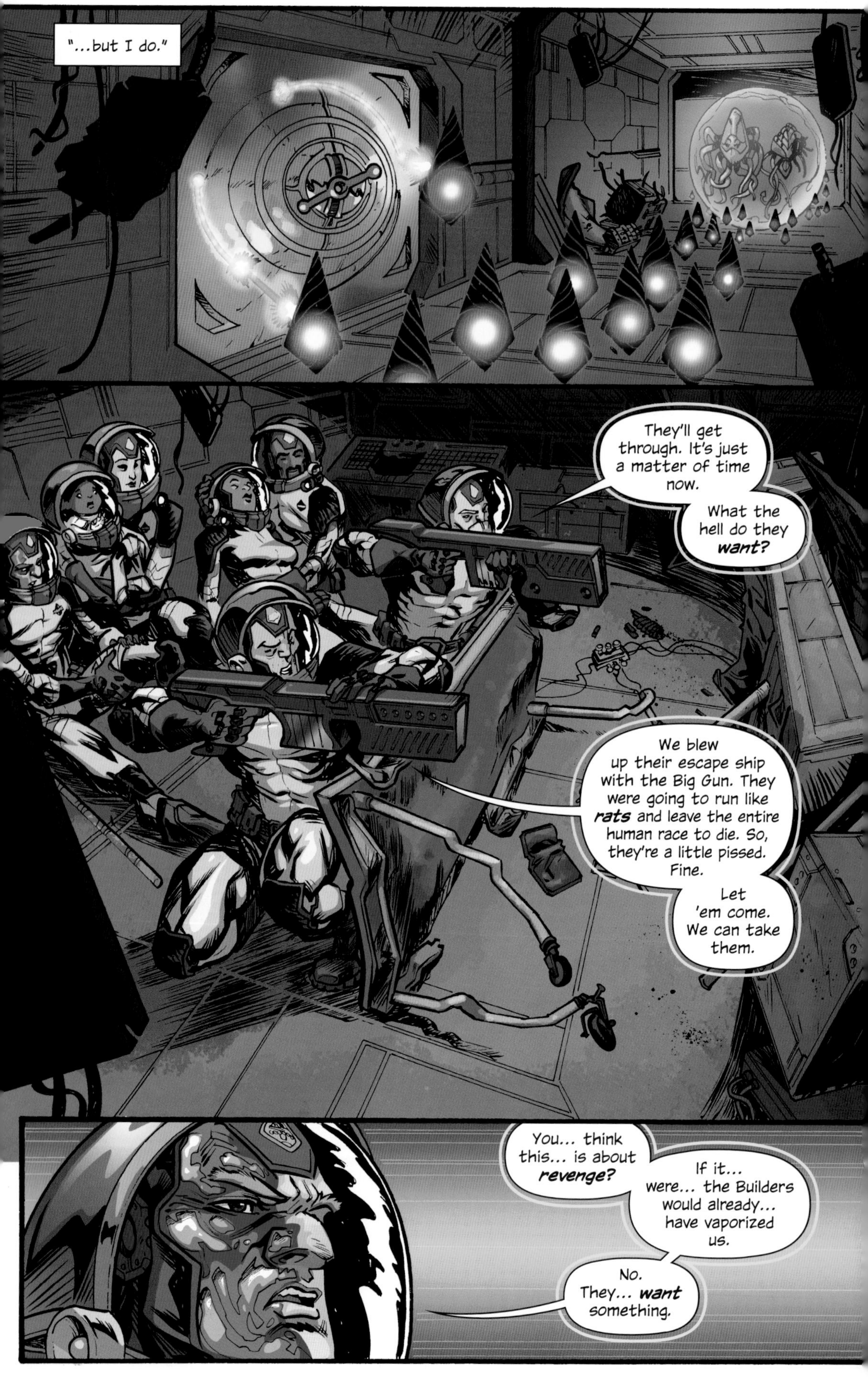
"...but I do."
They'll get through. It's just a matter of time now.
What the hell do they want?
We blew up their escape ship with the Big Gun. They were going to run like rats and leave the entire human race to die. So, they're a little pissed. Fine.
Let 'em come. We can take them.
You... think this... is about revenge?
If it... were... the Builders would already... have vaporized us.
No. They... want something.

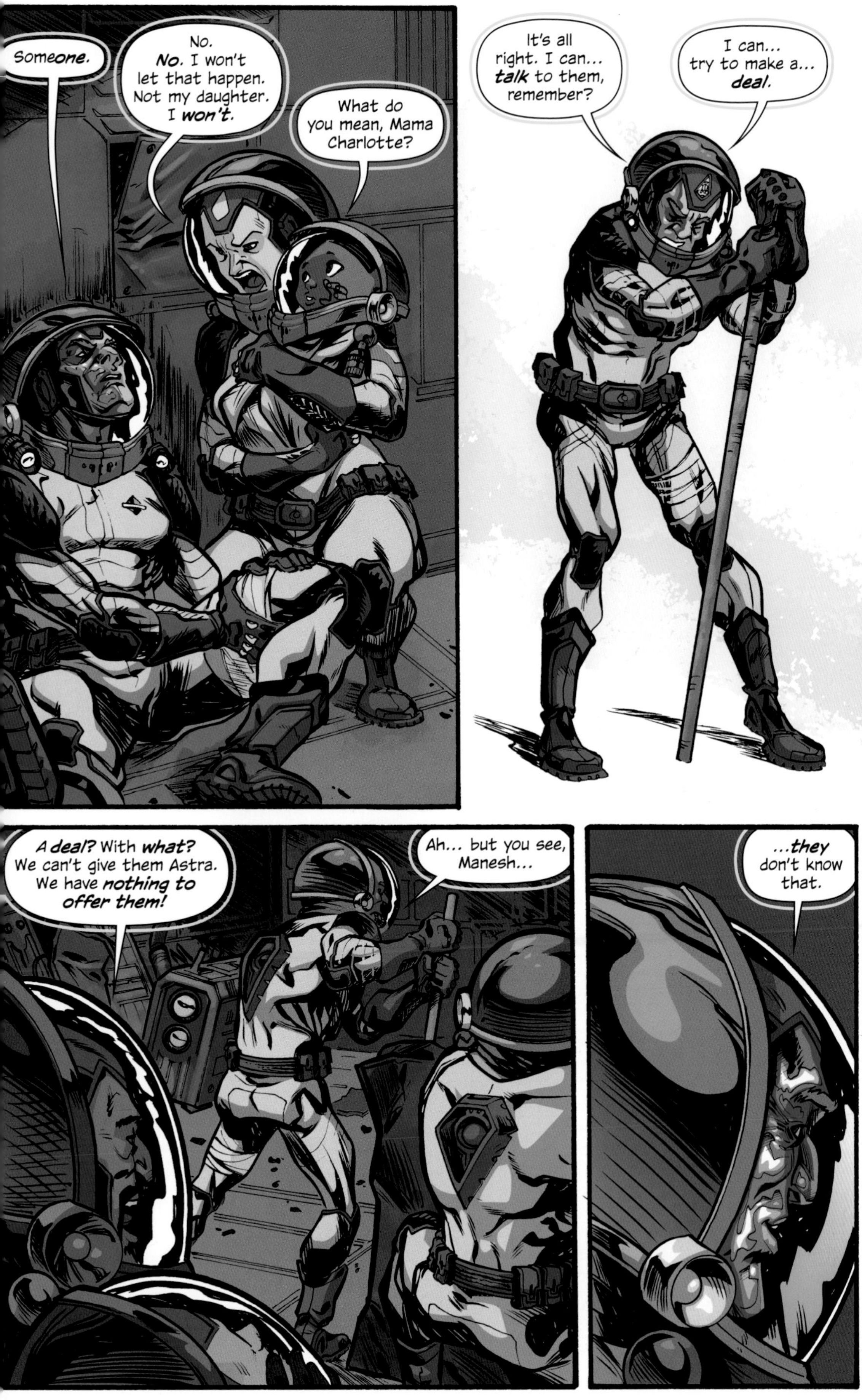
Someone.
No. No. I won't let that happen. Not my daughter. I won't.
What do you mean, Mama Charlotte?
It's all right. I can... talk to them, remember?
I can... try to make a... deal.
A deal? With what? We can't give them Astra. We have nothing to offer them!
Ah... but you see, Manesh...
...they don't know that.

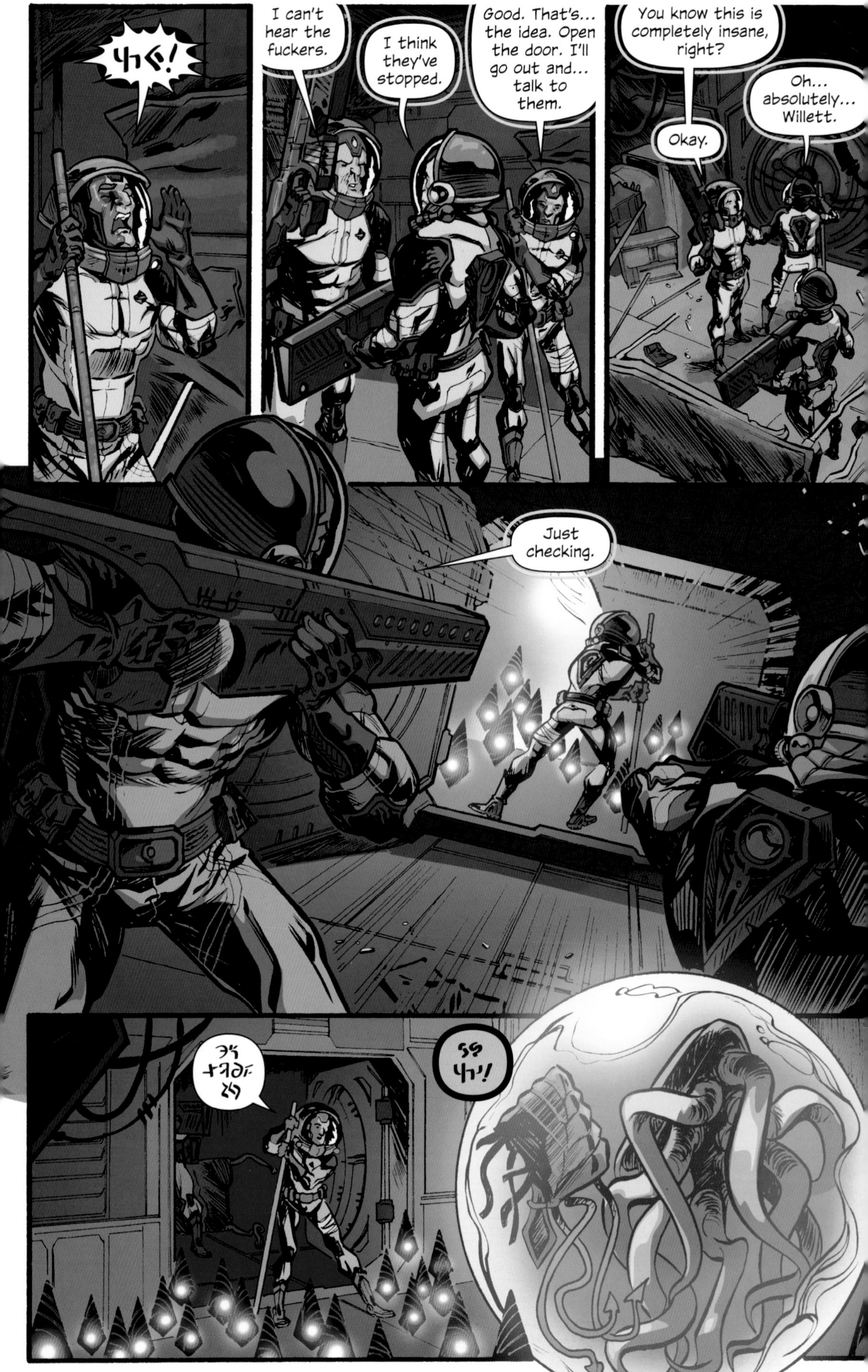
I can't hear the fuckers.
I think they've stopped.
Good. That's... the idea. Open the door. I'll go out and... talk to them.
You know this is completely insane, right?
Okay.
Oh... absolutely... Willett.
Just checking.

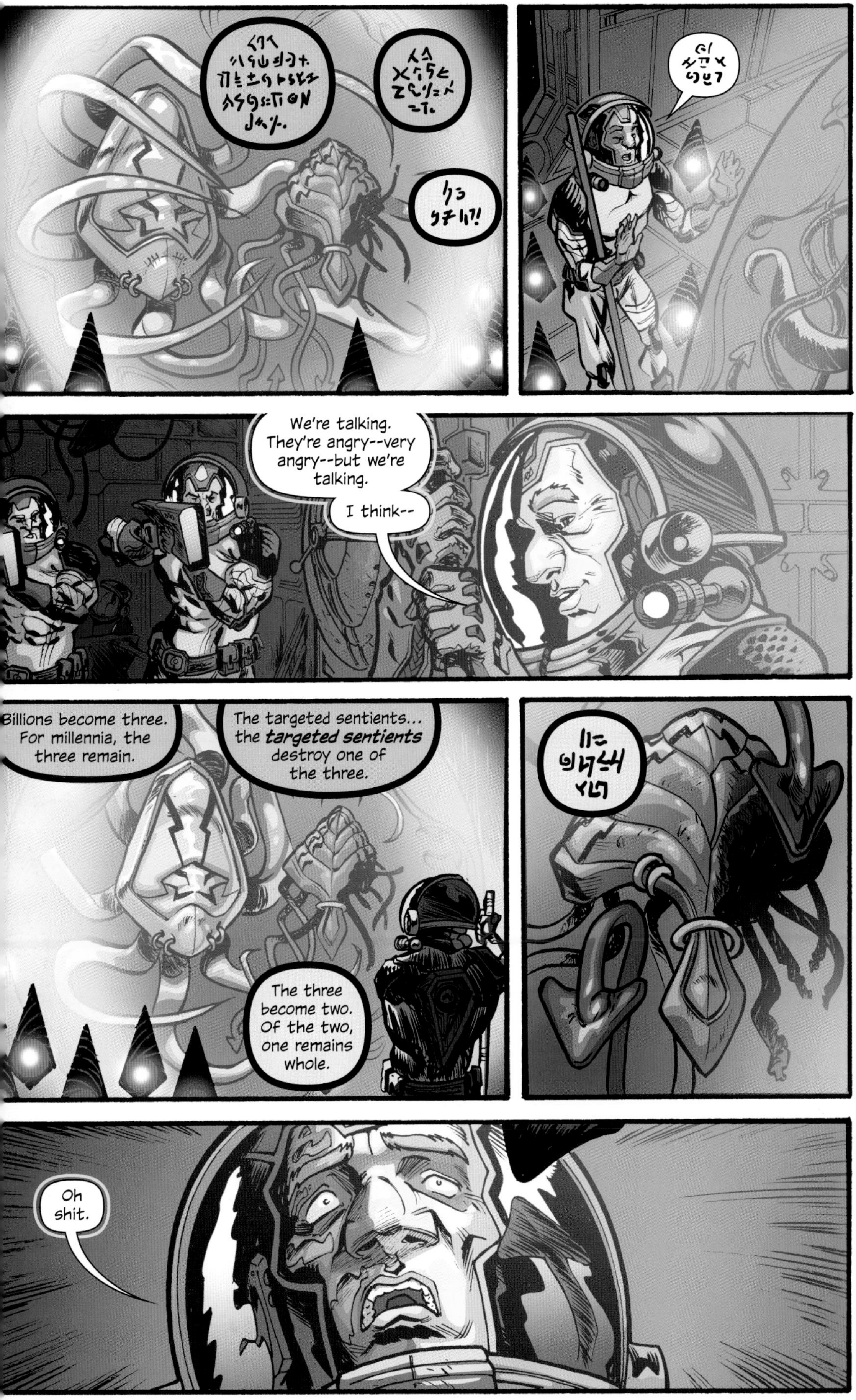
We're talking. They're angry--very angry--but we're talking.
I think--
Billions become three. For millennia, the three remain.
The targeted sentients... the ***targeted sentients*** destroy one of the three.
The three become two. Of the two, one remains whole.
Oh shit.

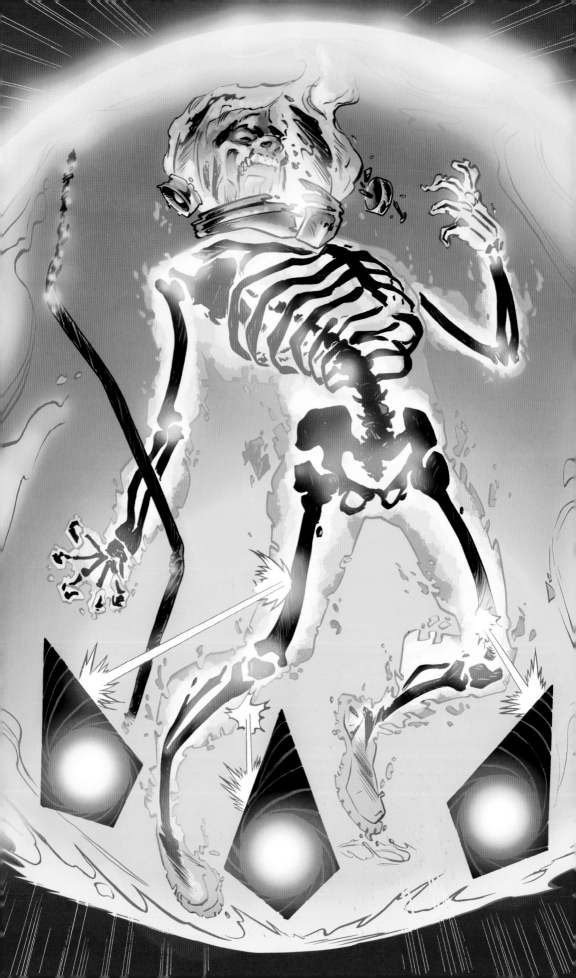

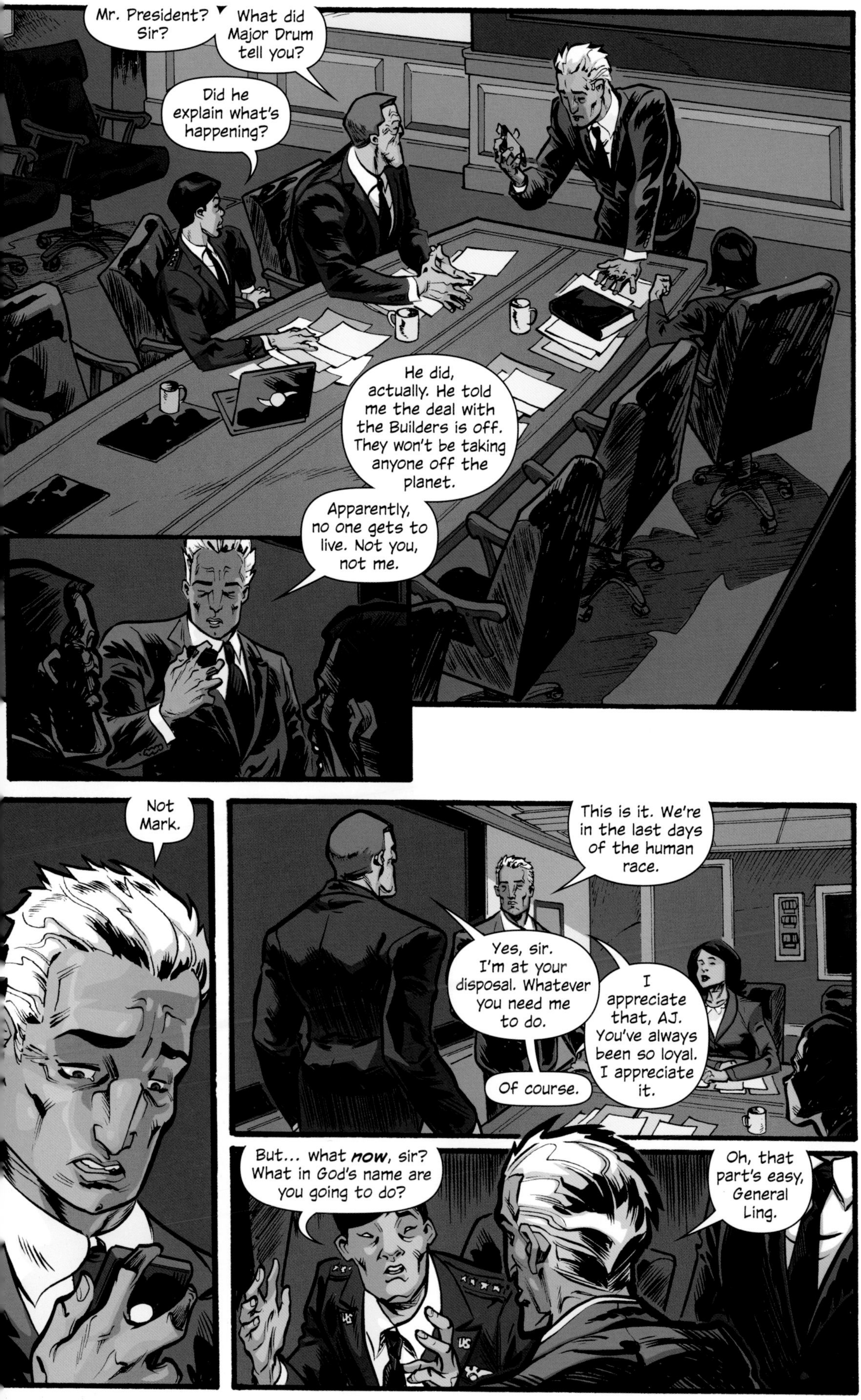
Mr. President? Sir?
What did Major Drum tell you?
Did he explain what's happening?
He did, actually. He told me the deal with the Builders is off. They won't be taking anyone off the planet.
Apparently, no one gets to live. Not you, not me.
Not Mark.
This is it. We're in the last days of the human race.
Yes, sir. I'm at your disposal. Whatever you need me to do.
I appreciate that, AJ. You've always been so loyal. I appreciate it.
Of course.
But... what *now*, sir? What in God's name are you going to do?
Oh, that part's easy, General Ling.

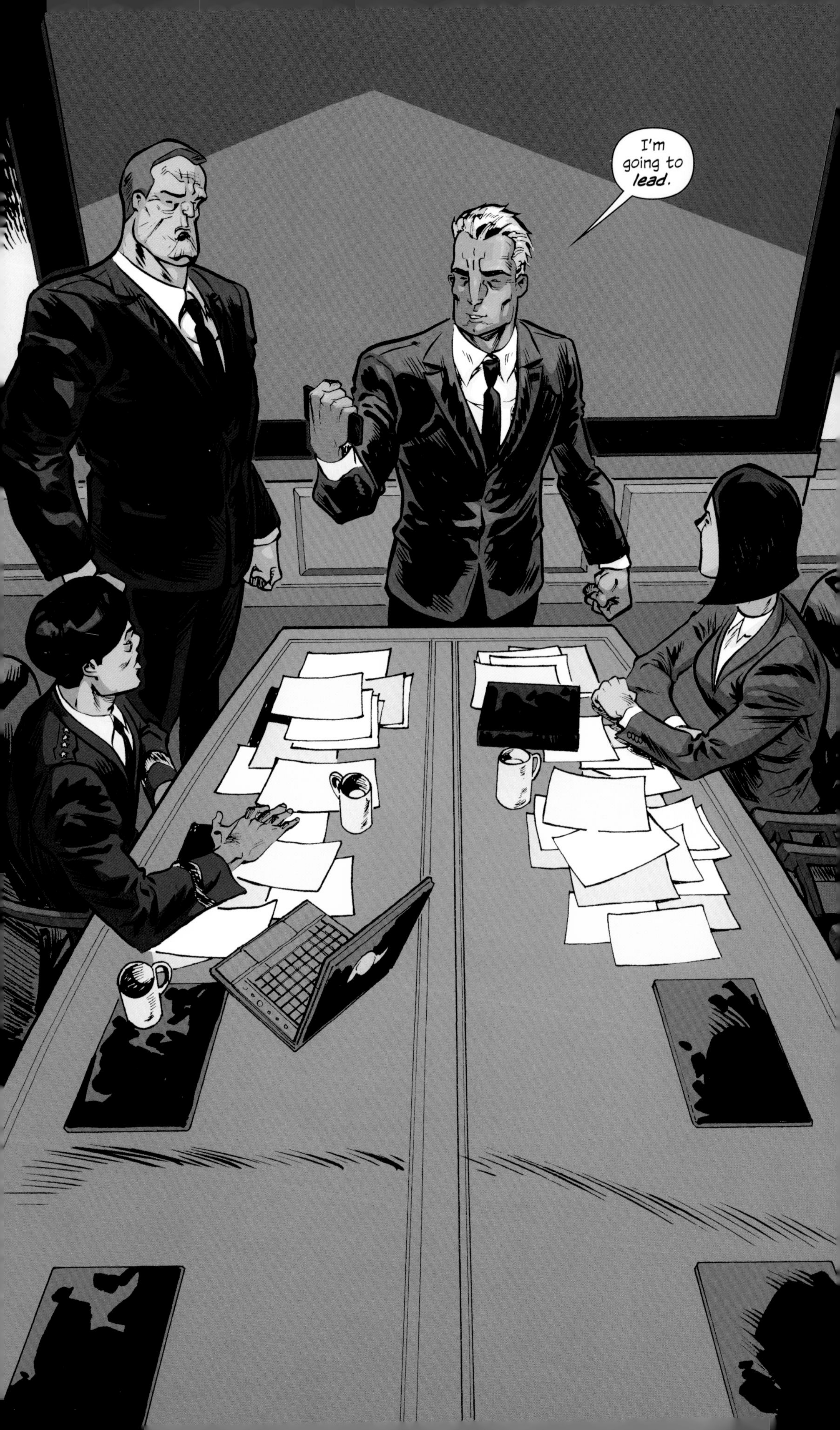
I'm going to *lead*.

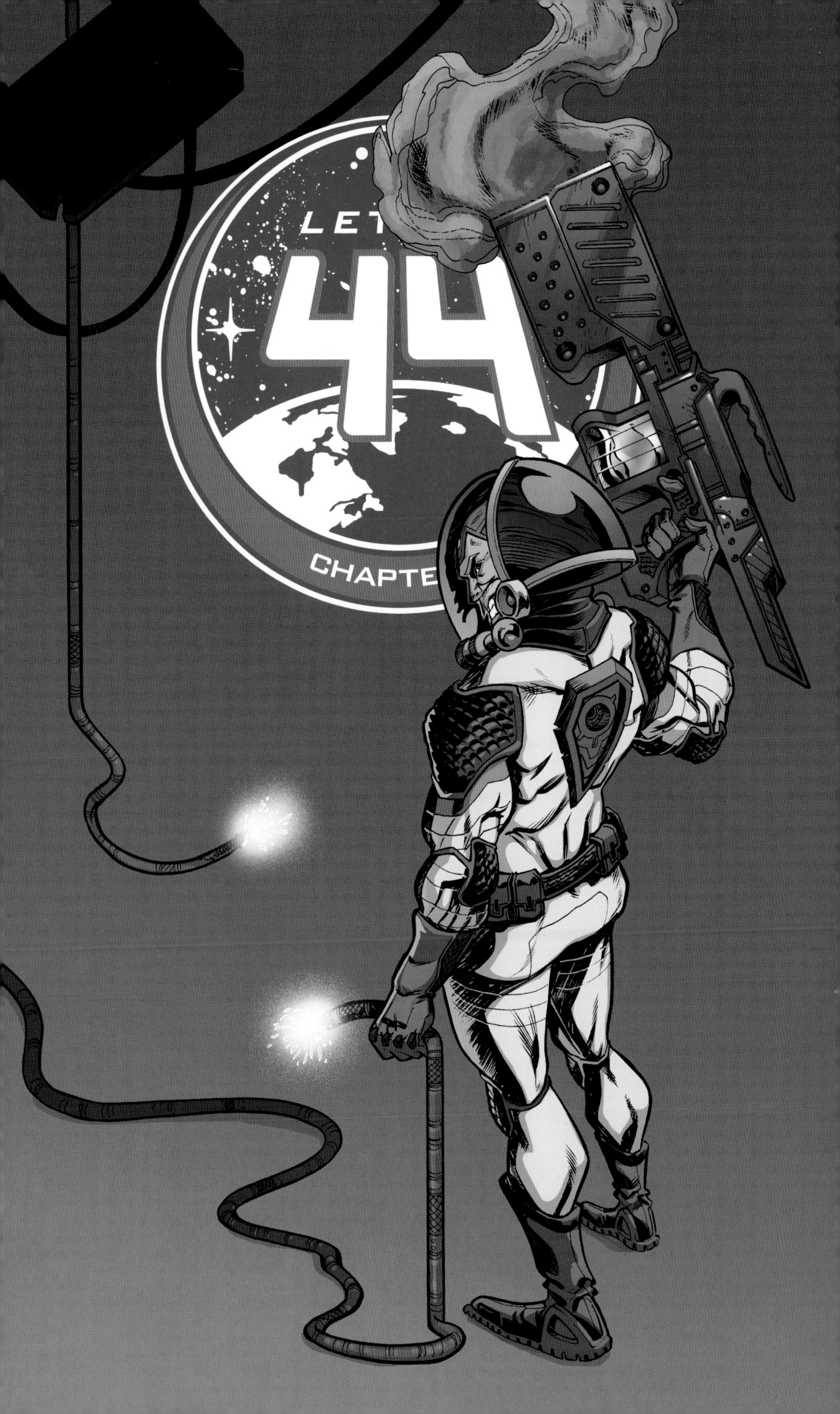
LET
44
CHAPTE

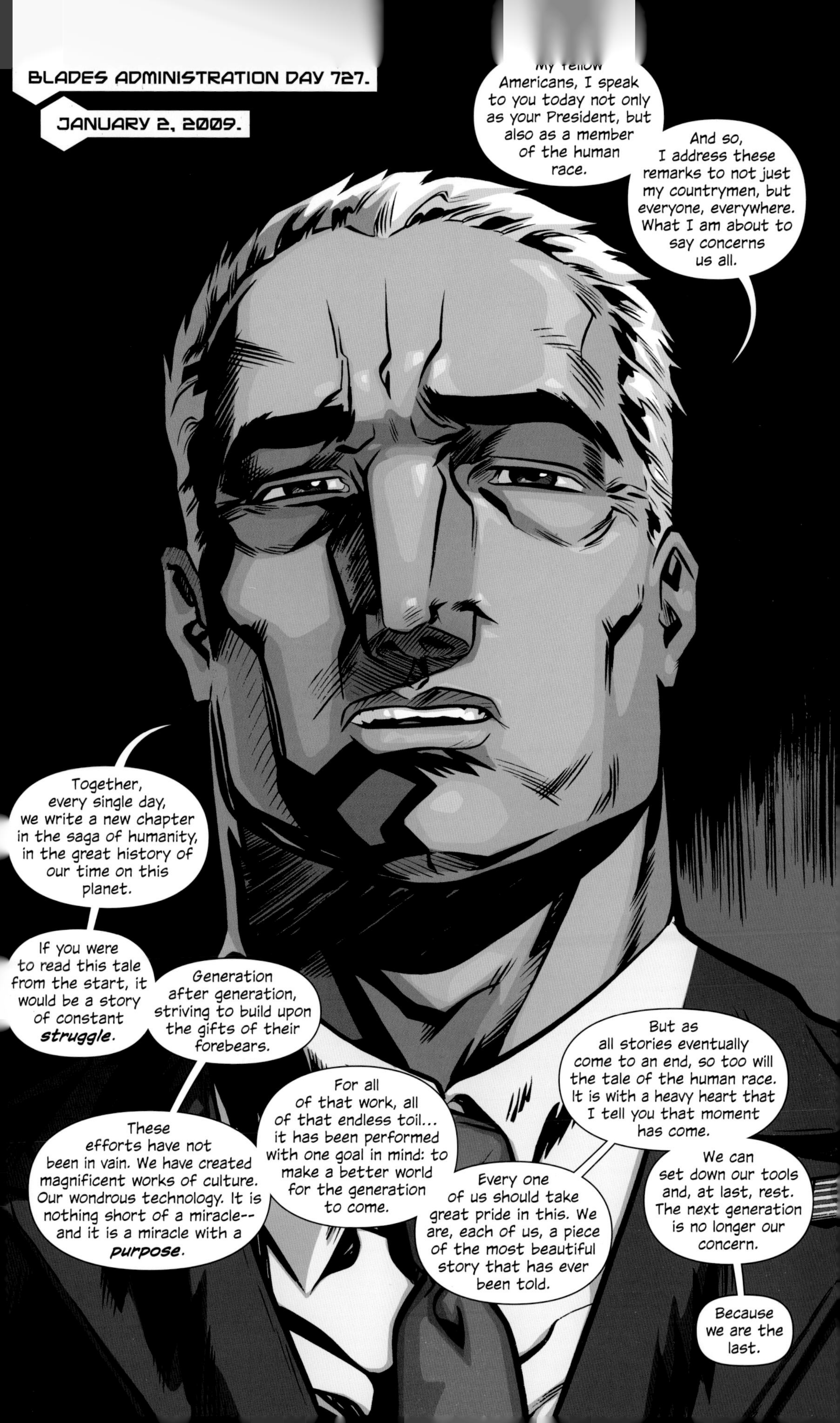
BLADES ADMINISTRATION DAY 727.
JANUARY 2, 2009.
My fellow Americans, I speak to you today not only as your President, but also as a member of the human race.
And so, I address these remarks to not just my countrymen, but everyone, everywhere. What I am about to say concerns us all.
Together, every single day, we write a new chapter in the saga of humanity, in the great history of our time on this planet.
If you were to read this tale from the start, it would be a story of constant ***struggle***.
Generation after generation, striving to build upon the gifts of their forebears.
These efforts have not been in vain. We have created magnificent works of culture. Our wondrous technology. It is nothing short of a miracle--and it is a miracle with a ***purpose***.
For all of that work, all of that endless toil... it has been performed with one goal in mind: to make a better world for the generation to come.
But as all stories eventually come to an end, so too will the tale of the human race. It is with a heavy heart that I tell you that moment has come.
Every one of us should take great pride in this. We are, each of us, a piece of the most beautiful story that has ever been told.
We can set down our tools and, at last, rest. The next generation is no longer our concern.
Because we are the last.

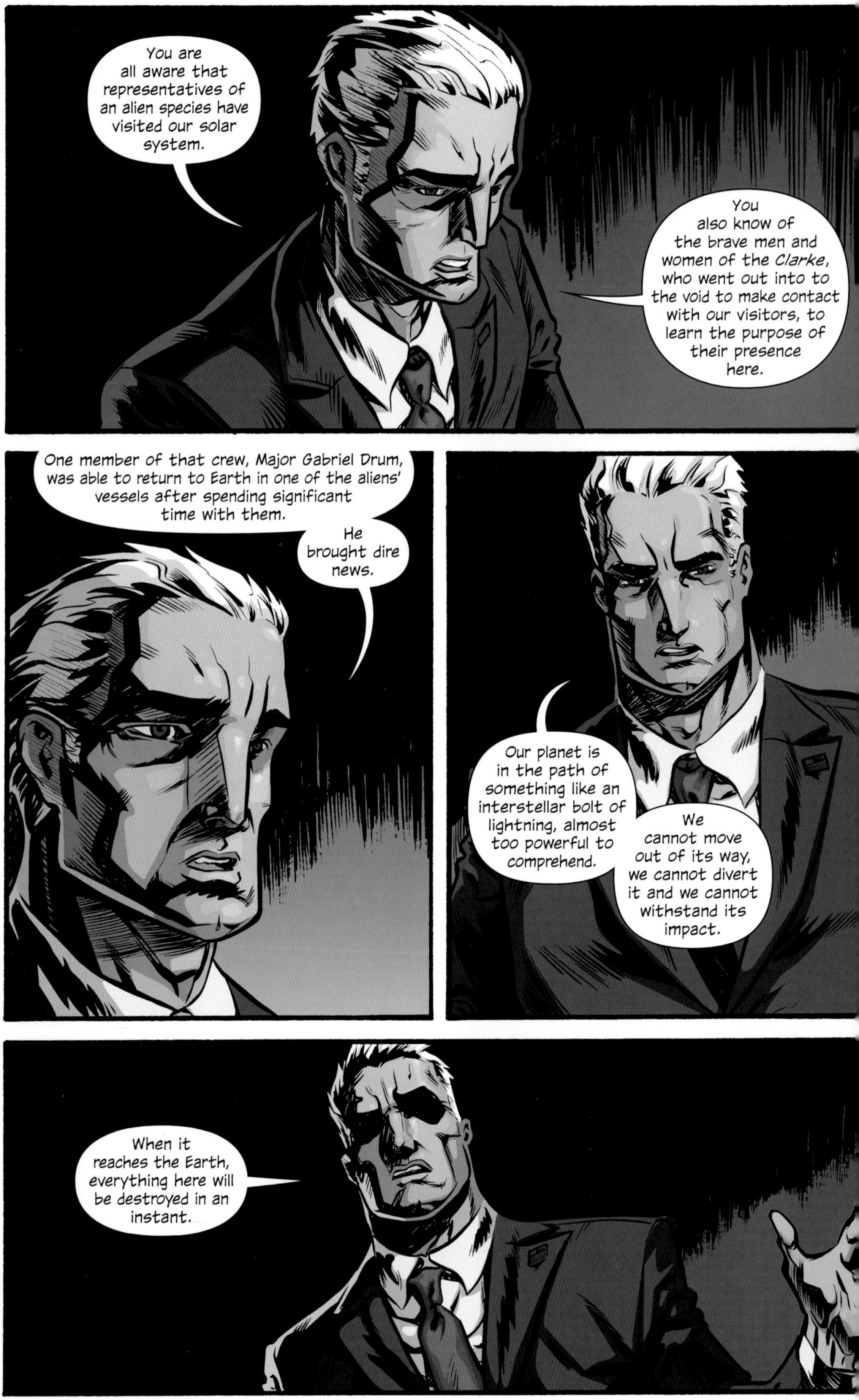
You are all aware that representatives of an alien species have visited our solar system.
You also know of the brave men and women of the *Clarke*, who went out into to the void to make contact with our visitors, to learn the purpose of their presence here.
One member of that crew, Major Gabriel Drum, was able to return to Earth in one of the aliens' vessels after spending significant time with them.
He brought dire news.
Our planet is in the path of something like an interstellar bolt of lightning, almost too powerful to comprehend.
We cannot move out of its way, we cannot divert it and we cannot withstand its impact.
When it reaches the Earth, everything here will be destroyed in an instant.

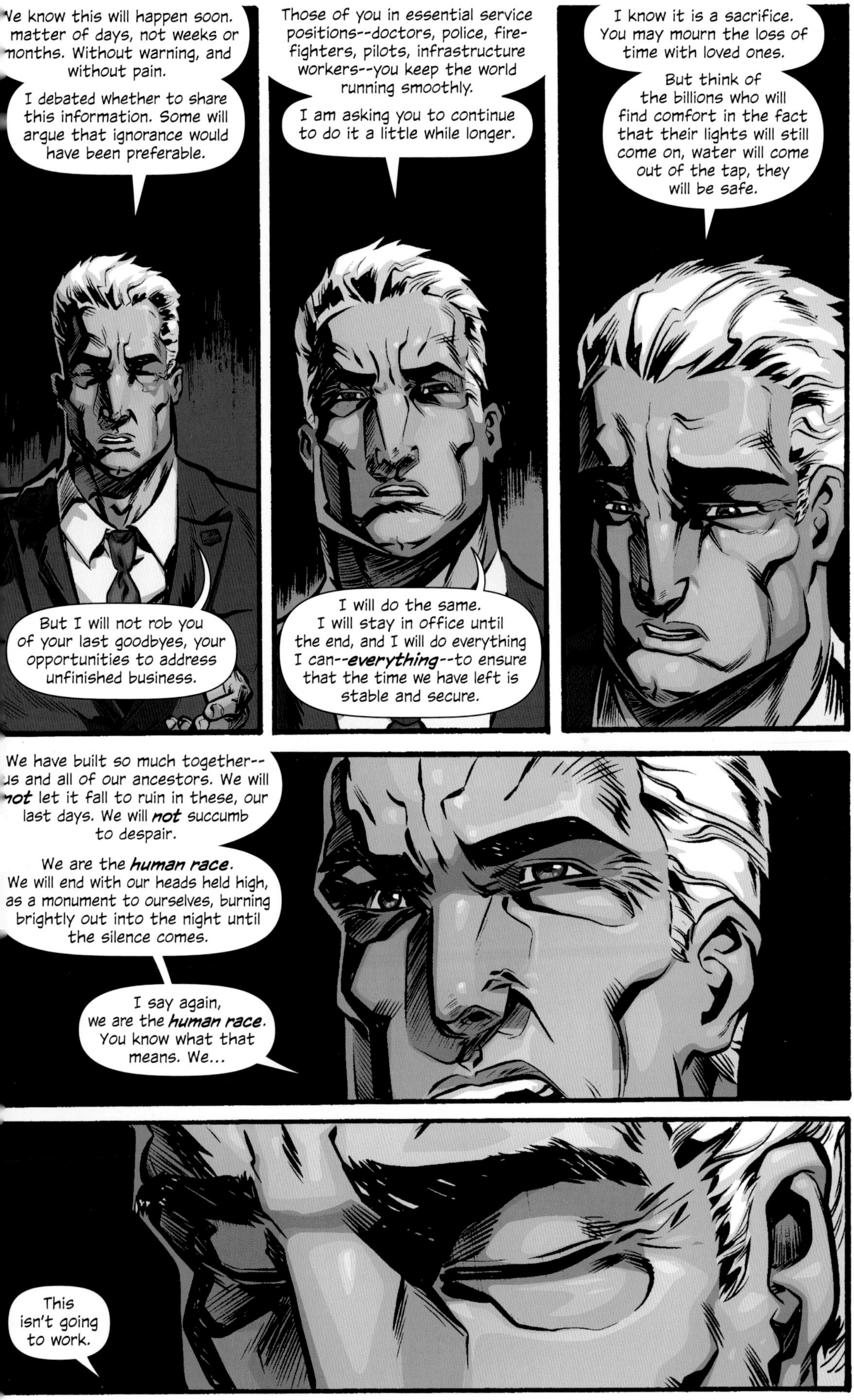
We know this will happen soon. matter of days, not weeks or months. Without warning, and without pain.
I debated whether to share this information. Some will argue that ignorance would have been preferable.
But I will not rob you of your last goodbyes, your opportunities to address unfinished business.
Those of you in essential service positions--doctors, police, fire-fighters, pilots, infrastructure workers--you keep the world running smoothly.
I am asking you to continue to do it a little while longer.
I will do the same. I will stay in office until the end, and I will do everything I can--*everything*--to ensure that the time we have left is stable and secure.
I know it is a sacrifice. You may mourn the loss of time with loved ones.
But think of the billions who will find comfort in the fact that their lights will still come on, water will come out of the tap, they will be safe.
We have built so much together--us and all of our ancestors. We will *not* let it fall to ruin in these, our last days. We will *not* succumb to despair.
We are the *human race*. We will end with our heads held high, as a monument to ourselves, burning brightly out into the night until the silence comes.
I say again, we are the *human race*. You know what that means. We...
This isn't going to work.

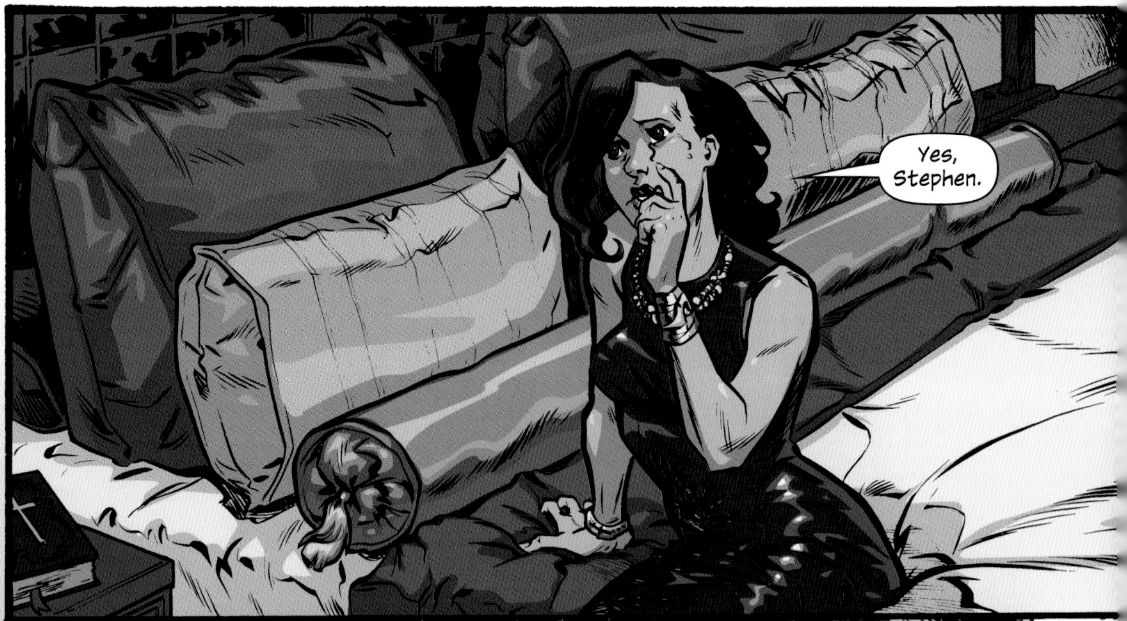
Yes, Stephen.

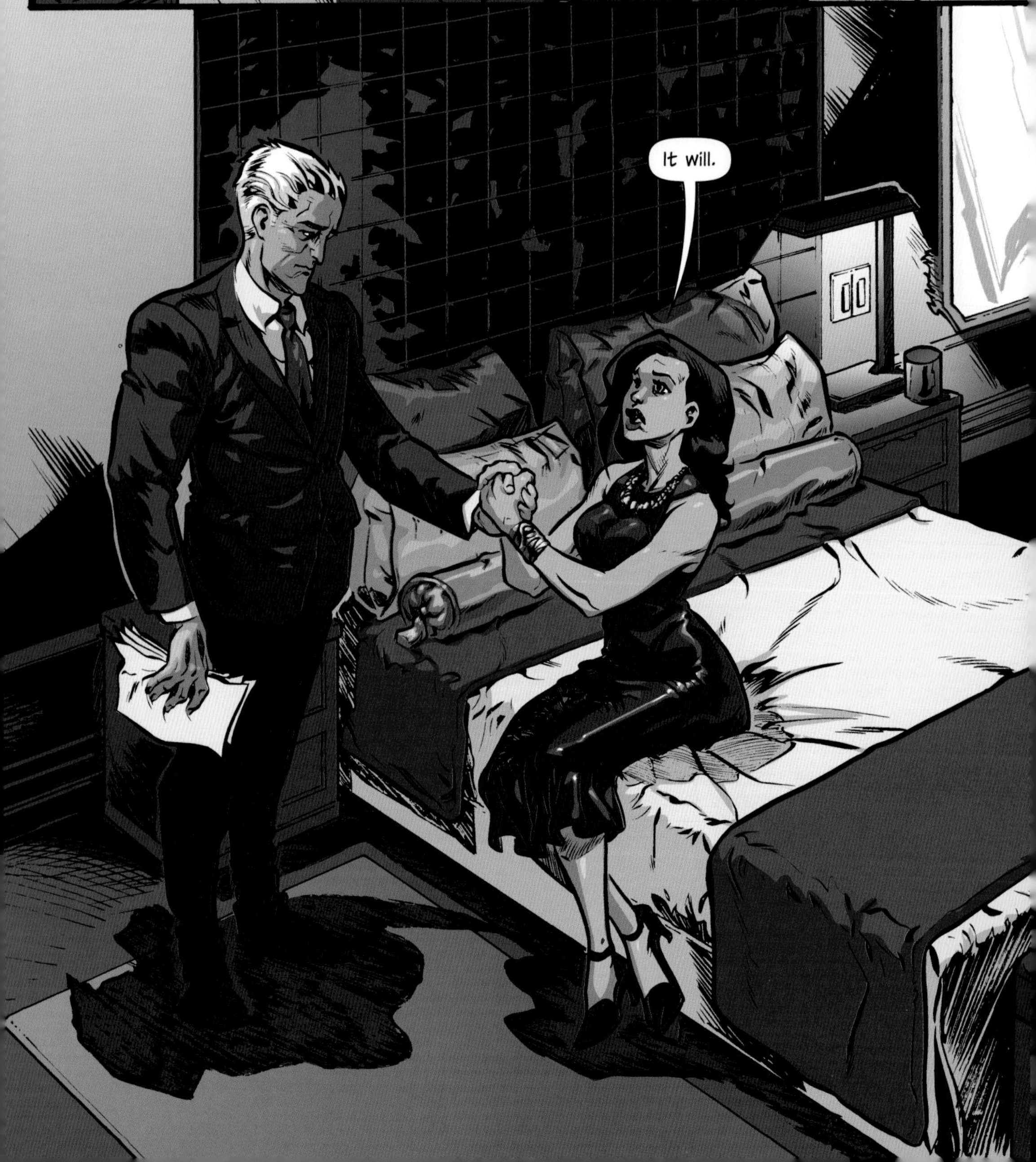
It will.

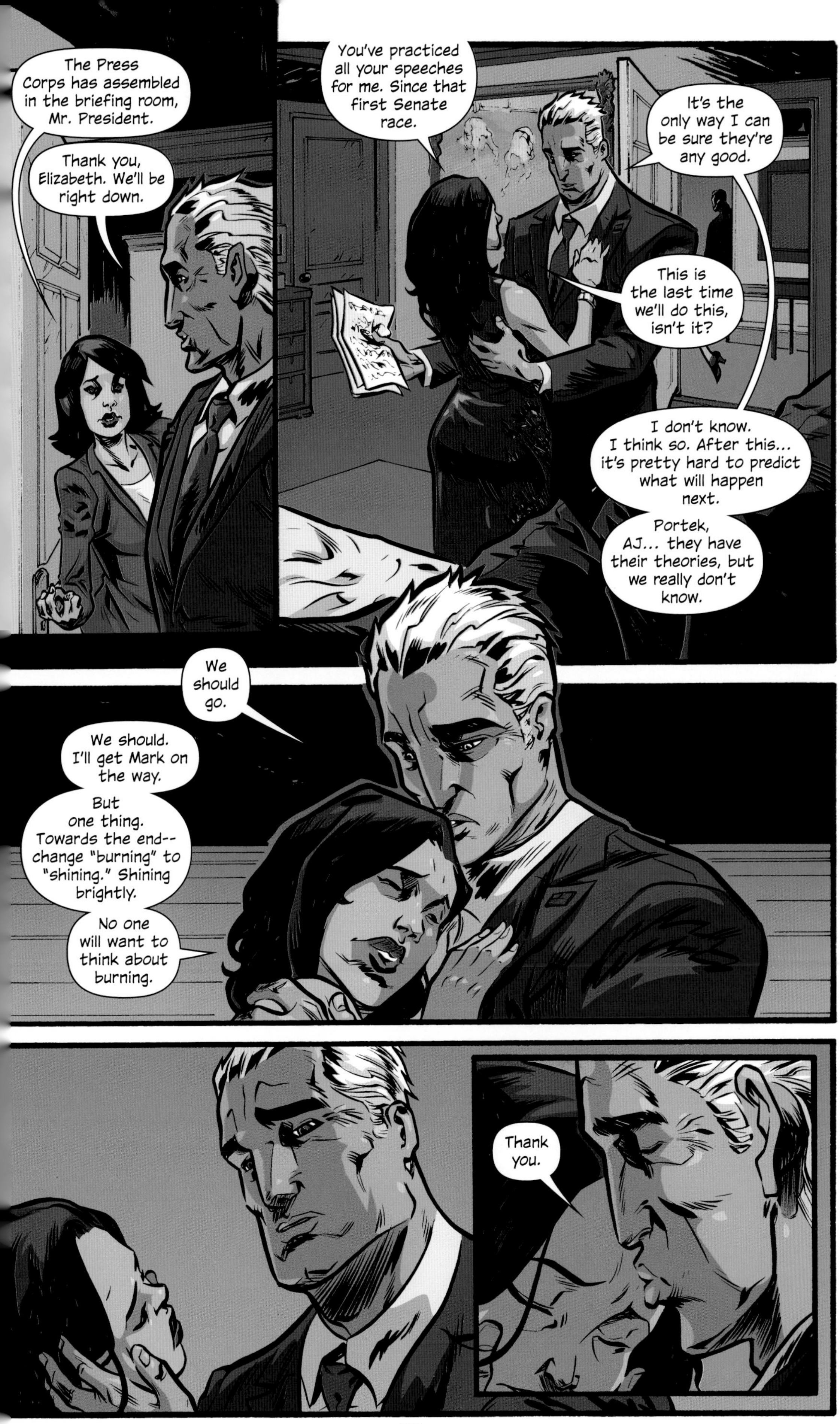
The Press Corps has assembled in the briefing room, Mr. President.
Thank you, Elizabeth. We'll be right down.
You've practiced all your speeches for me. Since that first Senate race.
It's the only way I can be sure they're any good.
This is the last time we'll do this, isn't it?
I don't know. I think so. After this... it's pretty hard to predict what will happen next.
Portek, AJ... they have their theories, but we really don't know.
We should go.
We should. I'll get Mark on the way.
But one thing. Towards the end--change "burning" to "shining." Shining brightly.
No one will want to think about burning.
Thank you.

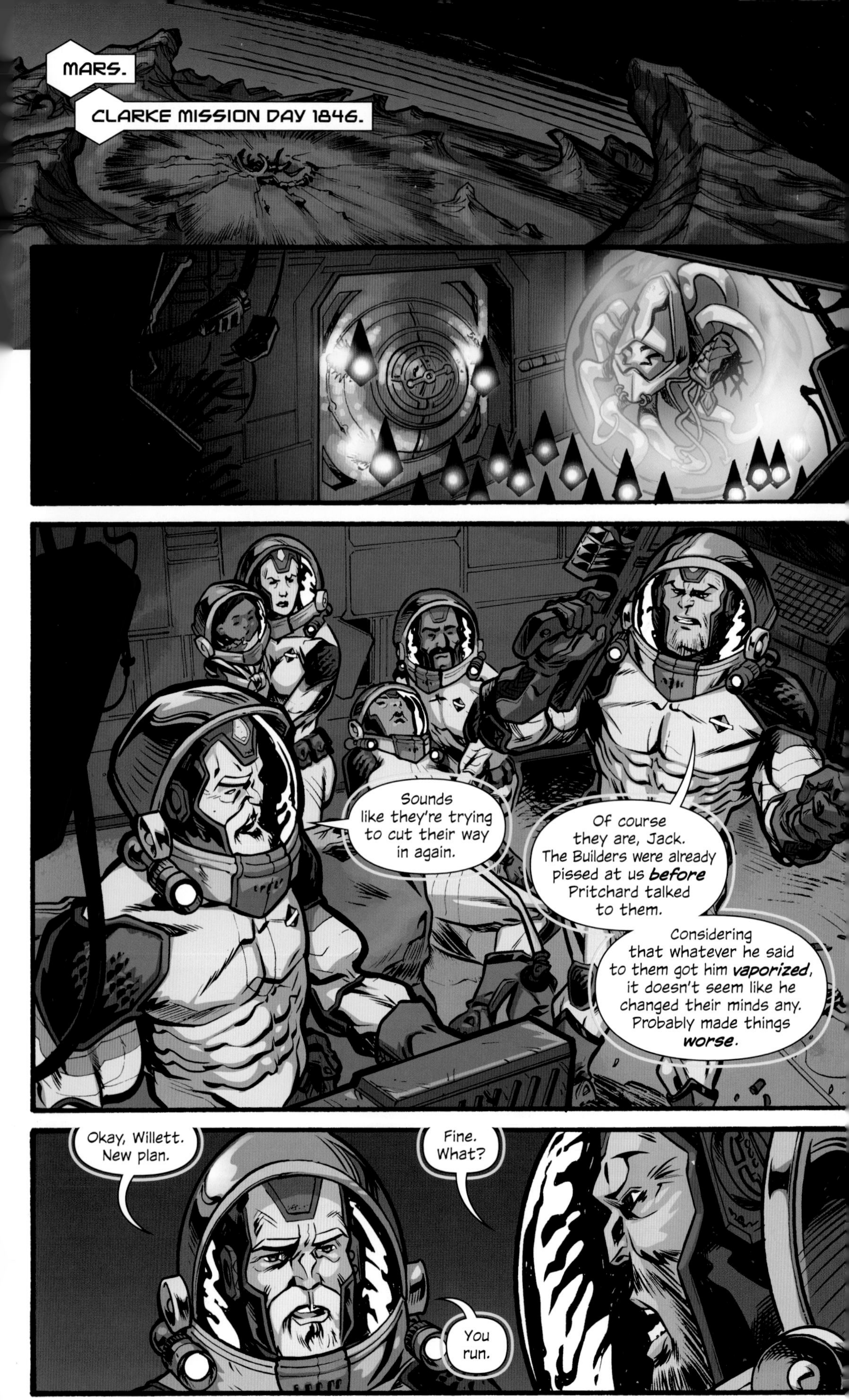
MARS.
CLARKE MISSION DAY 1846.
Sounds like they're trying to cut their way in again.
Of course they are, Jack. The Builders were already pissed at us *before* Pritchard talked to them.
Considering that whatever he said to them got him *vaporized*, it doesn't seem like he changed their minds any. Probably made things *worse*.
Okay, Willett. New plan.
Fine. What?
You run.

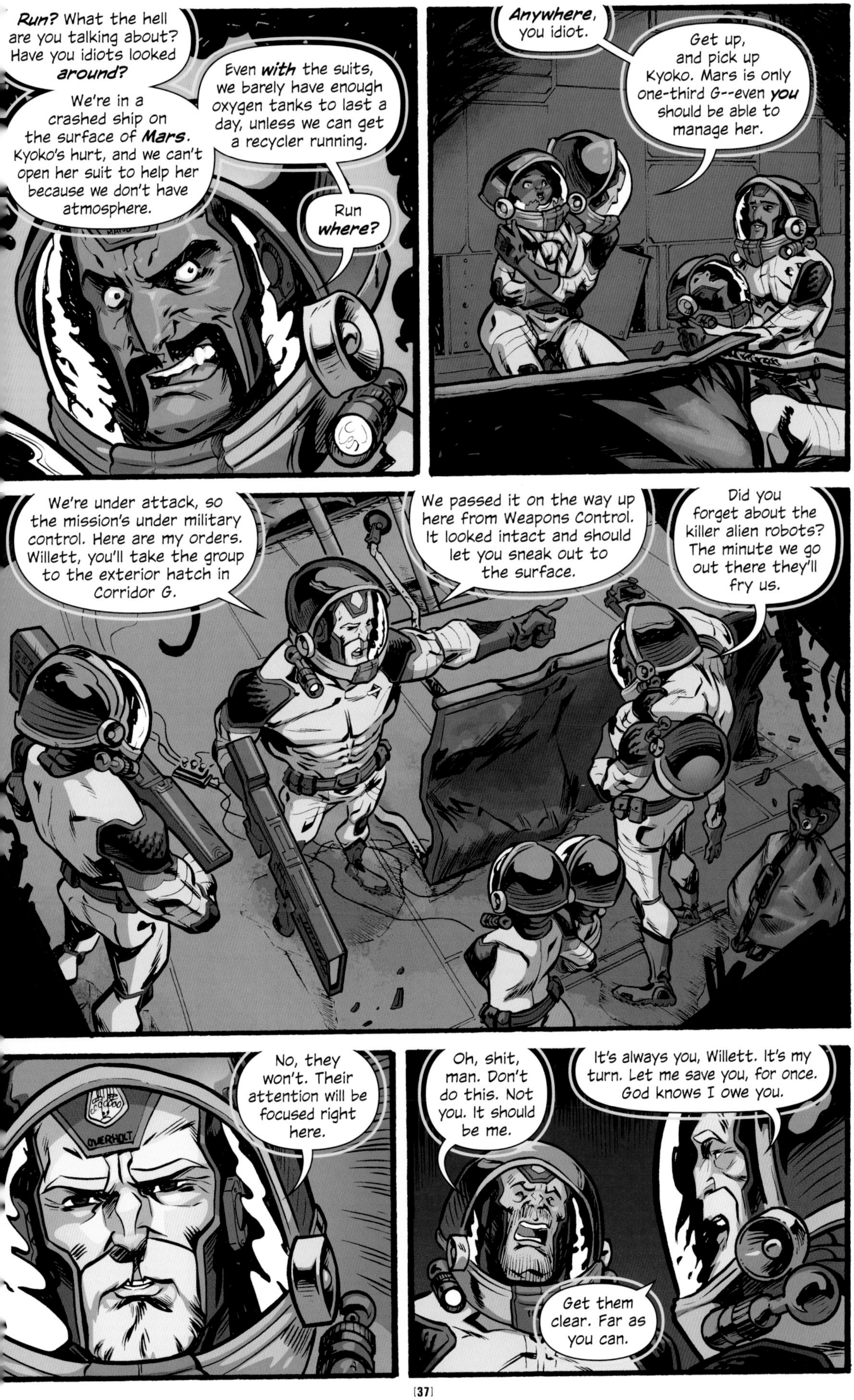

Run? What the hell are you talking about? Have you idiots looked around?
We're in a crashed ship on the surface of Mars. Kyoko's hurt, and we can't open her suit to help her because we don't have atmosphere.
Even with the suits, we barely have enough oxygen tanks to last a day, unless we can get a recycler running.
Run where?
Anywhere, you idiot.
Get up, and pick up Kyoko. Mars is only one-third G--even you should be able to manage her.
We're under attack, so the mission's under military control. Here are my orders. Willett, you'll take the group to the exterior hatch in Corridor G.
We passed it on the way up here from Weapons Control. It looked intact and should let you sneak out to the surface.
Did you forget about the killer alien robots? The minute we go out there they'll fry us.
No, they won't. Their attention will be focused right here.
Oh, shit, man. Don't do this. Not you. It should be me.
It's always you, Willett. It's my turn. Let me save you, for once. God knows I owe you.
Get them clear. Far as you can.

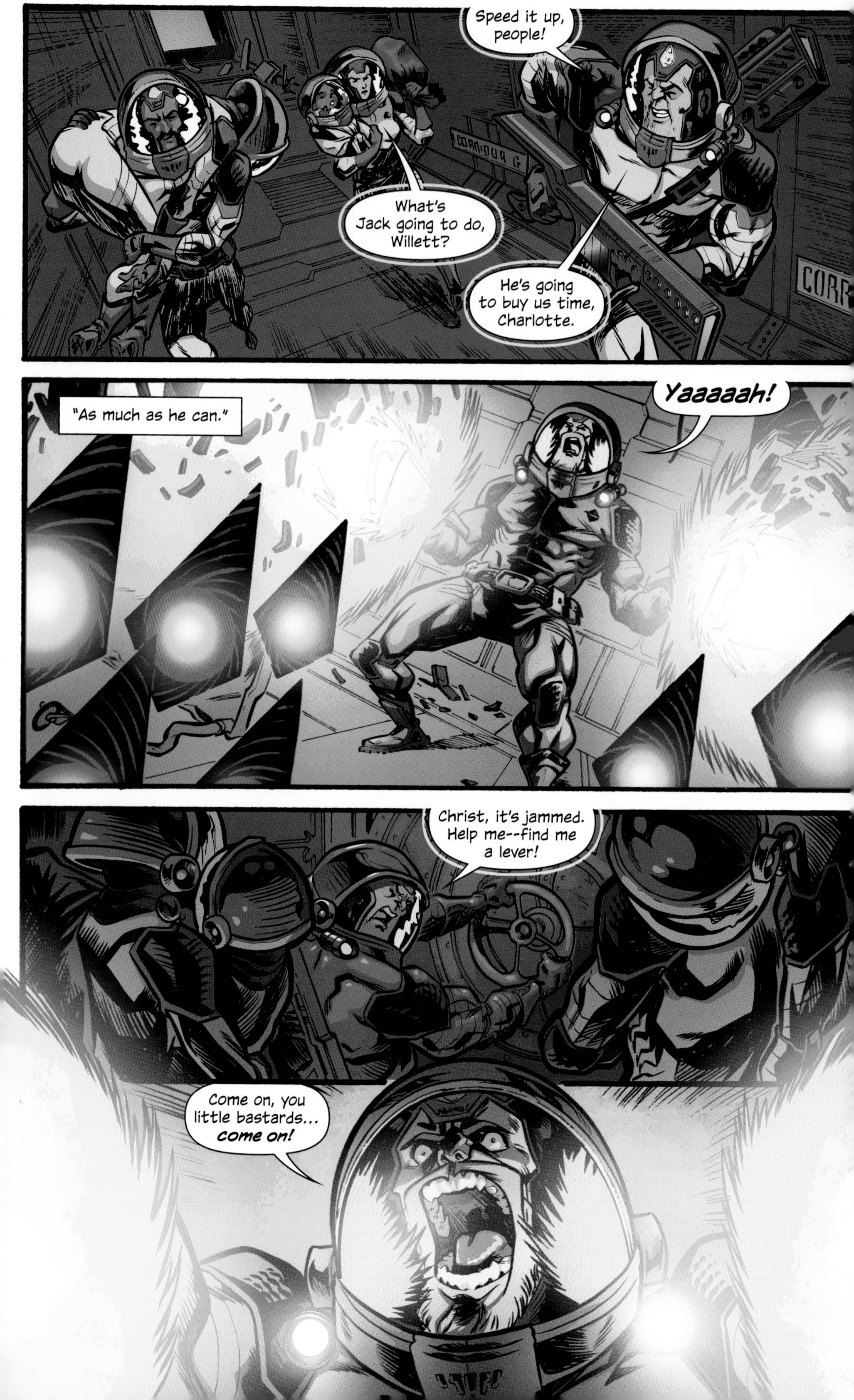
Speed it up, people!
What's Jack going to do, Willett?
He's going to buy us time, Charlotte.
"As much as he can."
Yaaaaah!
Christ, it's jammed. Help me--find me a lever!
Come on, you little bastards... come on!

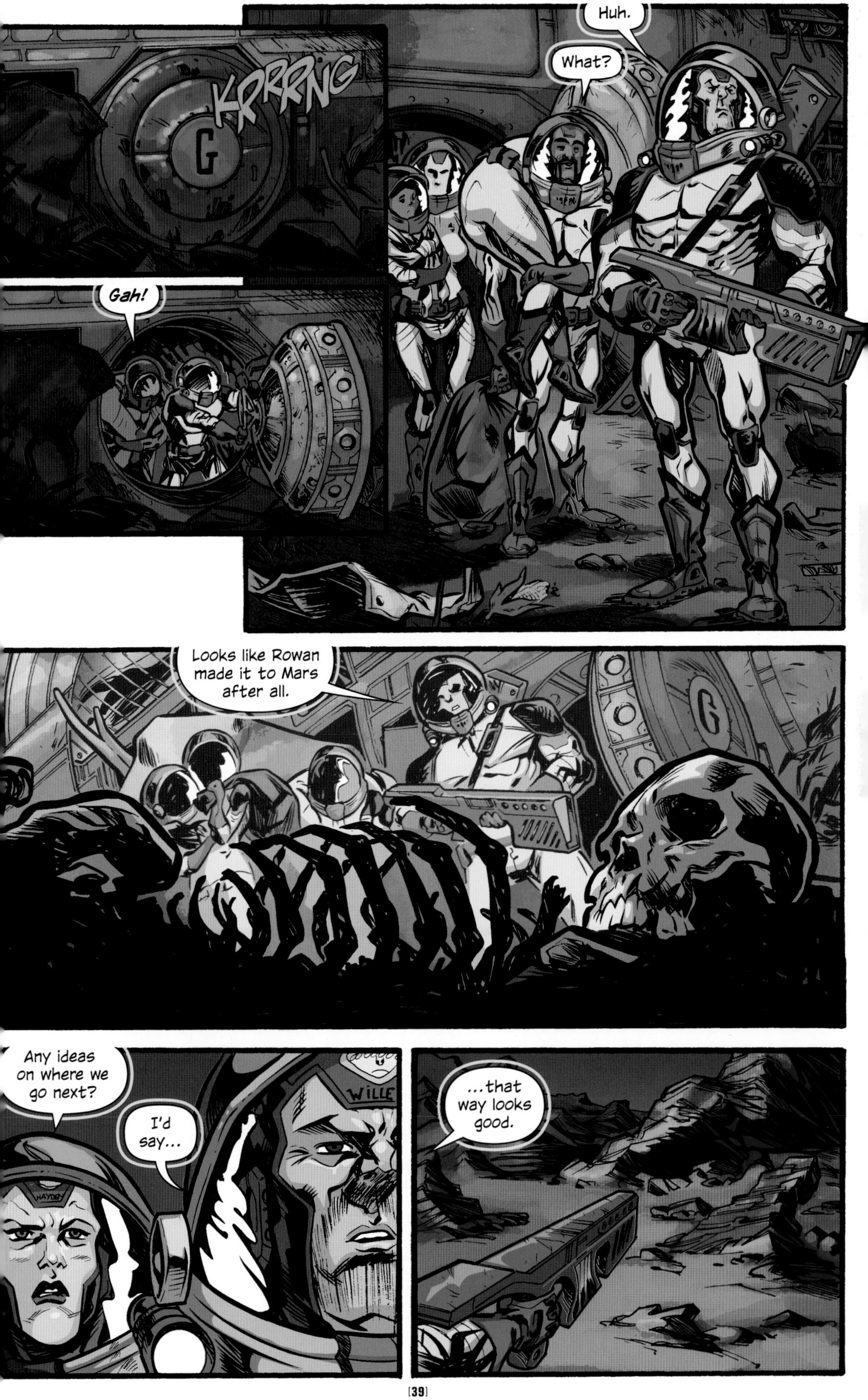
KRRRNG
Gah!
Huh.
What?
Looks like Rowan made it to Mars after all.
Any ideas on where we go next?
I'd say...
...that way looks good.

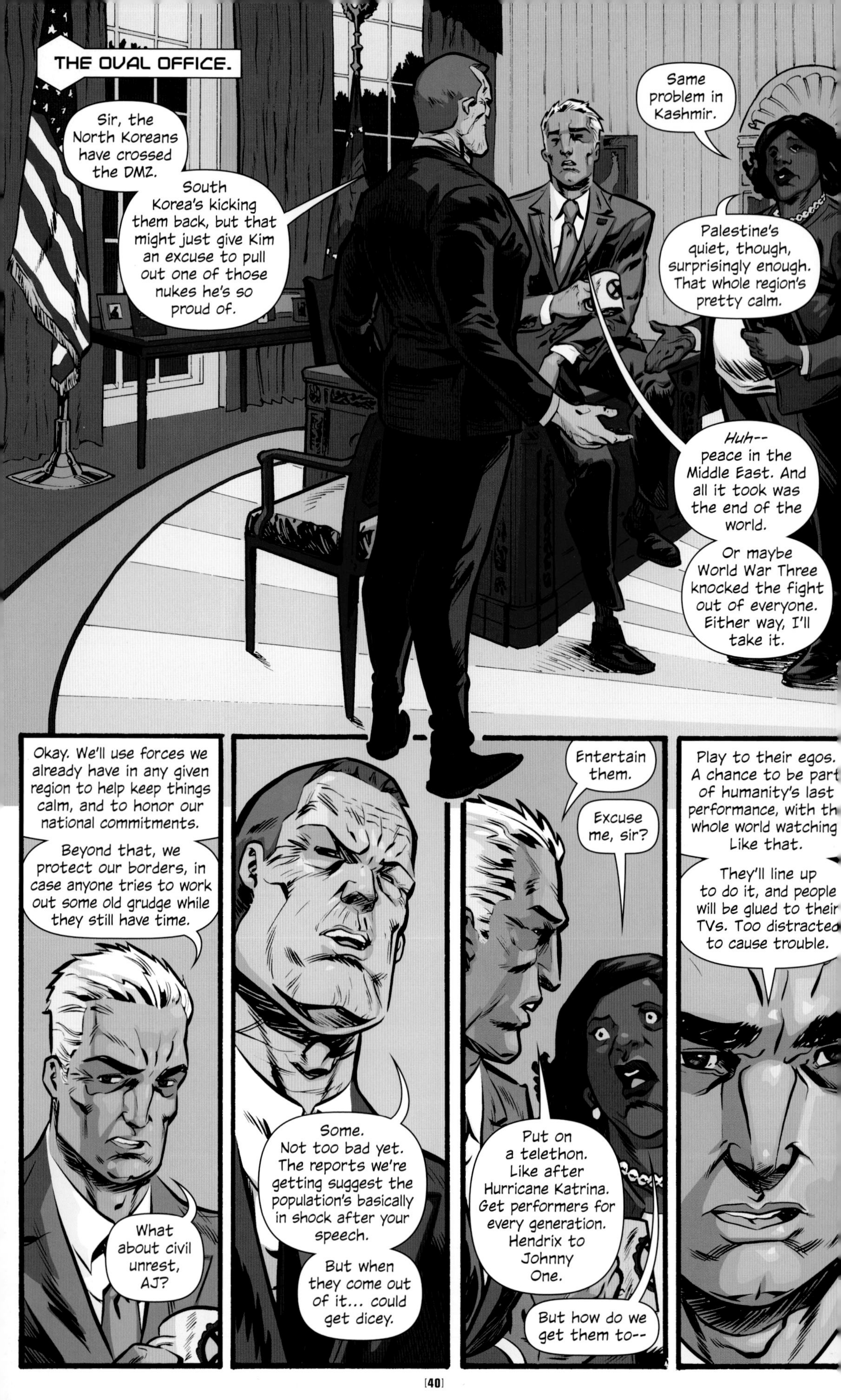
THE OVAL OFFICE.
Sir, the North Koreans have crossed the DMZ.
South Korea's kicking them back, but that might just give Kim an excuse to pull out one of those nukes he's so proud of.
Same problem in Kashmir.
Palestine's quiet, though, surprisingly enough. That whole region's pretty calm.
Huh-- peace in the Middle East. And all it took was the end of the world.
Or maybe World War Three knocked the fight out of everyone. Either way, I'll take it.
Okay. We'll use forces we already have in any given region to help keep things calm, and to honor our national commitments.
Beyond that, we protect our borders, in case anyone tries to work out some old grudge while they still have time.
What about civil unrest, AJ?
Some. Not too bad yet. The reports we're getting suggest the population's basically in shock after your speech.
But when they come out of it... could get dicey.
Entertain them.
Excuse me, sir?
Put on a telethon. Like after Hurricane Katrina. Get performers for every generation. Hendrix to Johnny One.
But how do we get them to--
Play to their egos. A chance to be part of humanity's last performance, with the whole world watching. Like that.
They'll line up to do it, and people will be glued to their TVs. Too distracted to cause trouble.

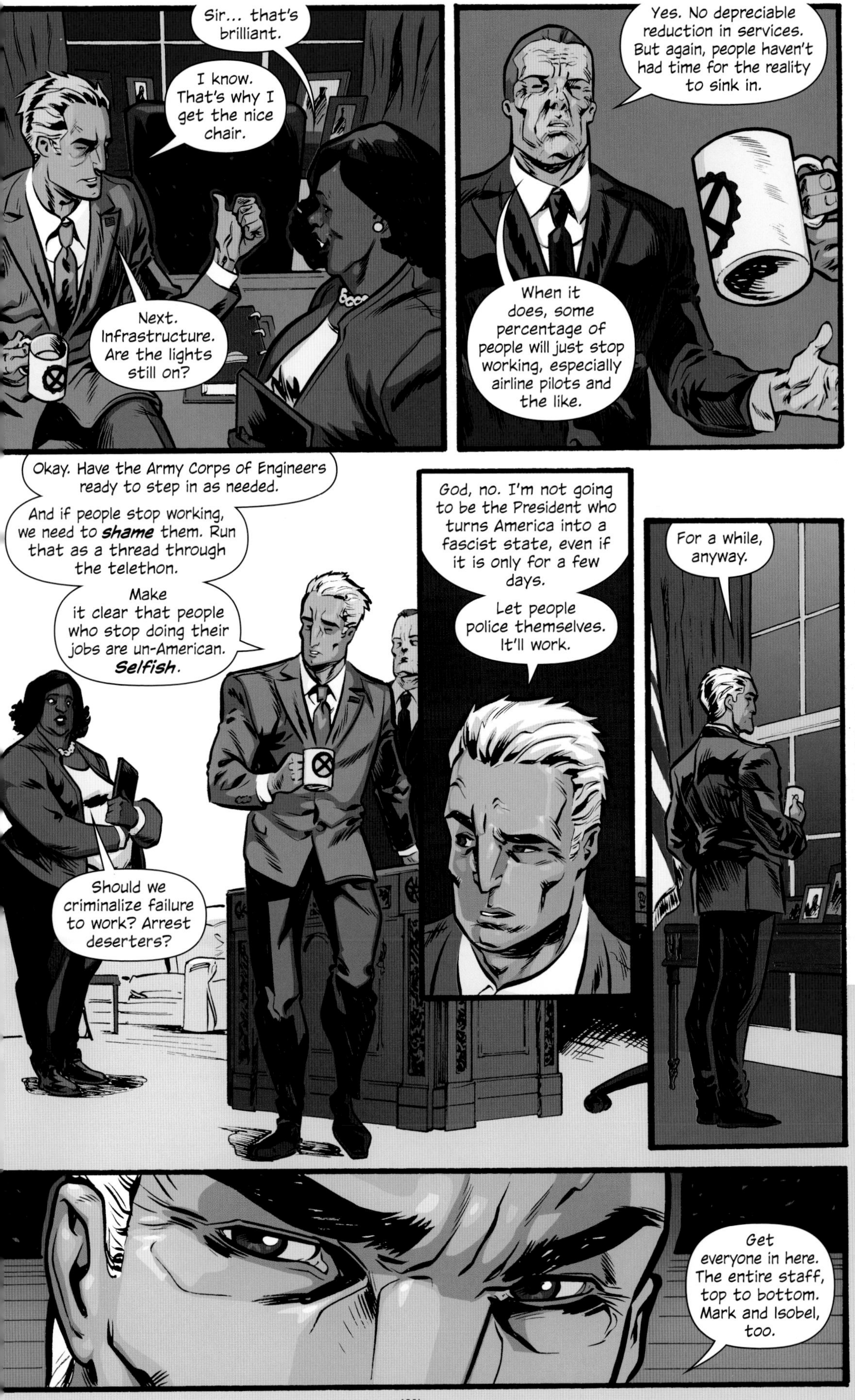
Sir... that's brilliant.
I know. That's why I get the nice chair.
Next. Infrastructure. Are the lights still on?
Yes. No depreciable reduction in services. But again, people haven't had time for the reality to sink in.
When it does, some percentage of people will just stop working, especially airline pilots and the like.
Okay. Have the Army Corps of Engineers ready to step in as needed.
And if people stop working, we need to shame them. Run that as a thread through the telethon.
Make it clear that people who stop doing their jobs are un-American. Selfish.
Should we criminalize failure to work? Arrest deserters?
God, no. I'm not going to be the President who turns America into a fascist state, even if it is only for a few days.
Let people police themselves. It'll work.
For a while, anyway.
Get everyone in here. The entire staff, top to bottom. Mark and Isobel, too.

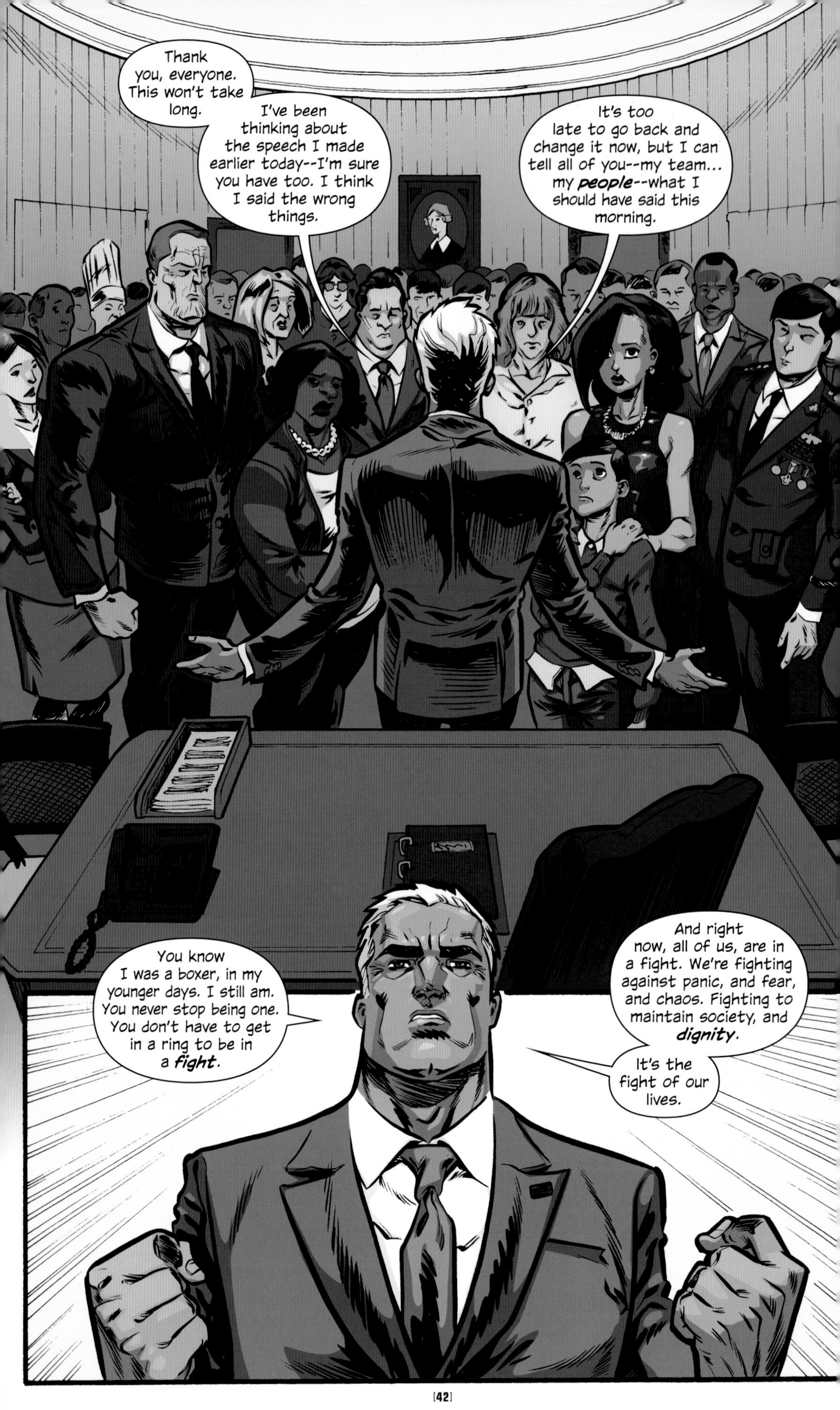

Thank you, everyone. This won't take long.
I've been thinking about the speech I made earlier today--I'm sure you have too. I think I said the wrong things.
It's too late to go back and change it now, but I can tell all of you--my team... my *people*--what I should have said this morning.
You know I was a boxer, in my younger days. I still am. You never stop being one. You don't have to get in a ring to be in a *fight*.
And right now, all of us, are in a fight. We're fighting against panic, and fear, and chaos. Fighting to maintain society, and *dignity*.
It's the fight of our lives.

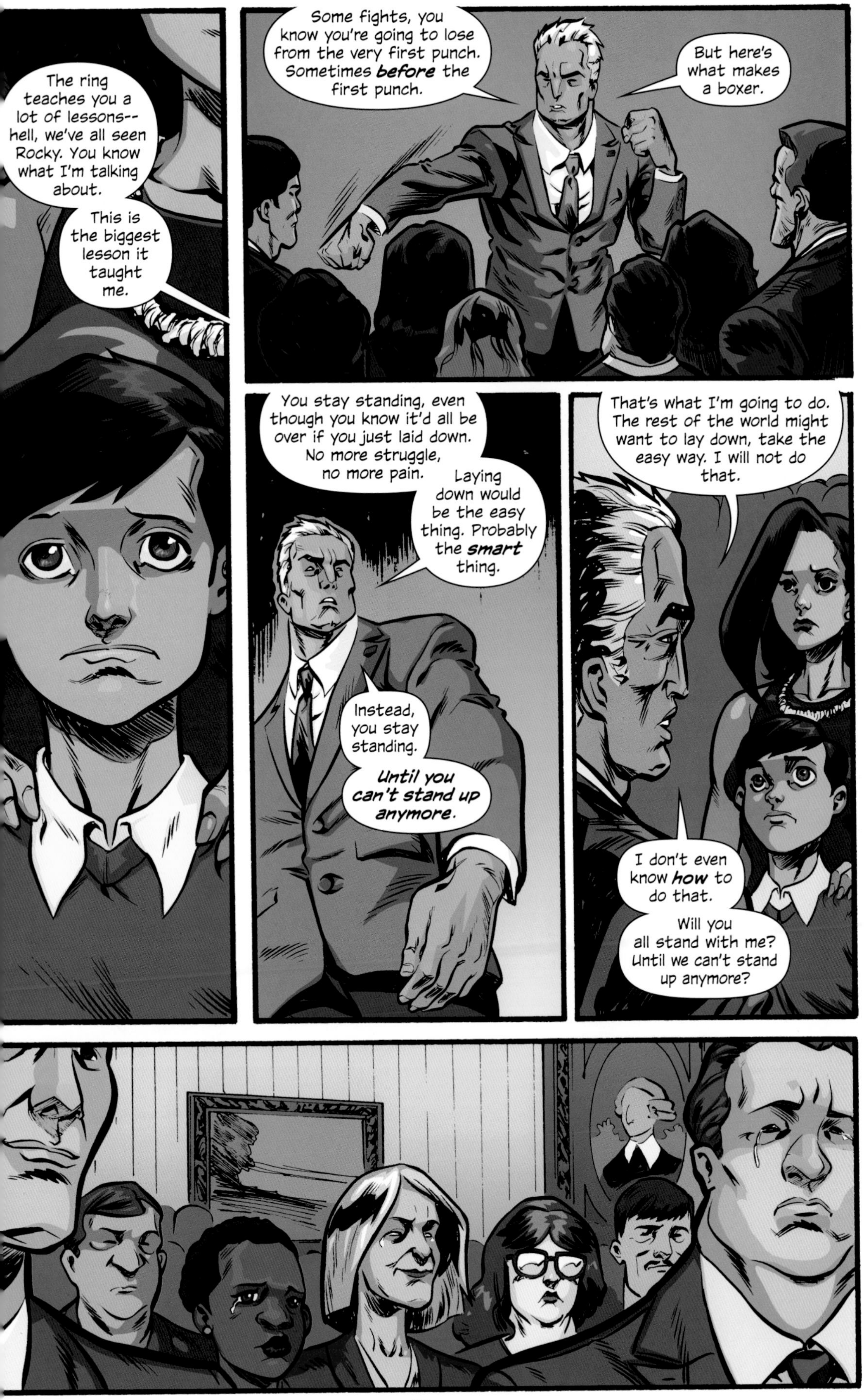

The ring teaches you a lot of lessons--hell, we've all seen Rocky. You know what I'm talking about.
This is the biggest lesson it taught me.
Some fights, you know you're going to lose from the very first punch. Sometimes *before* the first punch.
But here's what makes a boxer.
You stay standing, even though you know it'd all be over if you just laid down. No more struggle, no more pain.
Laying down would be the easy thing. Probably the *smart* thing.
Instead, you stay standing.
Until you can't stand up anymore.
That's what I'm going to do. The rest of the world might want to lay down, take the easy way. I will not do that.
I don't even know *how* to do that.
Will you all stand with me? Until we can't stand up anymore?

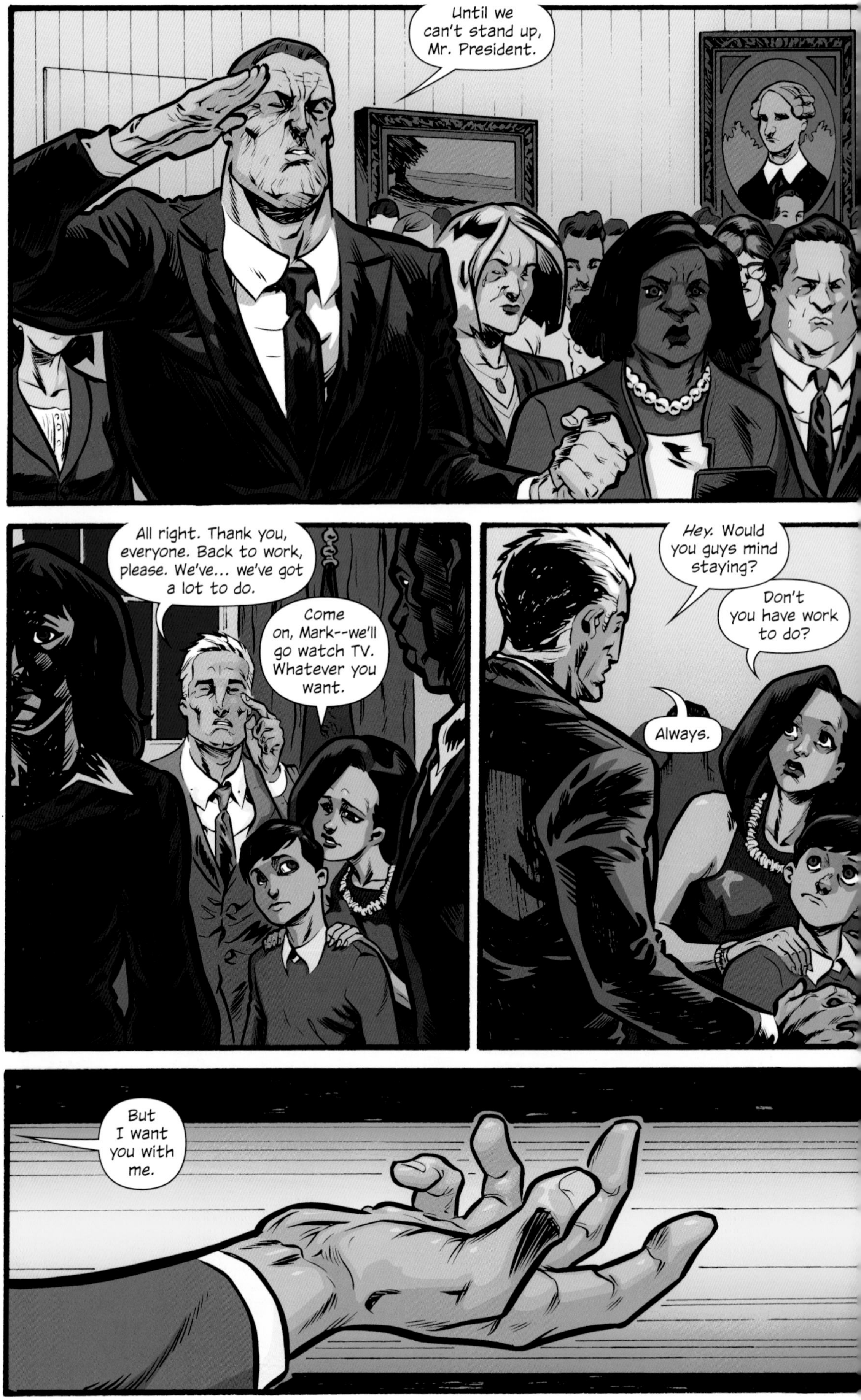
Until we can't stand up, Mr. President.
All right. Thank you, everyone. Back to work, please. We've... we've got a lot to do.
Come on, Mark--we'll go watch TV. Whatever you want.
Hey. Would you guys mind staying?
Don't you have work to do?
Always.
But I want you with me.

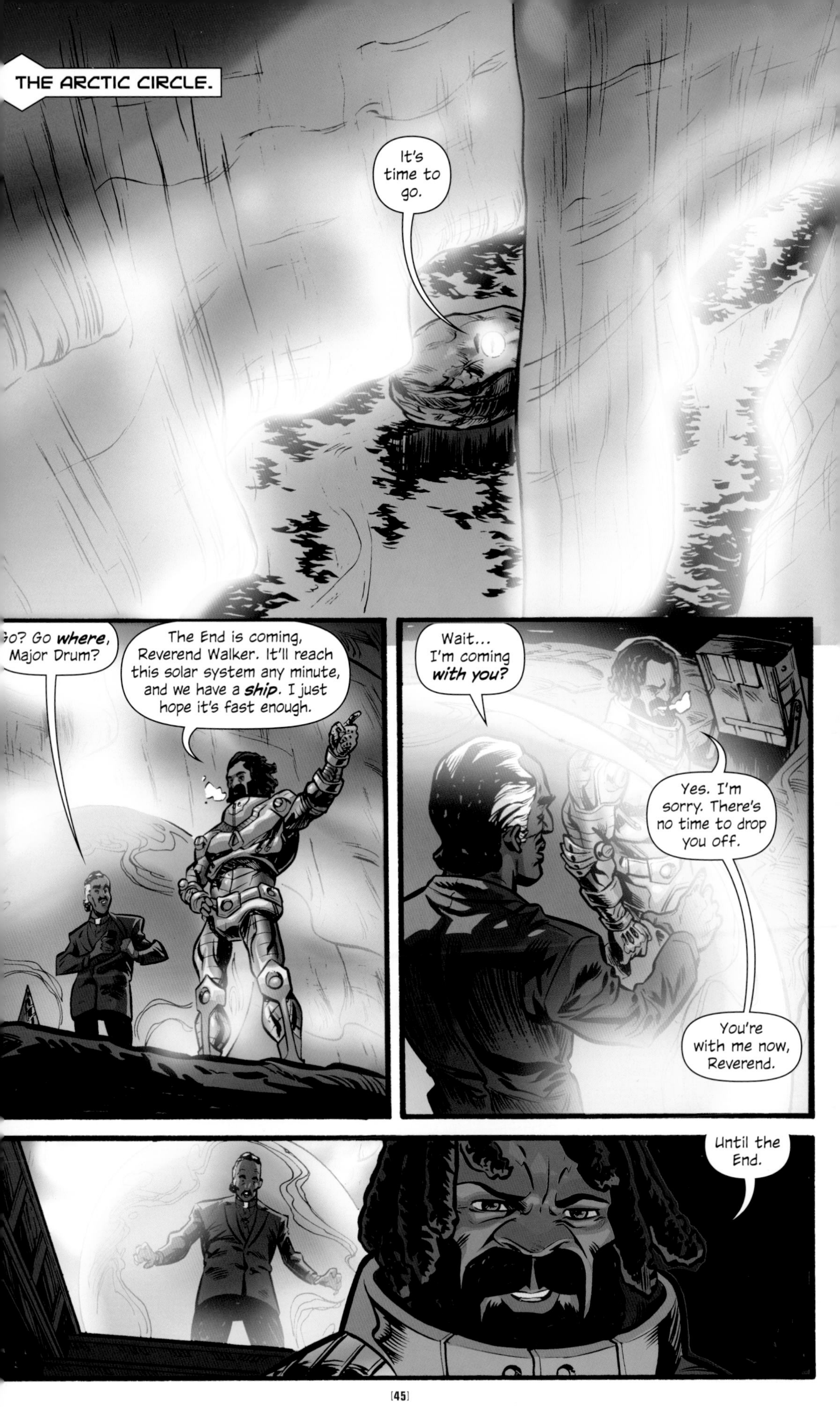

THE ARCTIC CIRCLE.
It's time to go.
Go? Go *where*, Major Drum?
The End is coming, Reverend Walker. It'll reach this solar system any minute, and we have a *ship*. I just hope it's fast enough.
Wait... I'm coming *with you?*
Yes. I'm sorry. There's no time to drop you off.
You're with me now, Reverend.
Until the End.

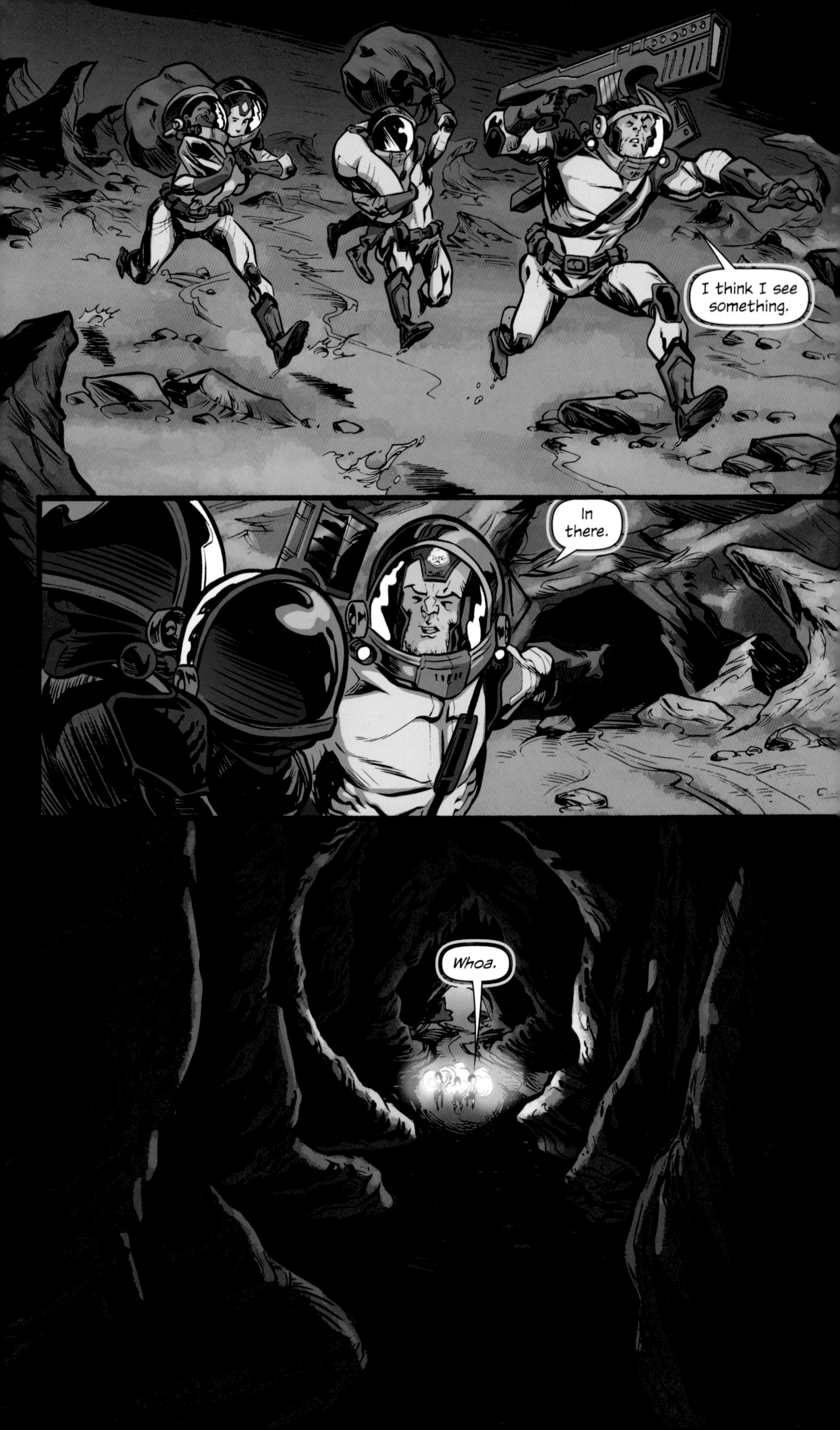
I think I see something.
In there.
Whoa.

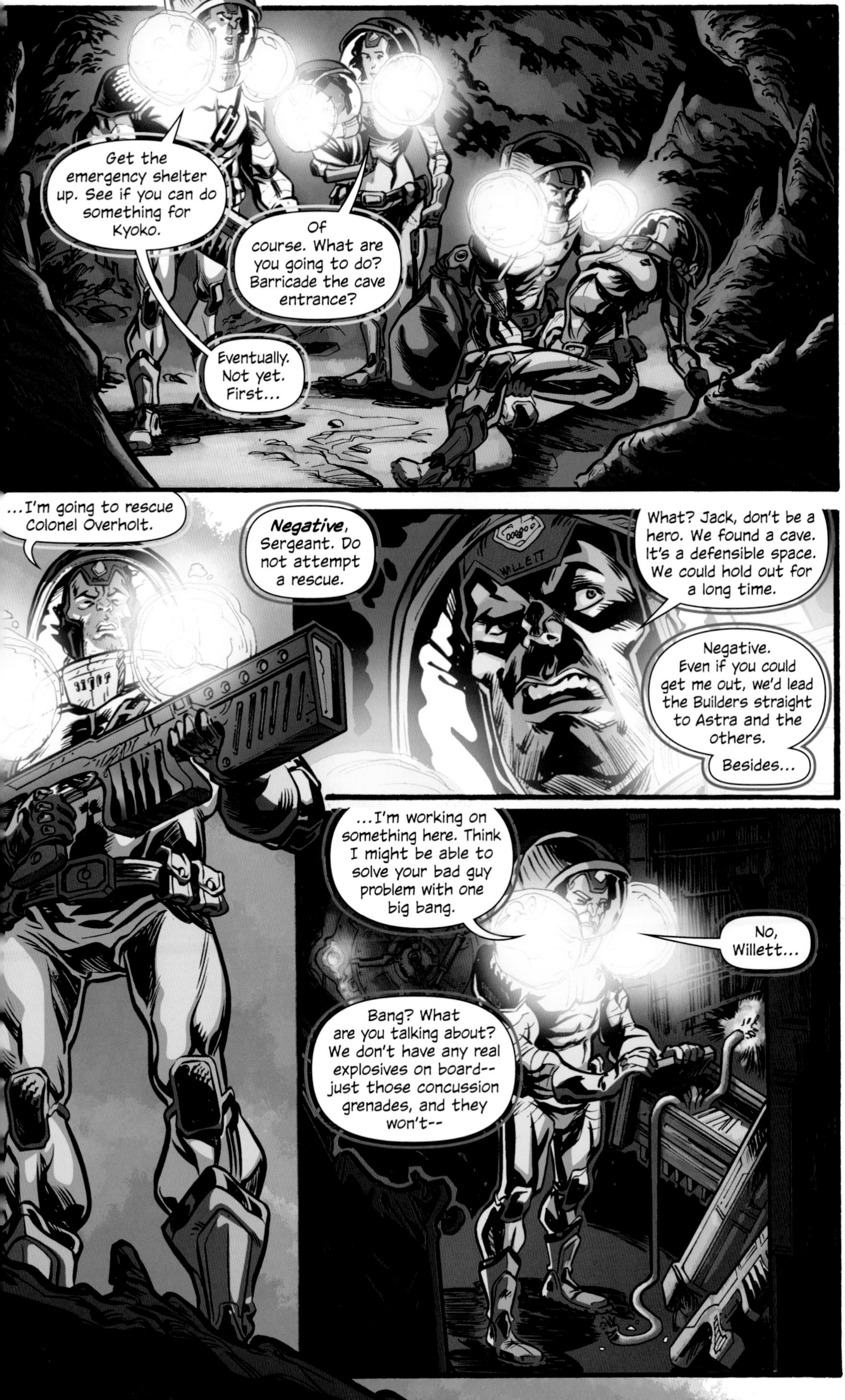
Get the emergency shelter up. See if you can do something for Kyoko.
Of course. What are you going to do? Barricade the cave entrance?
Eventually. Not yet. First...
...I'm going to rescue Colonel Overholt.
Negative, Sergeant. Do not attempt a rescue.
What? Jack, don't be a hero. We found a cave. It's a defensible space. We could hold out for a long time.
Negative. Even if you could get me out, we'd lead the Builders straight to Astra and the others.
Besides...
...I'm working on something here. Think I might be able to solve your bad guy problem with one big bang.
No, Willett...
Bang? What are you talking about? We don't have any real explosives on board-- just those concussion grenades, and they won't--

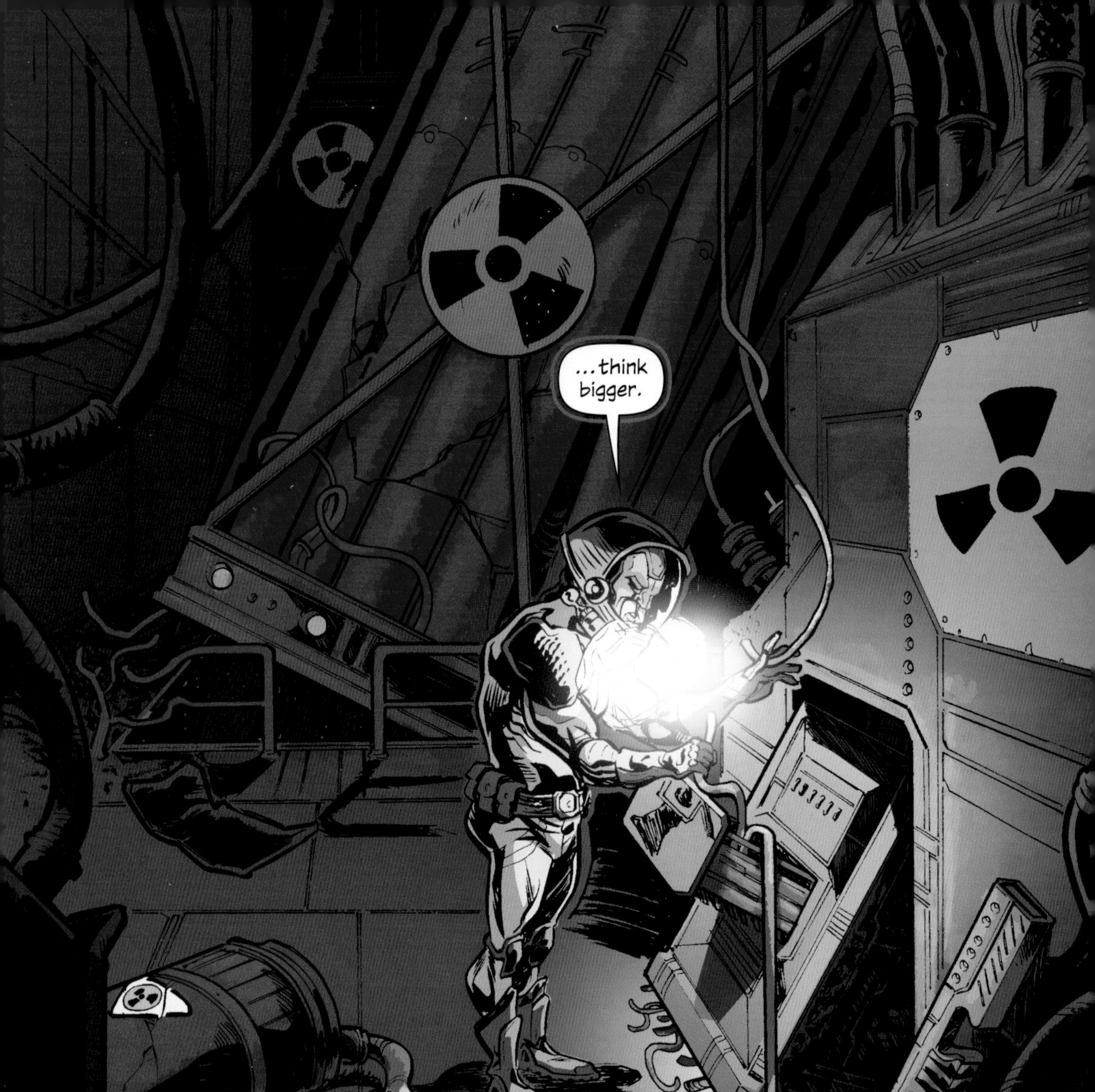
...think bigger.

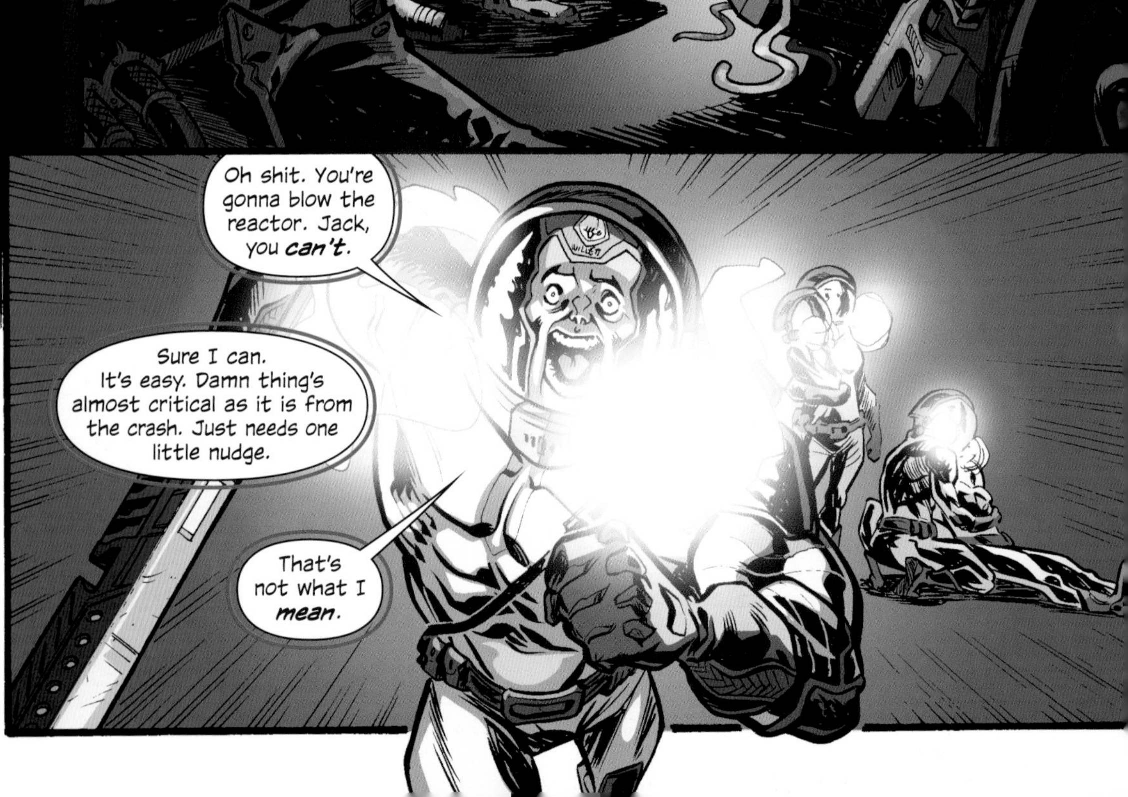
Oh shit. You're gonna blow the reactor. Jack, you *can't*.
Sure I can. It's easy. Damn thing's almost critical as it is from the crash. Just needs one little nudge.
That's not what I *mean*.

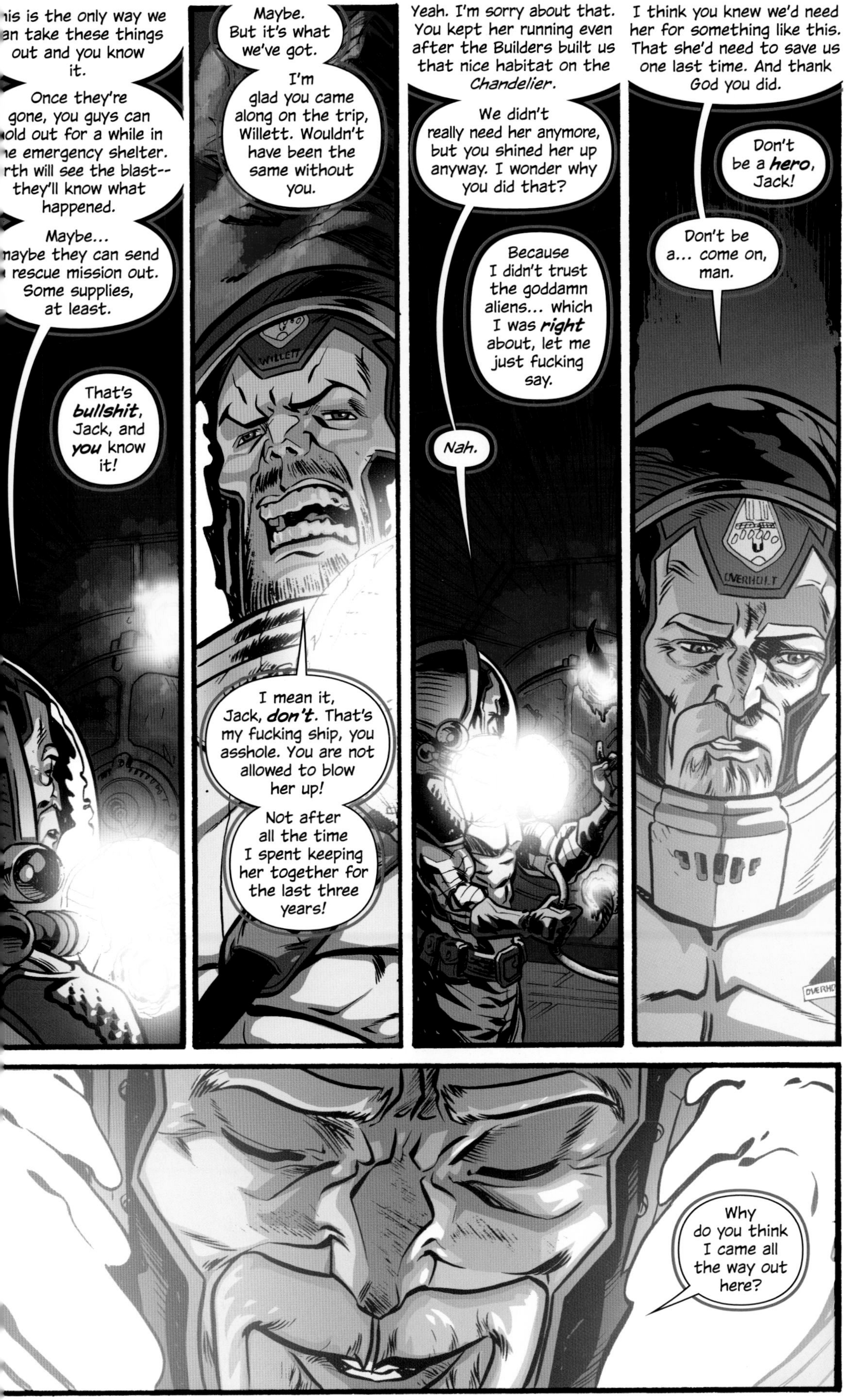

is is the only way we an take these things out and you know it.
Once they're gone, you guys can old out for a while in e emergency shelter. rth will see the blast-- they'll know what happened.
Maybe... naybe they can send rescue mission out. Some supplies, at least.
That's bullshit, Jack, and you know it!
Maybe. But it's what we've got.
I'm glad you came along on the trip, Willett. Wouldn't have been the same without you.
WILLETT
I mean it, Jack, don't. That's my fucking ship, you asshole. You are not allowed to blow her up!
Not after all the time I spent keeping her together for the last three years!
Yeah. I'm sorry about that. You kept her running even after the Builders built us that nice habitat on the Chandelier.
We didn't really need her anymore, but you shined her up anyway. I wonder why you did that?
Because I didn't trust the goddamn aliens... which I was right about, let me just fucking say.
Nah.
I think you knew we'd need her for something like this. That she'd need to save us one last time. And thank God you did.
Don't be a hero, Jack!
Don't be a... come on, man.
OVERHOLT
Why do you think I came all the way out here?

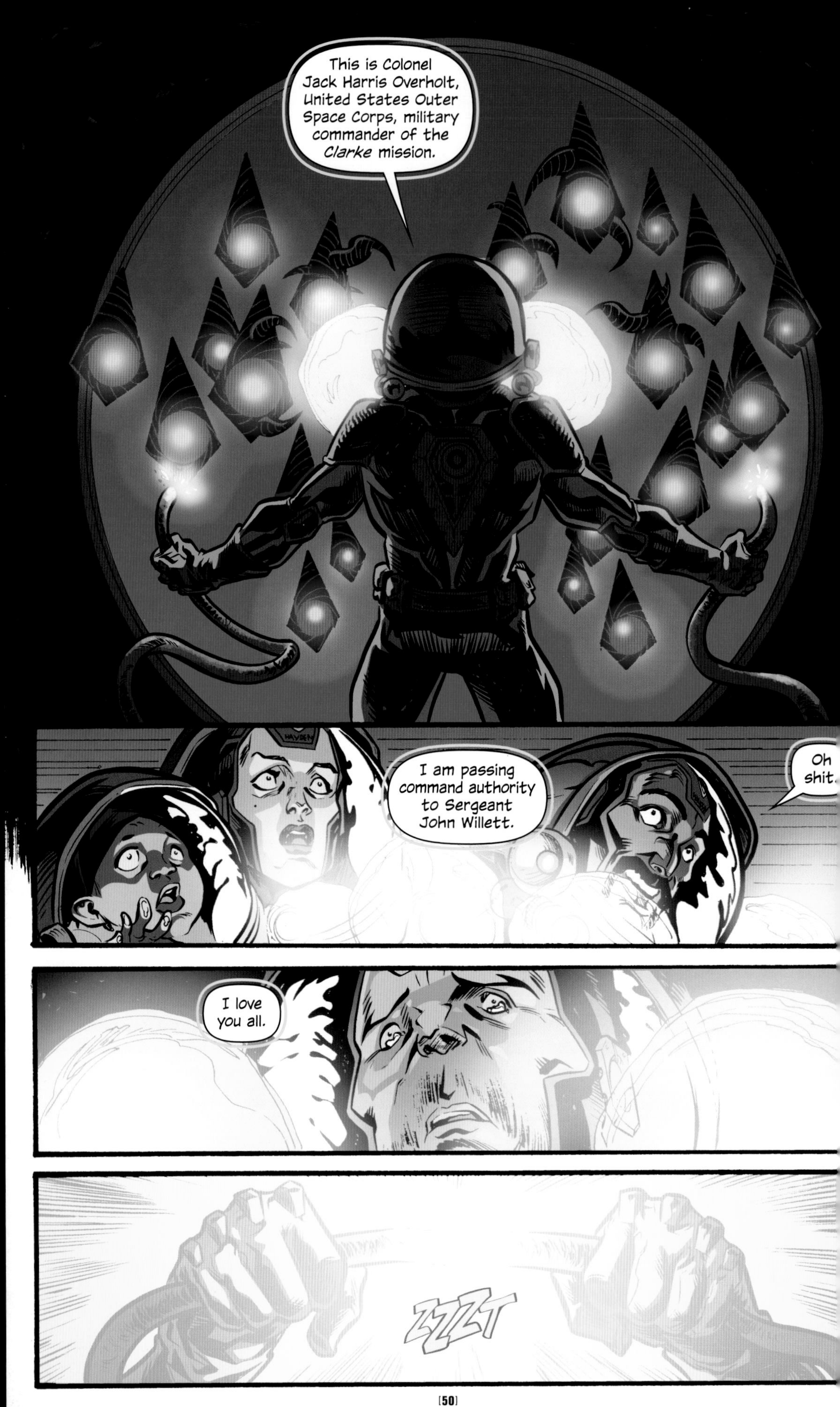
This is Colonel Jack Harris Overholt, United States Outer Space Corps, military commander of the *Clarke* mission.
HAYDEN
I am passing command authority to Sergeant John Willett.
Oh shit.
I love you all.
ZZZT

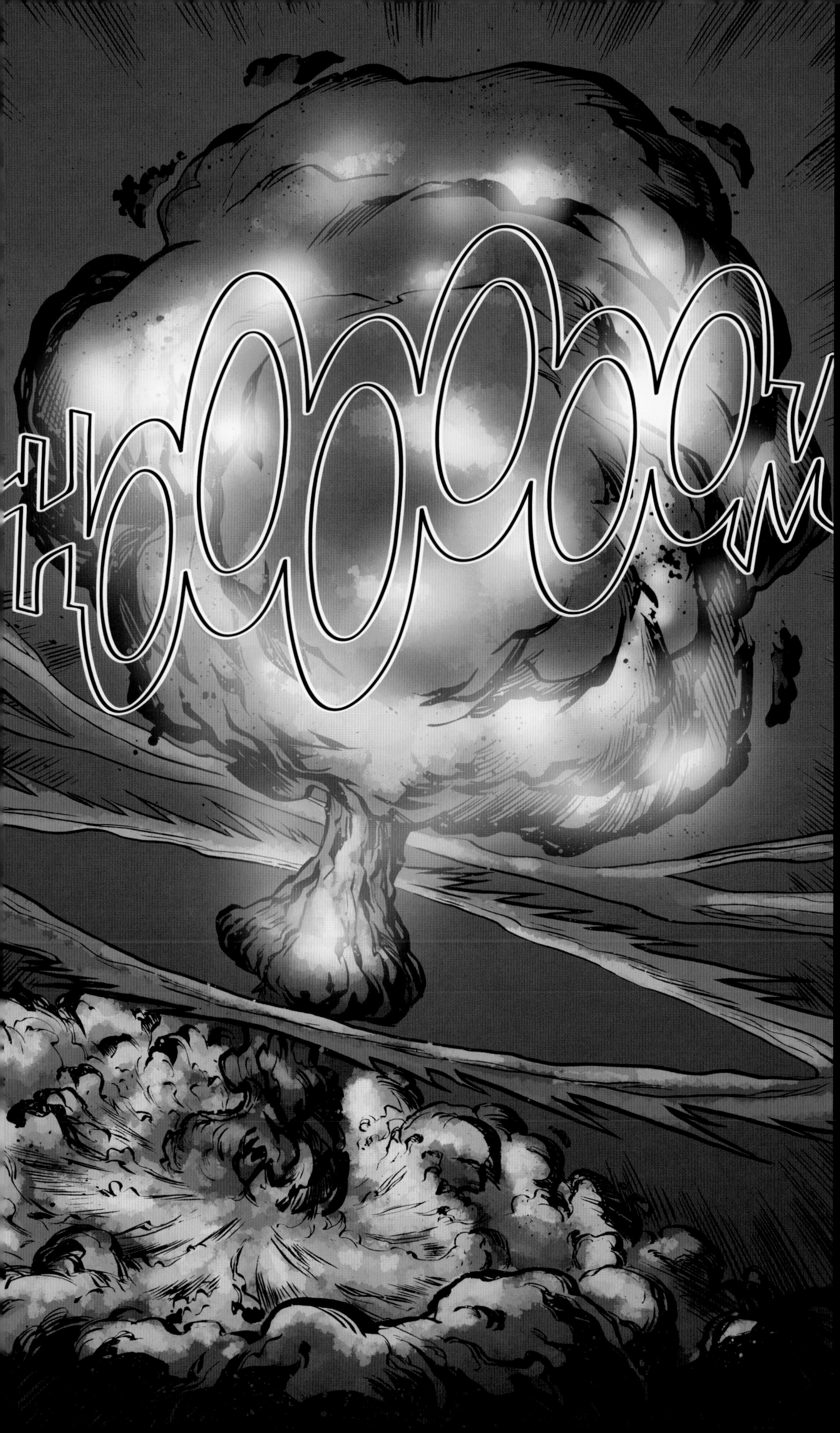

INNER OORT CLOUD.

NINETY ASTRONOMICAL UNITS FROM EARTH.

DWARF PLANET, DESIGNATION "SEDNA".

13,463,808,362.19 KILOMETERS FROM EARTH.

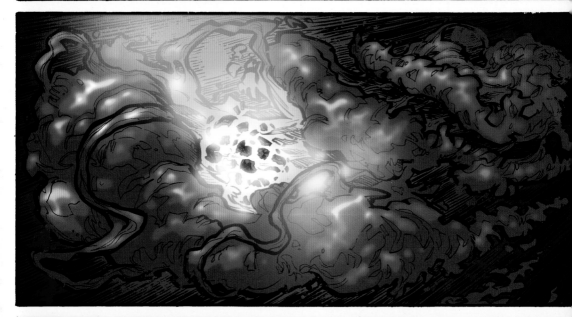

TWELVE LIGHT-HOURS FROM EARTH.

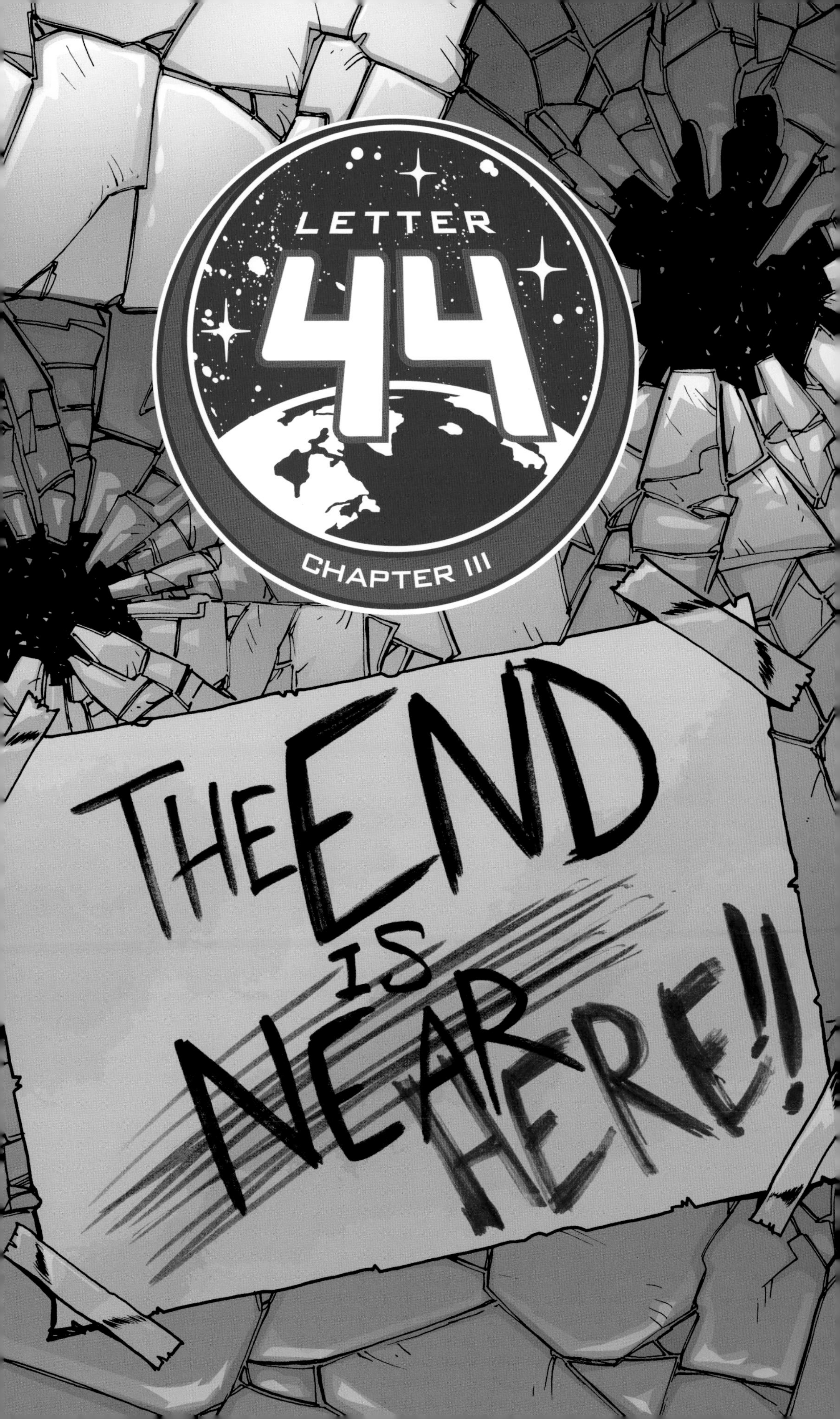
LETTER
44
CHAPTER III
THE END IS NEAR HERE!!

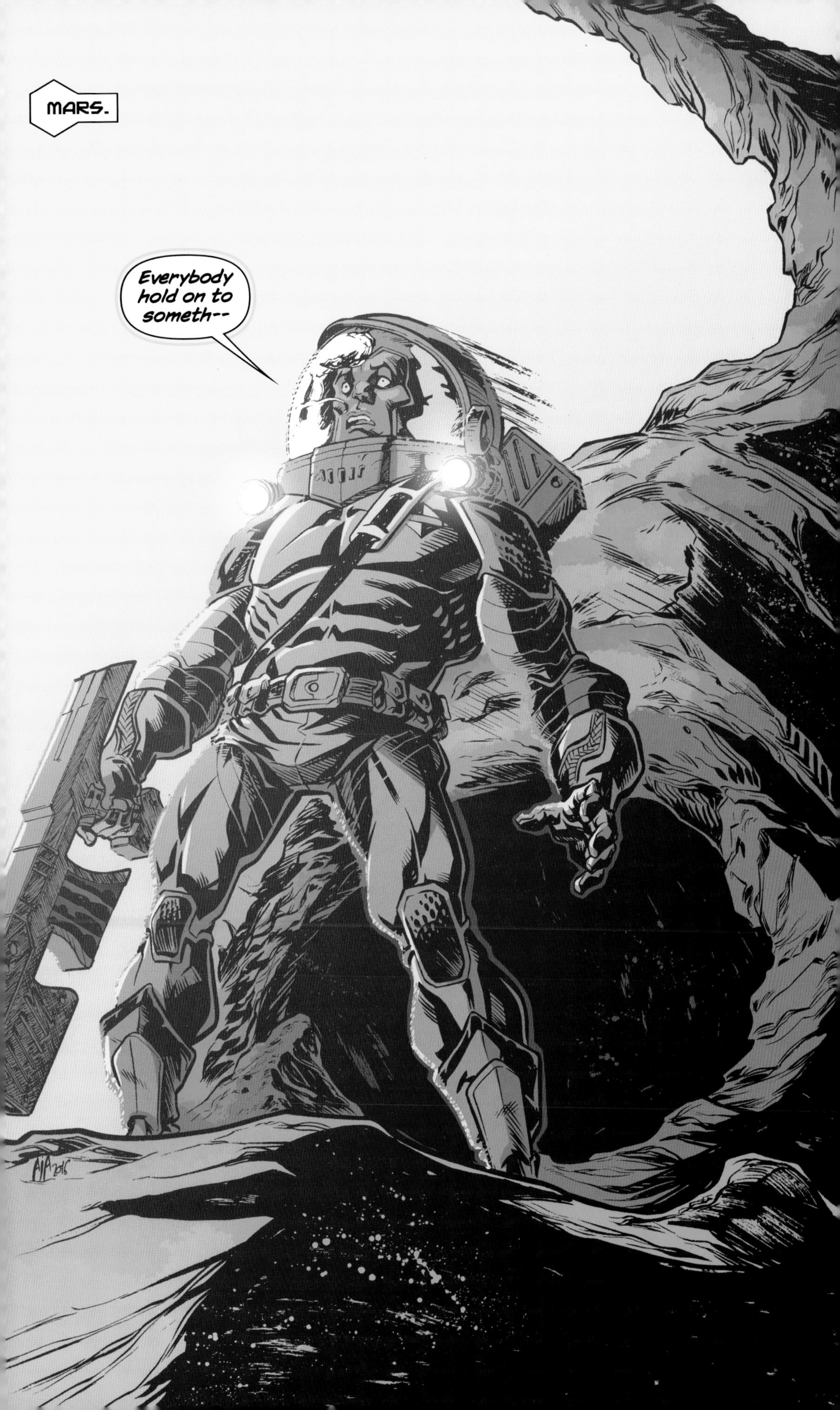
MARS.
Everybody hold on to someth--
AJA 2016

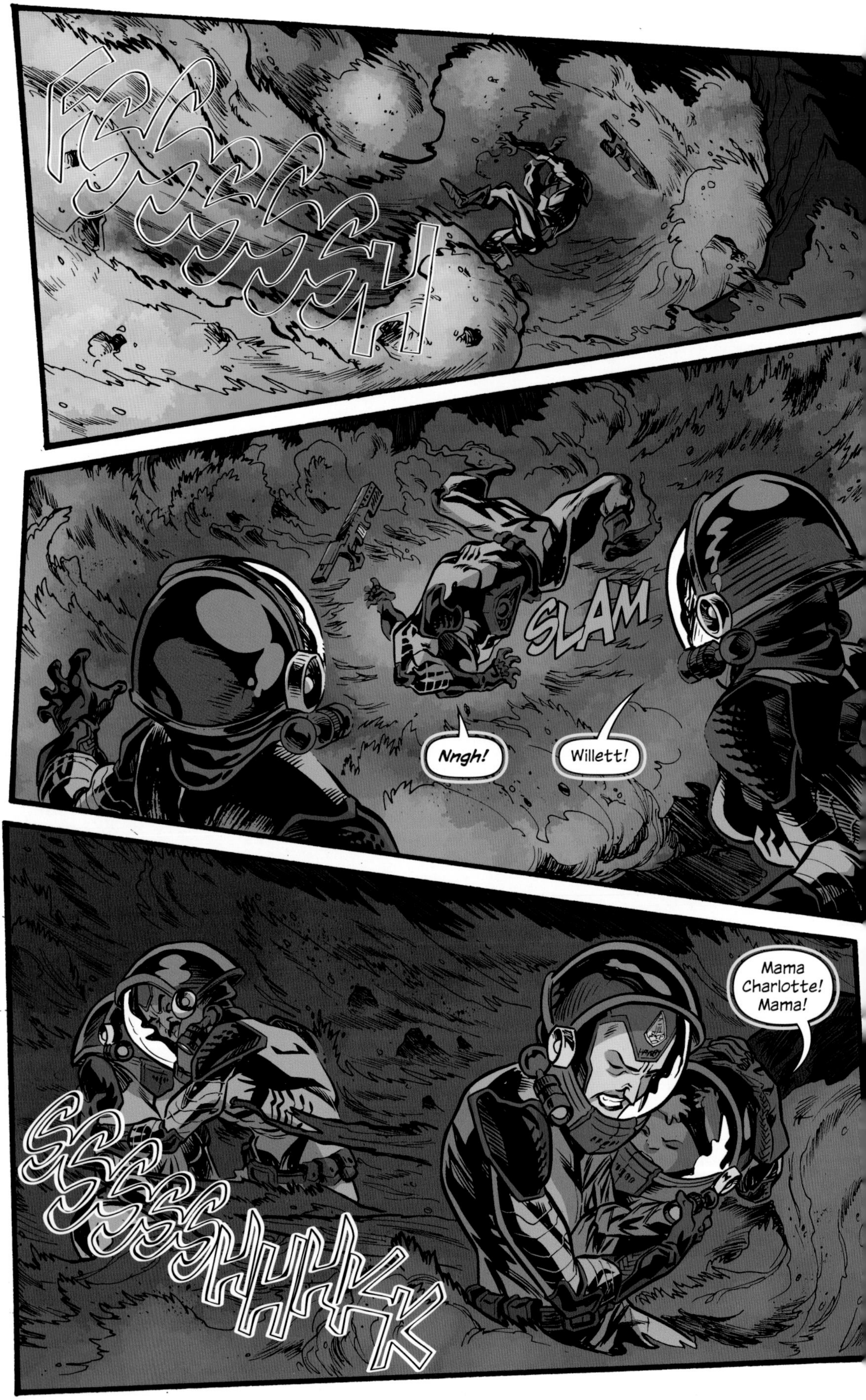
FSSSSSSSSH
SLAM
Nngh!
Willett!
Mama Charlotte! Mama!
SSSSSHHHKK

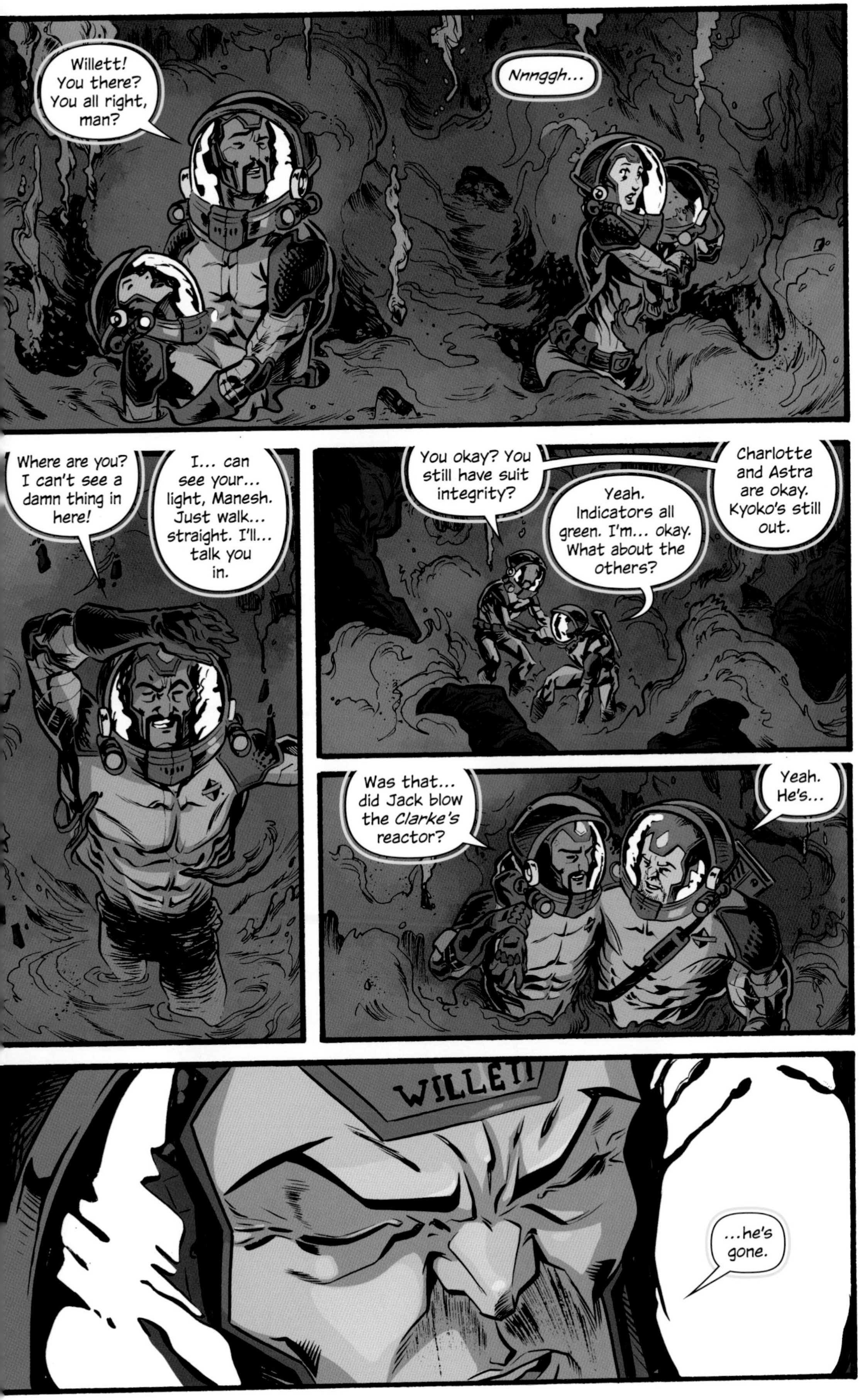
Willett! You there? You all right, man?
Nnnggh...
Where are you? I can't see a damn thing in here!
I... can see your... light, Manesh. Just walk... straight. I'll... talk you in.
You okay? You still have suit integrity?
Yeah. Indicators all green. I'm... okay. What about the others?
Charlotte and Astra are okay. Kyoko's still out.
Was that... did Jack blow the *Clarke's* reactor?
Yeah. He's...
WILLETT
...he's gone.

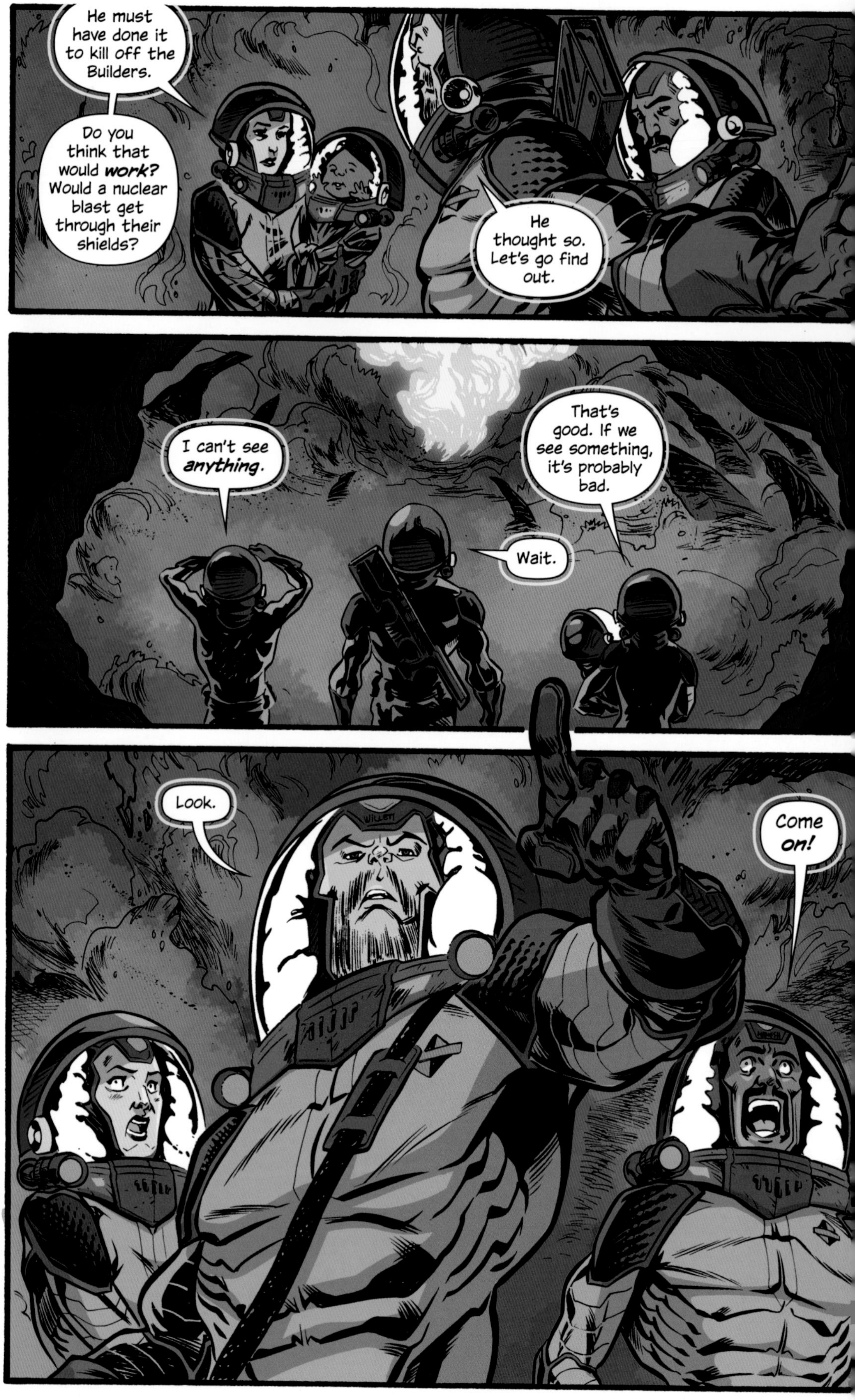
He must have done it to kill off the Builders.
Do you think that would work? Would a nuclear blast get through their shields?
He thought so. Let's go find out.
I can't see anything.
That's good. If we see something, it's probably bad.
Wait.
Look.
Come on!

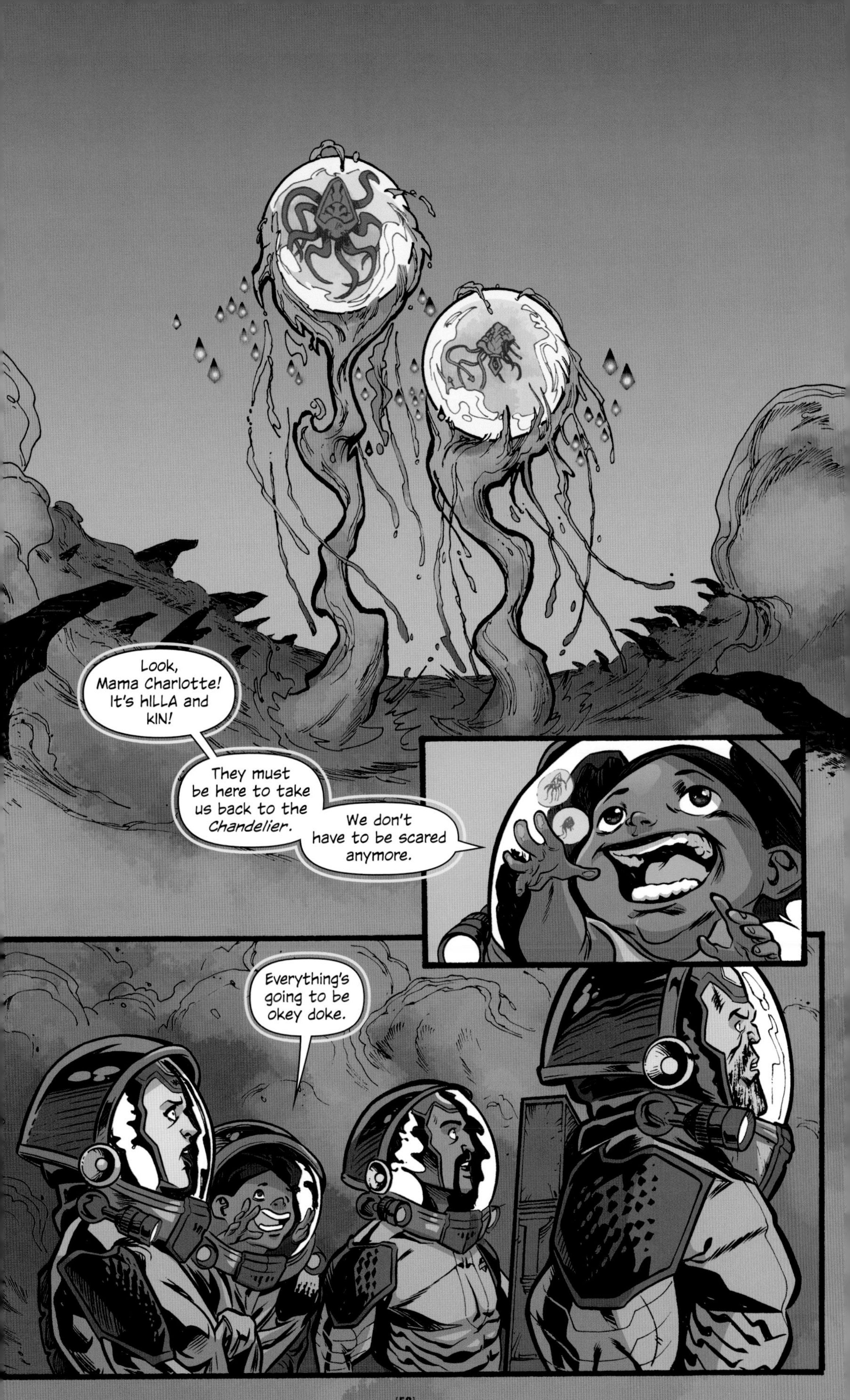
Look, Mama Charlotte! It's hILLA and kIN!
They must be here to take us back to the *Chandelier*.
We don't have to be scared anymore.
Everything's going to be okey doke.

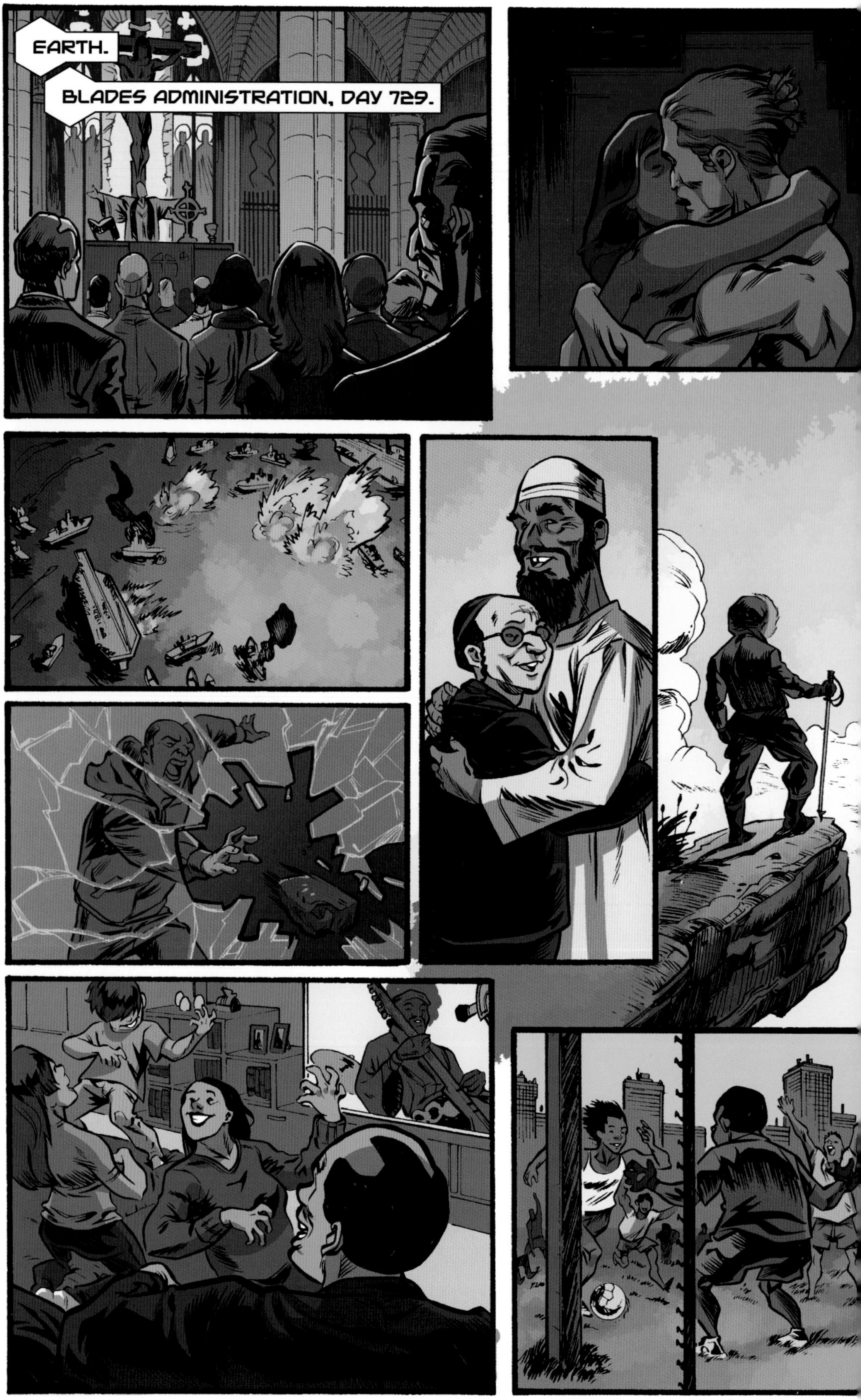
EARTH.
BLADES ADMINISTRATION, DAY 729.

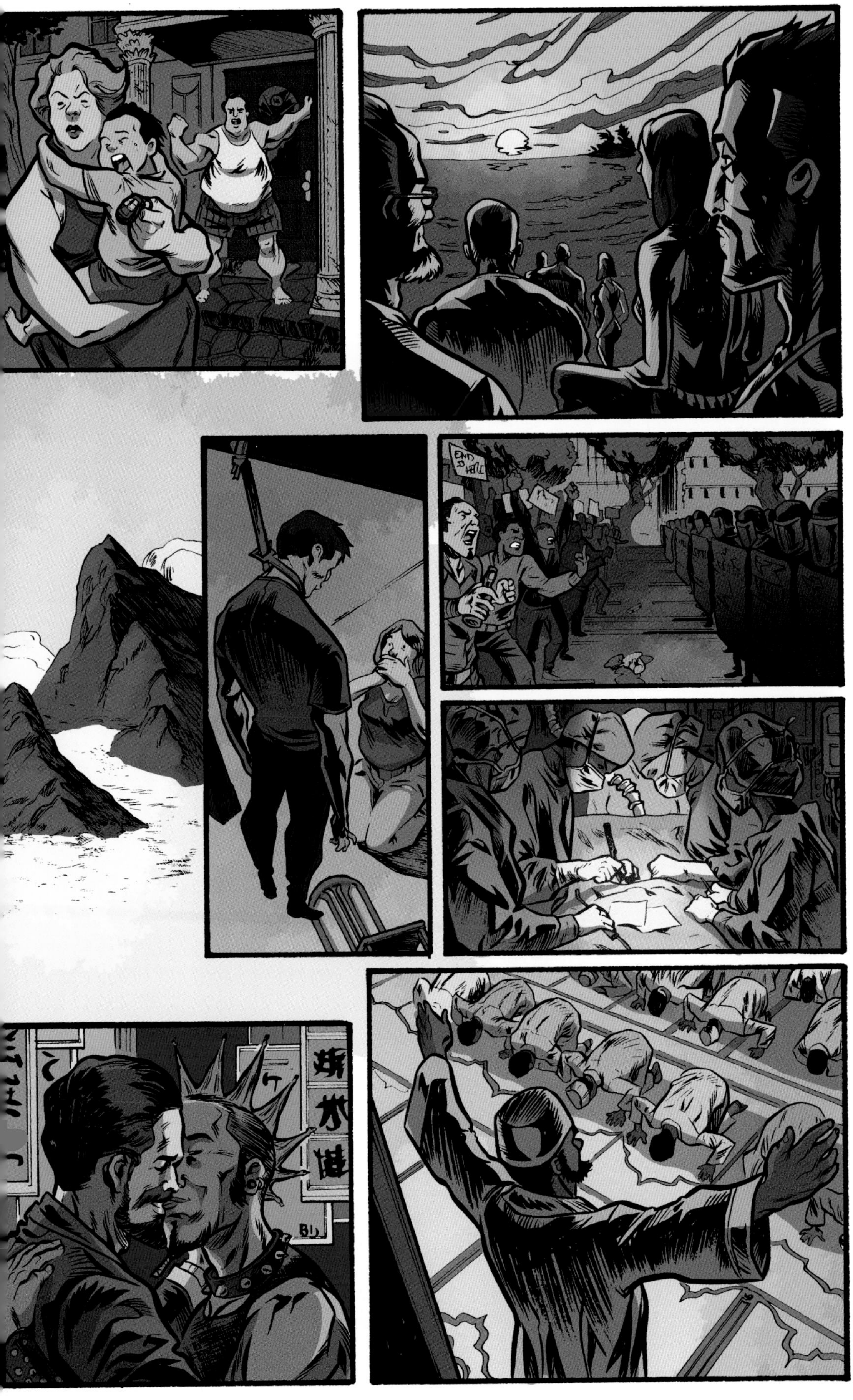

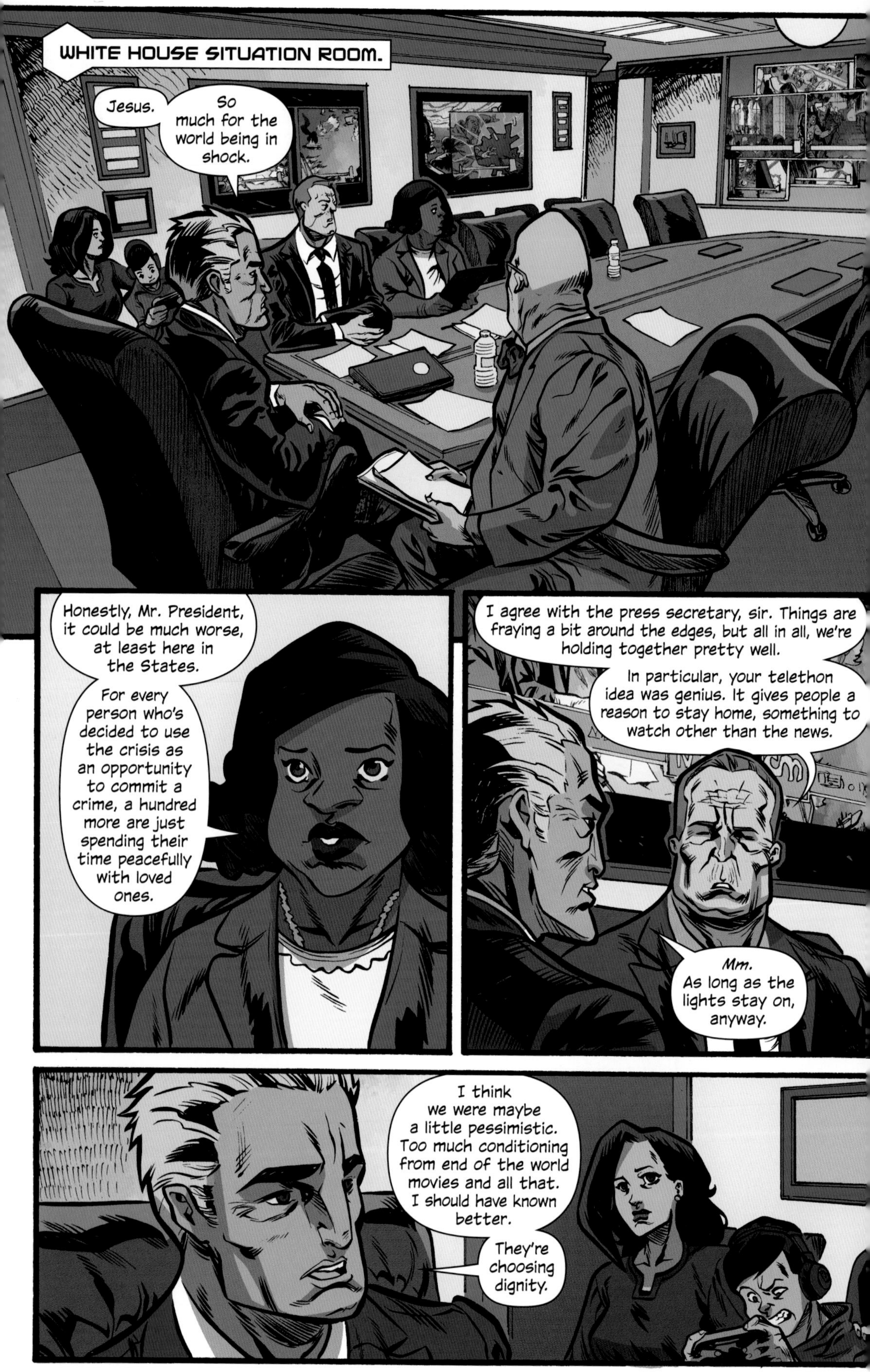
WHITE HOUSE SITUATION ROOM.
Jesus.
So much for the world being in shock.
Honestly, Mr. President, it could be much worse, at least here in the States.
For every person who's decided to use the crisis as an opportunity to commit a crime, a hundred more are just spending their time peacefully with loved ones.
I agree with the press secretary, sir. Things are fraying a bit around the edges, but all in all, we're holding together pretty well.
In particular, your telethon idea was genius. It gives people a reason to stay home, something to watch other than the news.
Mm. As long as the lights stay on, anyway.
I think we were maybe a little pessimistic. Too much conditioning from end of the world movies and all that. I should have known better.
They're choosing dignity.

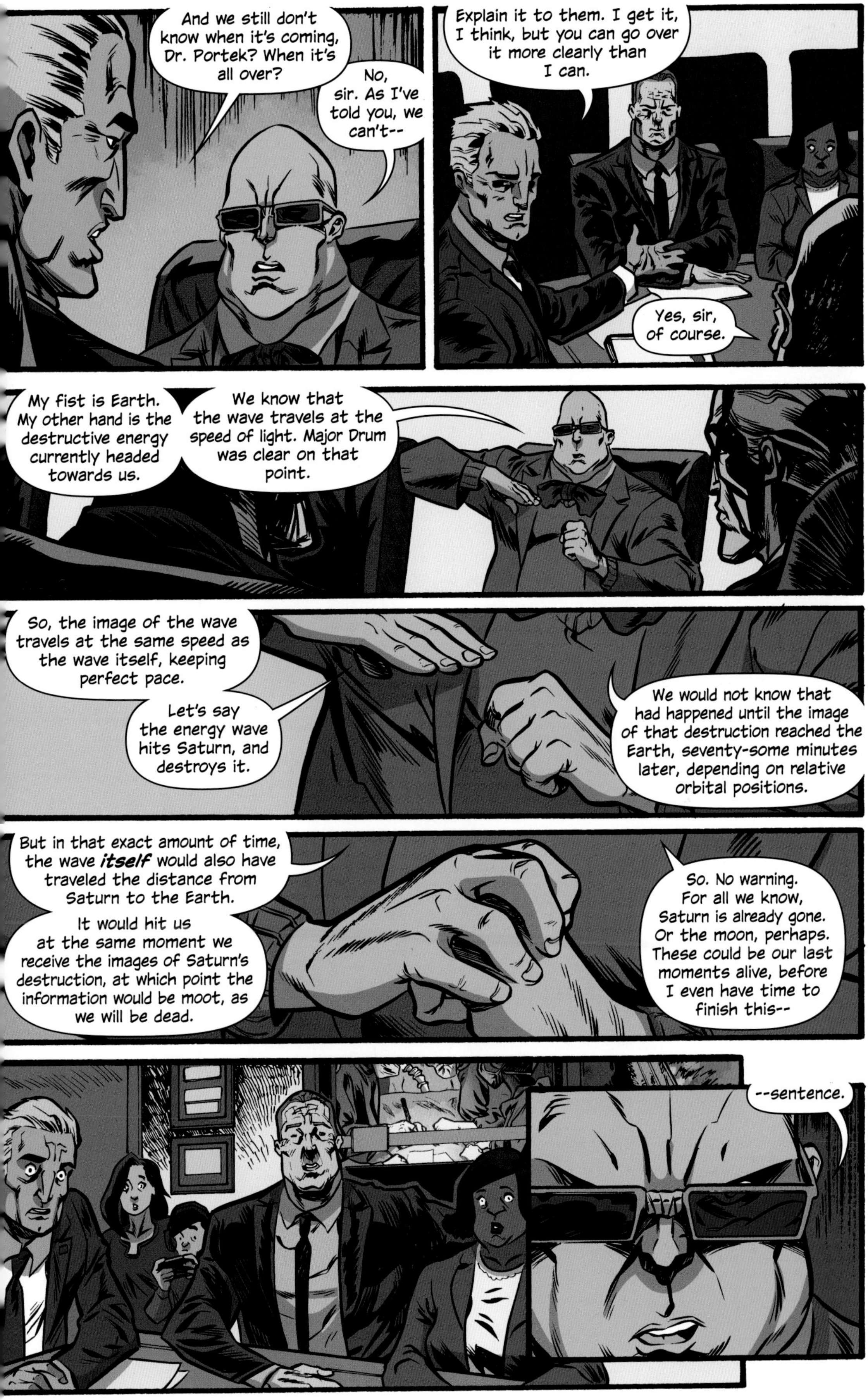

And we still don't know when it's coming, Dr. Portek? When it's all over?
No, sir. As I've told you, we can't--
Explain it to them. I get it, I think, but you can go over it more clearly than I can.
Yes, sir, of course.
My fist is Earth. My other hand is the destructive energy currently headed towards us.
We know that the wave travels at the speed of light. Major Drum was clear on that point.
So, the image of the wave travels at the same speed as the wave itself, keeping perfect pace.
Let's say the energy wave hits Saturn, and destroys it.
We would not know that had happened until the image of that destruction reached the Earth, seventy-some minutes later, depending on relative orbital positions.
But in that exact amount of time, the wave *itself* would also have traveled the distance from Saturn to the Earth.
It would hit us at the same moment we receive the images of Saturn's destruction, at which point the information would be moot, as we will be dead.
So. No warning. For all we know, Saturn is already gone. Or the moon, perhaps. These could be our last moments alive, before I even have time to finish this--
--sentence.

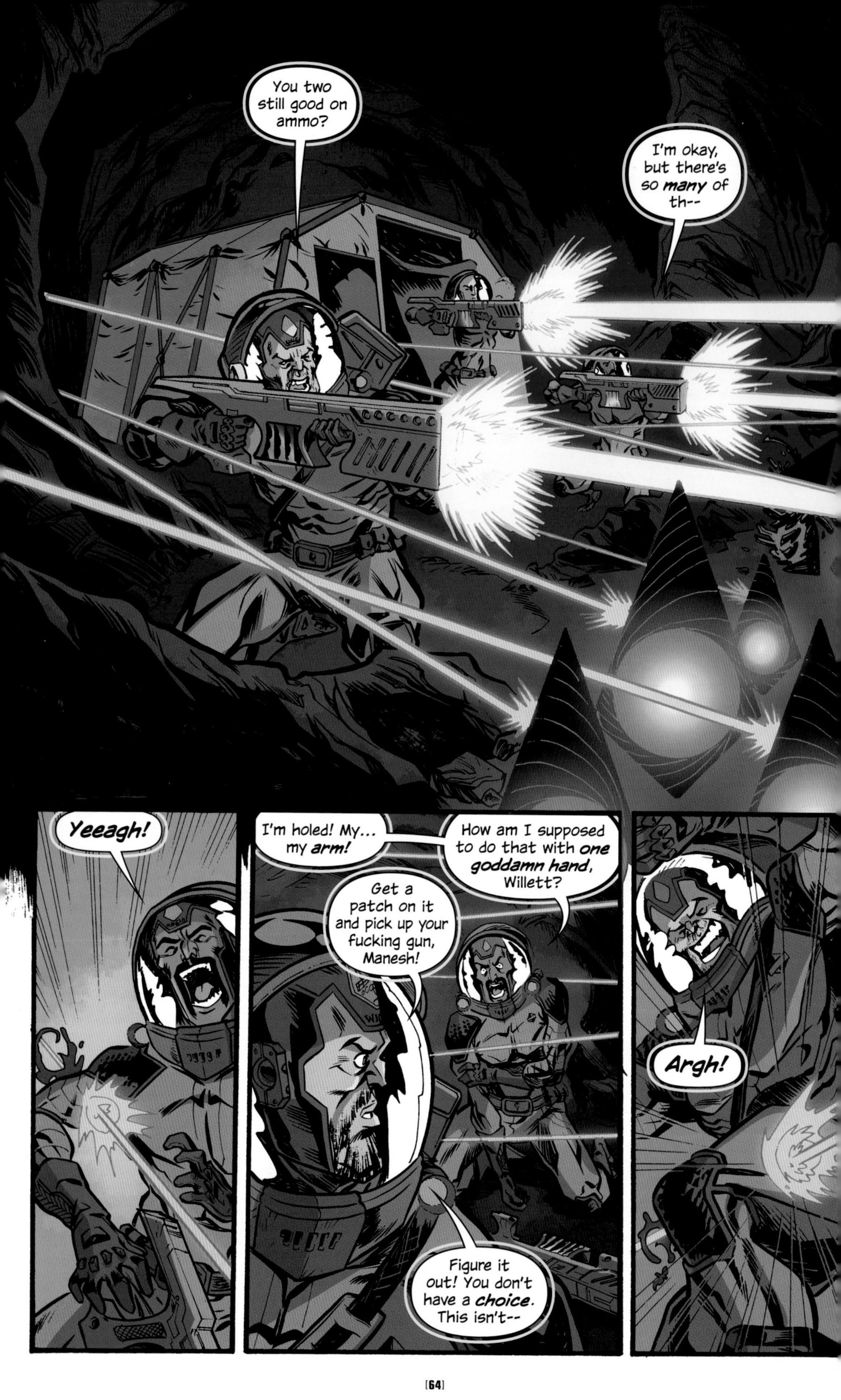

You two still good on ammo?
I'm okay, but there's so *many* of th--
Yeeagh!
I'm holed! My... my *arm!*
Get a patch on it and pick up your fucking gun, Manesh!
How am I supposed to do that with *one goddamn hand*, Willett?
Figure it out! You don't have a *choice*. This isn't--
Argh!

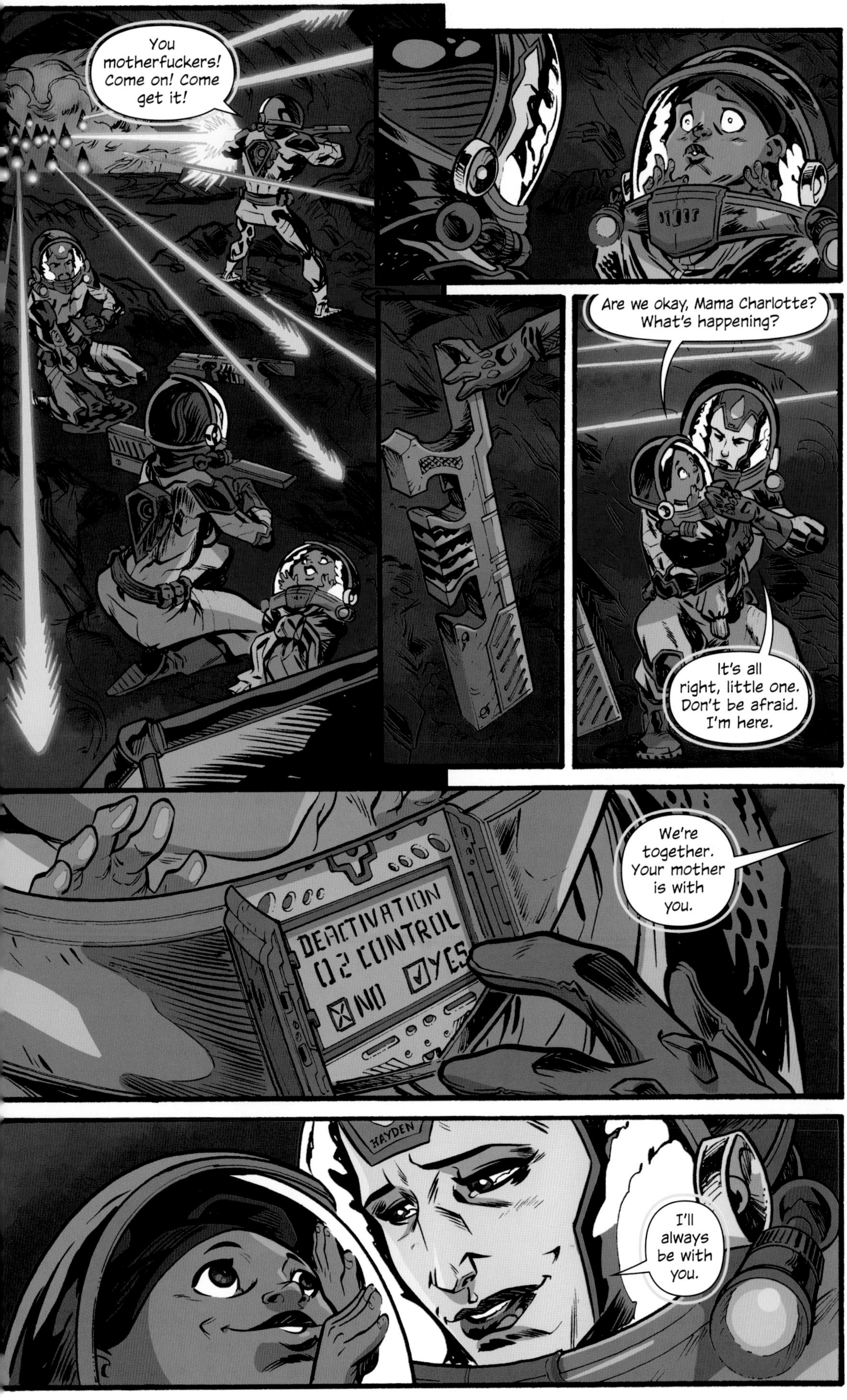
You motherfuckers! Come on! Come get it!
Are we okay, Mama Charlotte? What's happening?
It's all right, little one. Don't be afraid. I'm here.
DEACTIVATION
O2 CONTROL
NO
YES
We're together. Your mother is with you.
HAYDEN
I'll always be with you.

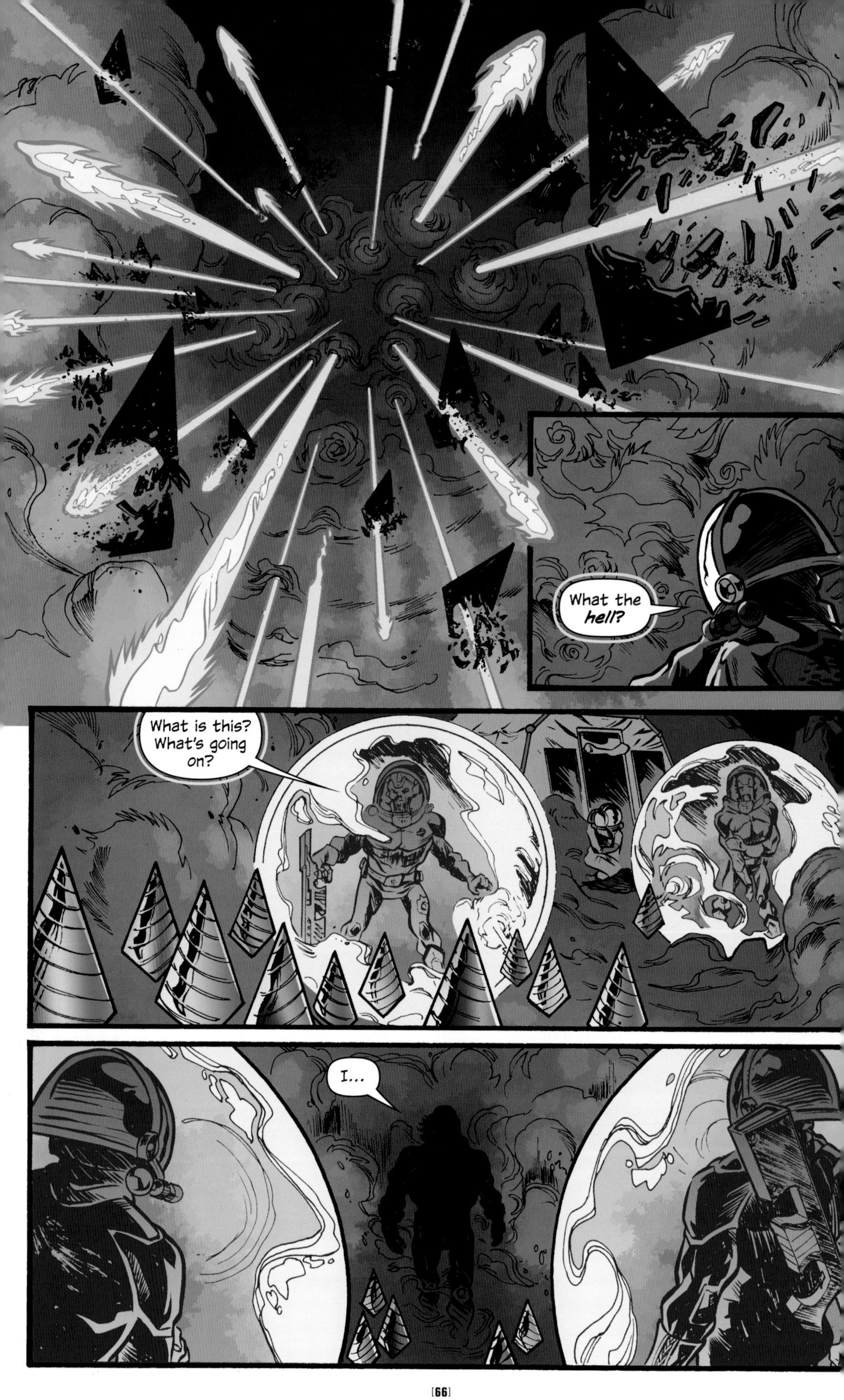
What the *hell?*
What is this? What's going on?
I...

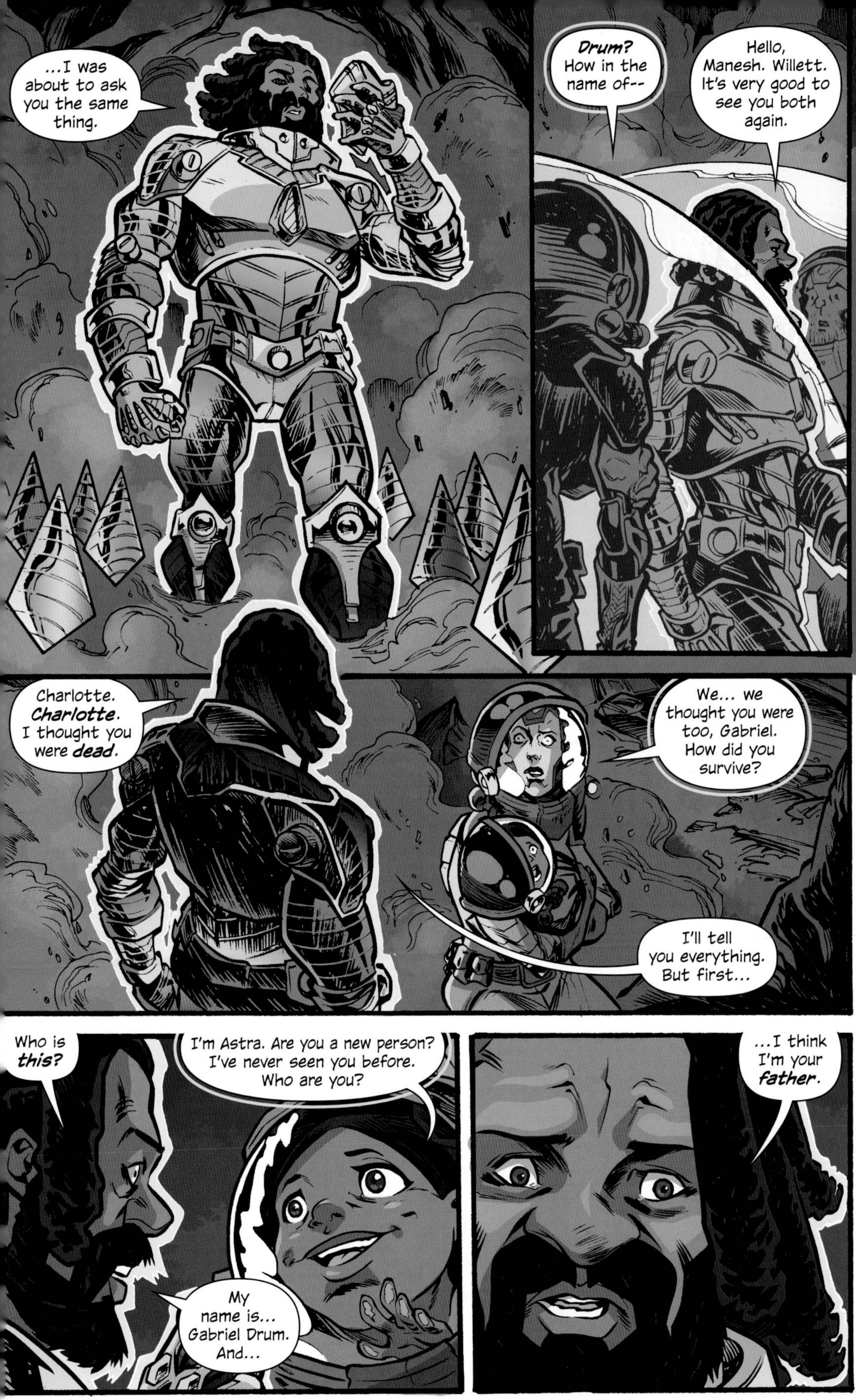
...I was about to ask you the same thing.
Drum? How in the name of--
Hello, Manesh. Willett. It's very good to see you both again.
Charlotte. Charlotte. I thought you were dead.
We... we thought you were too, Gabriel. How did you survive?
I'll tell you everything. But first...
Who is this?
I'm Astra. Are you a new person? I've never seen you before. Who are you?
My name is... Gabriel Drum. And...
...I think I'm your father.

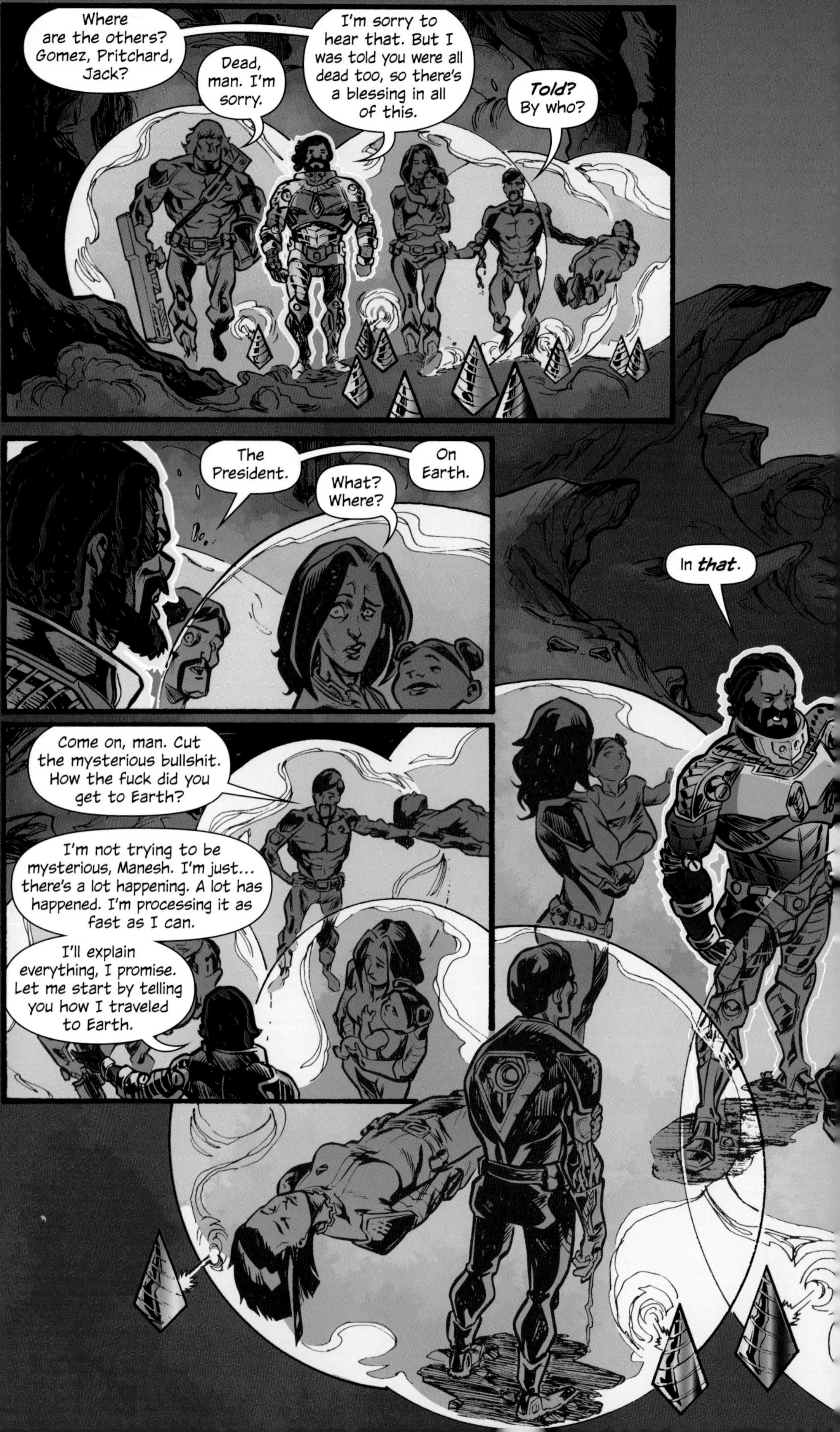
Where are the others? Gomez, Pritchard, Jack?
Dead, man. I'm sorry.
I'm sorry to hear that. But I was told you were all dead too, so there's a blessing in all of this.
Told? By who?
The President.
On Earth.
What? Where?
In *that*.
Come on, man. Cut the mysterious bullshit. How the fuck did you get to Earth?
I'm not trying to be mysterious, Manesh. I'm just... there's a lot happening. A lot has happened. I'm processing it as fast as I can.
I'll explain everything, I promise. Let me start by telling you how I traveled to Earth.

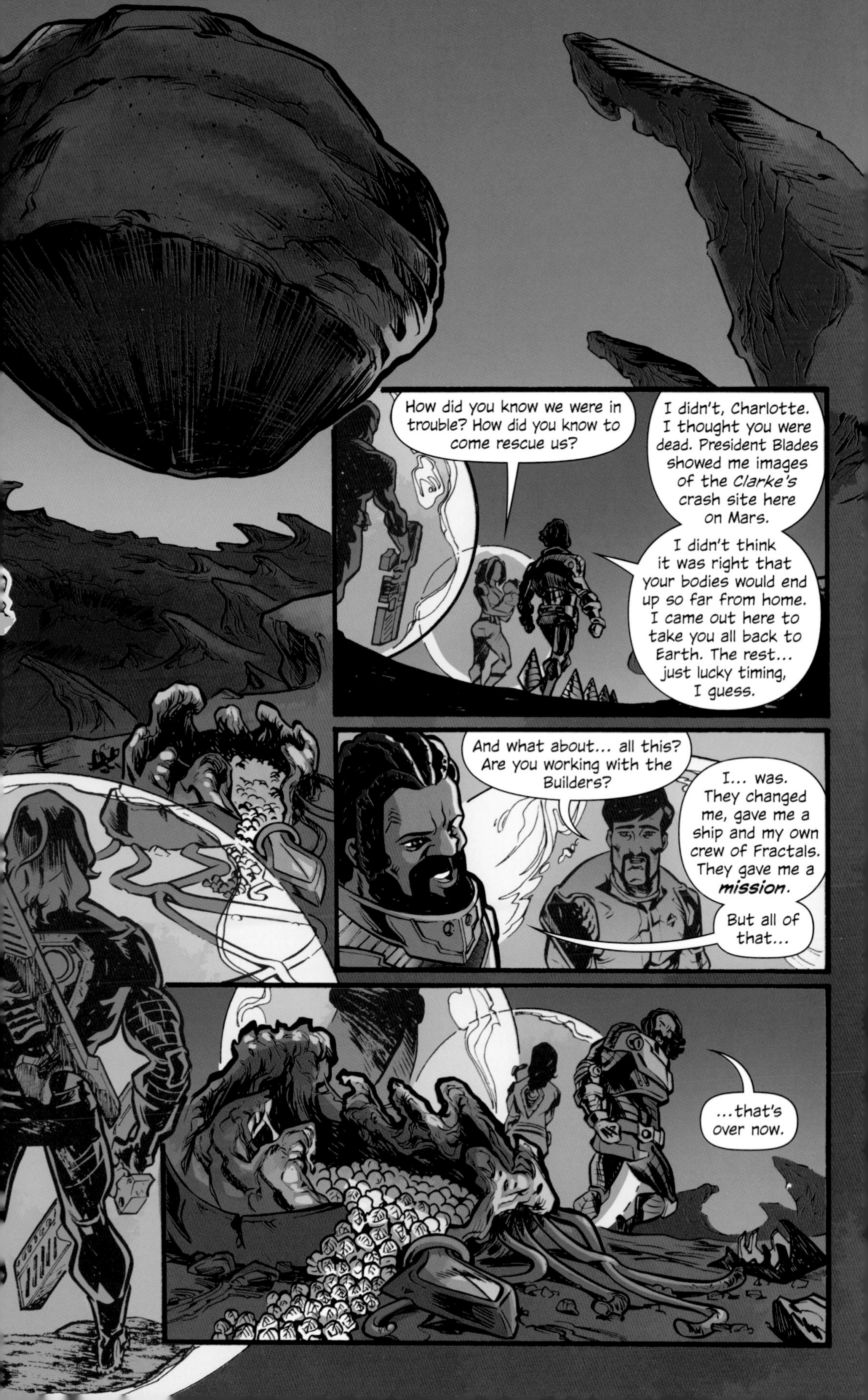
How did you know we were in trouble? How did you know to come rescue us?
I didn't, Charlotte. I thought you were dead. President Blades showed me images of the *Clarke's* crash site here on Mars.
I didn't think it was right that your bodies would end up so far from home. I came out here to take you all back to Earth. The rest... just lucky timing, I guess.
And what about... all this? Are you working with the Builders?
I... was. They changed me, gave me a ship and my own crew of Fractals. They gave me a ***mission***.
But all of that...
...that's over now.

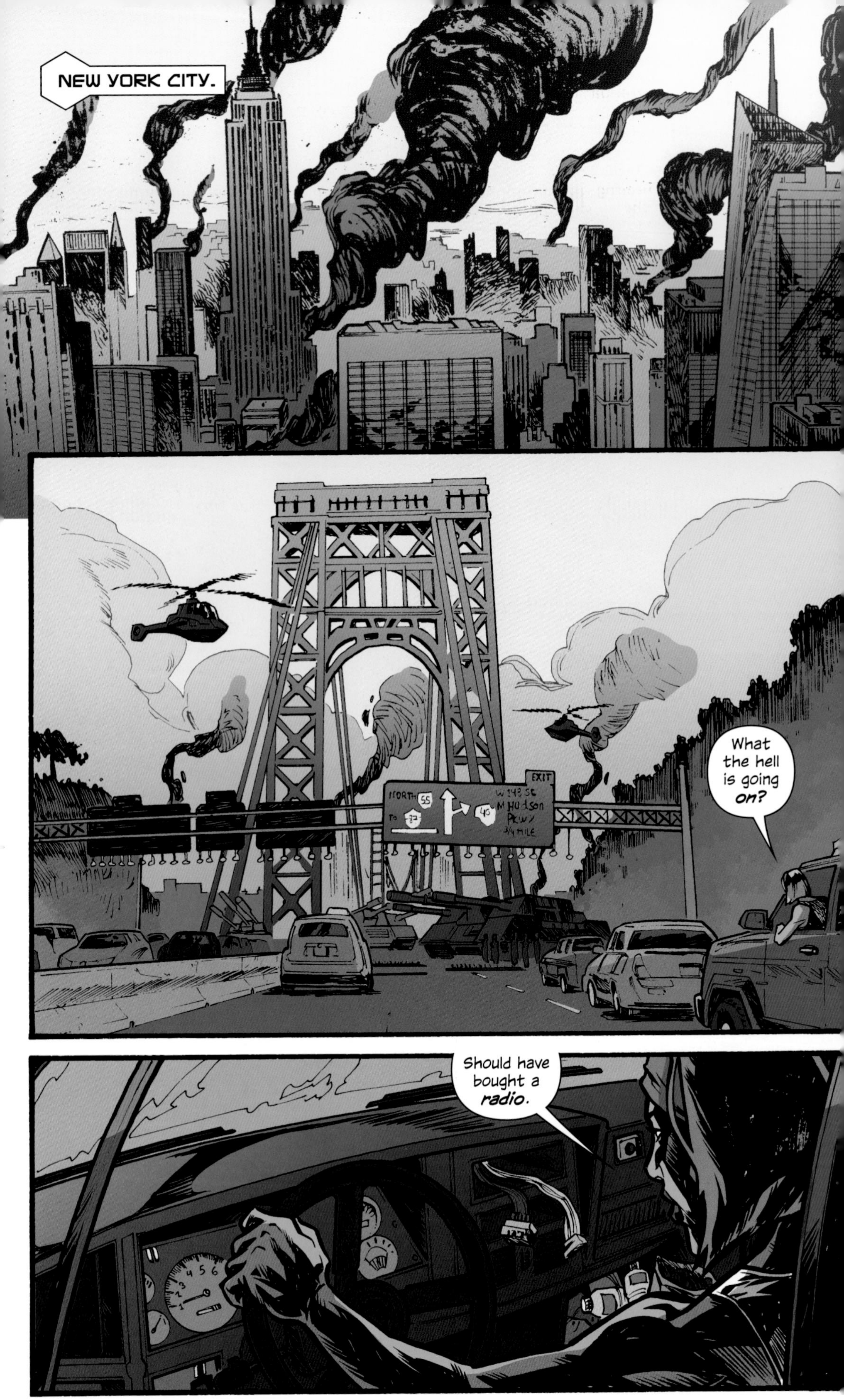
NEW YORK CITY.
What the hell is going *on?*
Should have bought a *radio.*

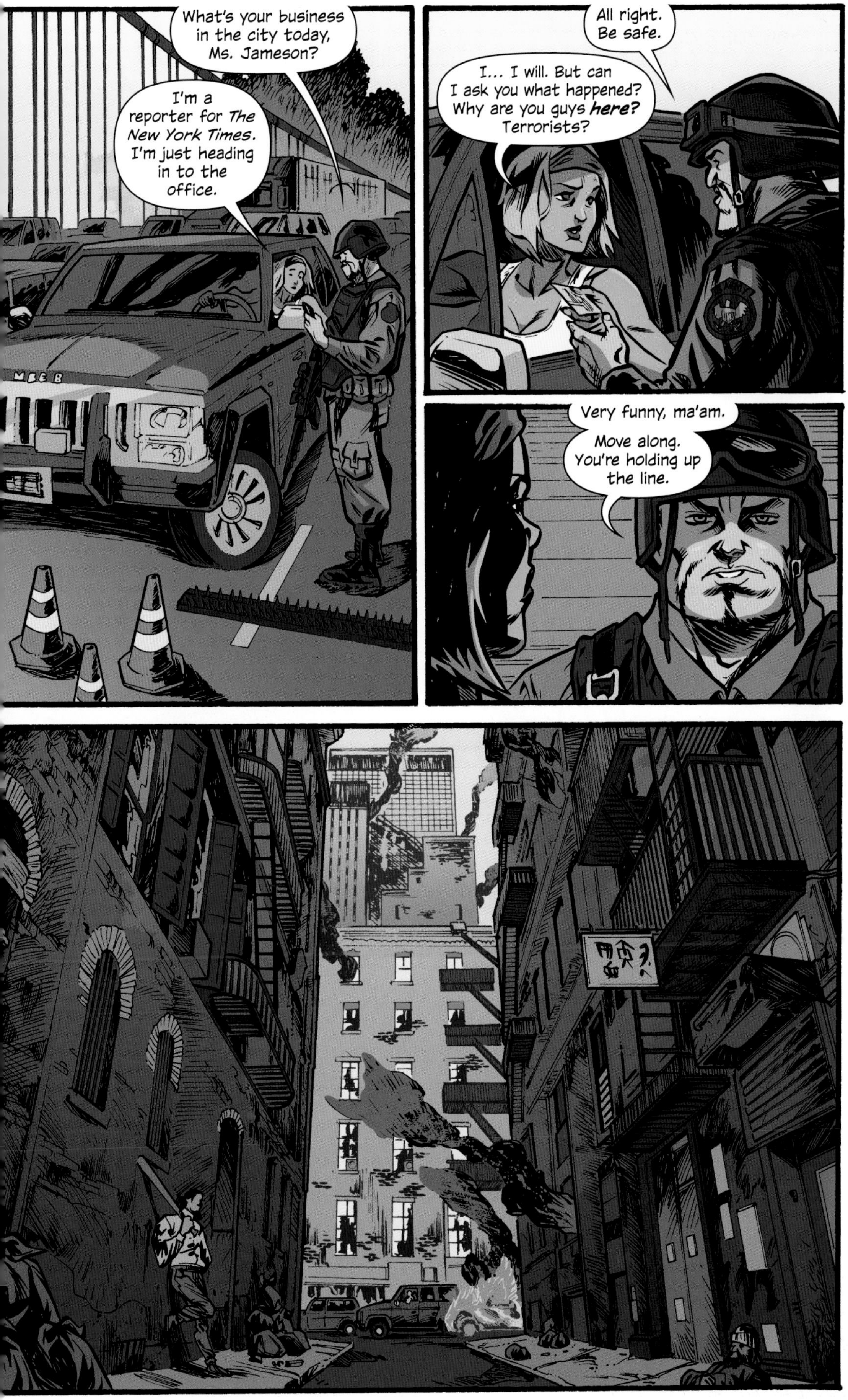
What's your business in the city today, Ms. Jameson?
I'm a reporter for *The New York Times.* I'm just heading in to the office.
All right. Be safe.
I... I will. But can I ask you what happened? Why are you guys ***here?*** Terrorists?
Very funny, ma'am.
Move along. You're holding up the line.

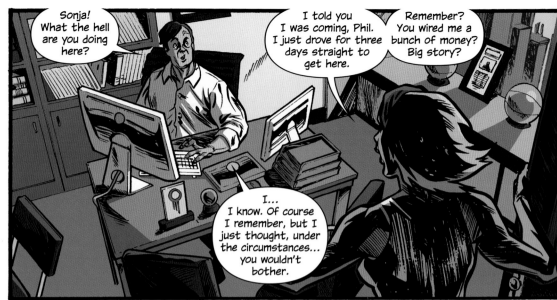

Sonja! What the hell are you doing here?

I told you I was coming, Phil. I just drove for three days straight to get here.

Remember? You wired me a bunch of money? Big story?

I... I know. Of course I remember, but I just thought, under the circumstances... you wouldn't bother.

Wouldn't **bother?** Francis Carroll--the former **President**--kidnapped me and held me hostage in a nuclear bunker.

He had **thousands** of people there. He told us the **world** had ended, that an **asteroid** had hit. He was setting himself up like some kind of... **savior.**

Oh, Sonja, I'm not sure I--

I'm telling you the **truth**. I was **there**. And that's not all.

He caused the wars in Iraq and Afghanistan. He made sure Blades won. It's all about the aliens in the asteroid belt. He had this elaborate **plan**, and--

Sonja... enough. I'm sure it would have been the biggest story of all time, but right now...

Phil, please. **What's going on?**

I drove straight through from Nevada, and my car didn't have a radio. What are you **talking** about?

Oh, Jesus. Brace yourself, all right?

The New York Times

PRESIDENT BLADES: WE ARE THE LAST.

I'm sorry to be the one to tell you this...

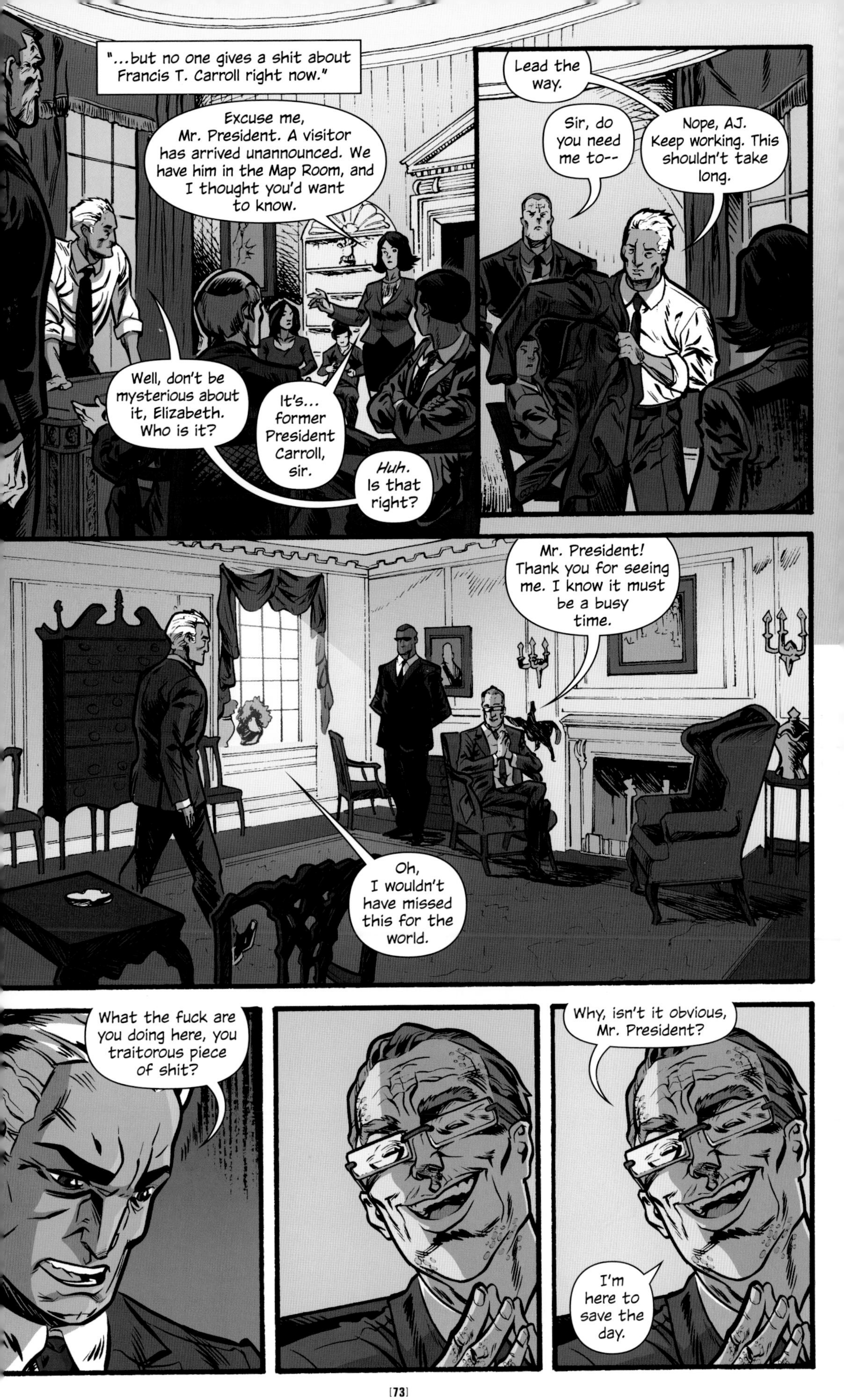
"...but no one gives a shit about Francis T. Carroll right now."
Excuse me, Mr. President. A visitor has arrived unannounced. We have him in the Map Room, and I thought you'd want to know.
Well, don't be mysterious about it, Elizabeth. Who is it?
It's... former President Carroll, sir.
Huh. Is that right?
Lead the way.
Sir, do you need me to--
Nope, AJ. Keep working. This shouldn't take long.
Mr. President! Thank you for seeing me. I know it must be a busy time.
Oh, I wouldn't have missed this for the world.
What the fuck are you doing here, you traitorous piece of shit?
Why, isn't it obvious, Mr. President?
I'm here to save the day.

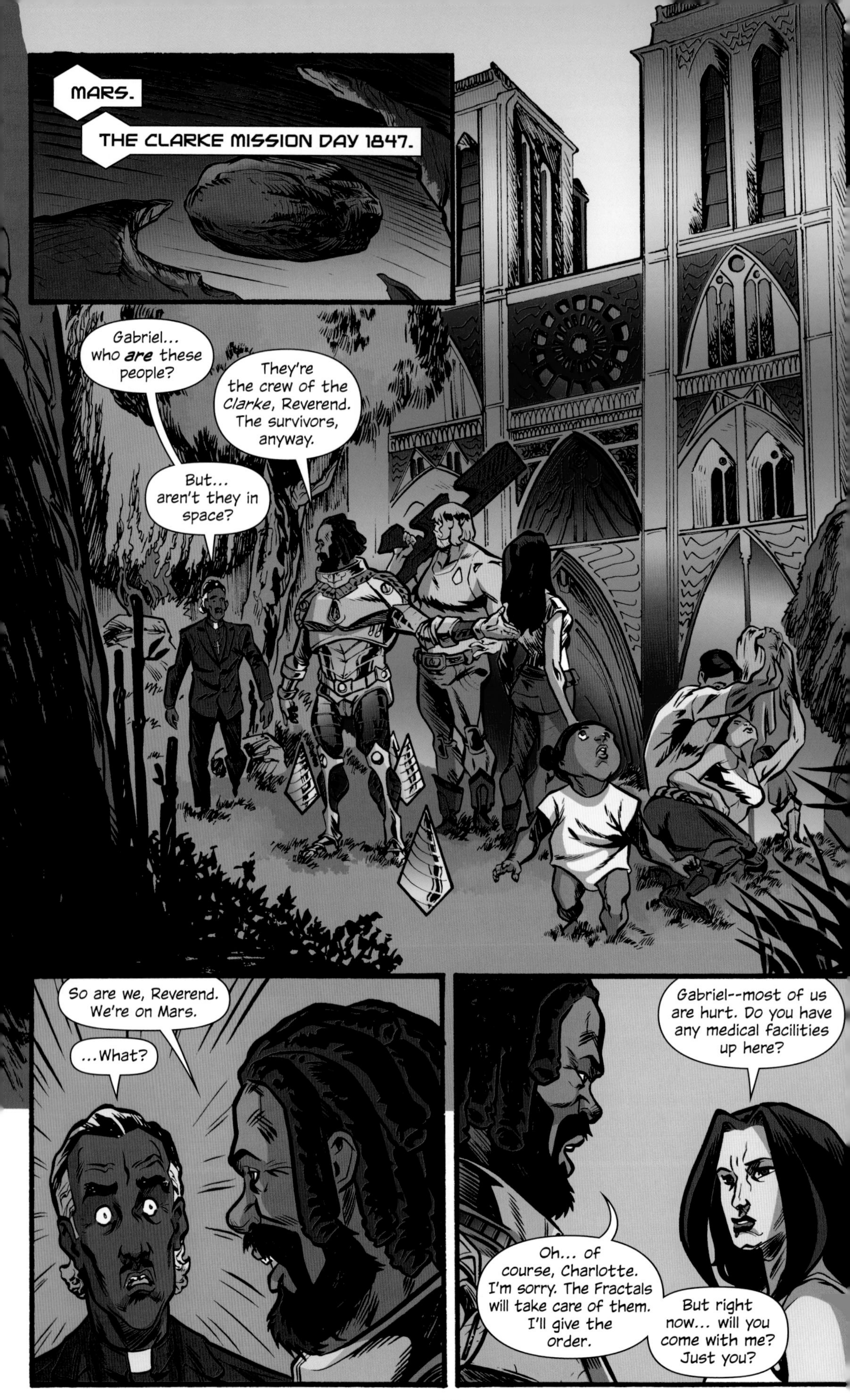
MARS.
THE CLARKE MISSION DAY 1847.
Gabriel... who *are* these people?
They're the crew of the *Clarke*, Reverend. The survivors, anyway.
But... aren't they in space?
So are we, Reverend. We're on Mars.
...What?
Gabriel--most of us are hurt. Do you have any medical facilities up here?
Oh... of course, Charlotte. I'm sorry. The Fractals will take care of them. I'll give the order.
But right now... will you come with me? Just you?

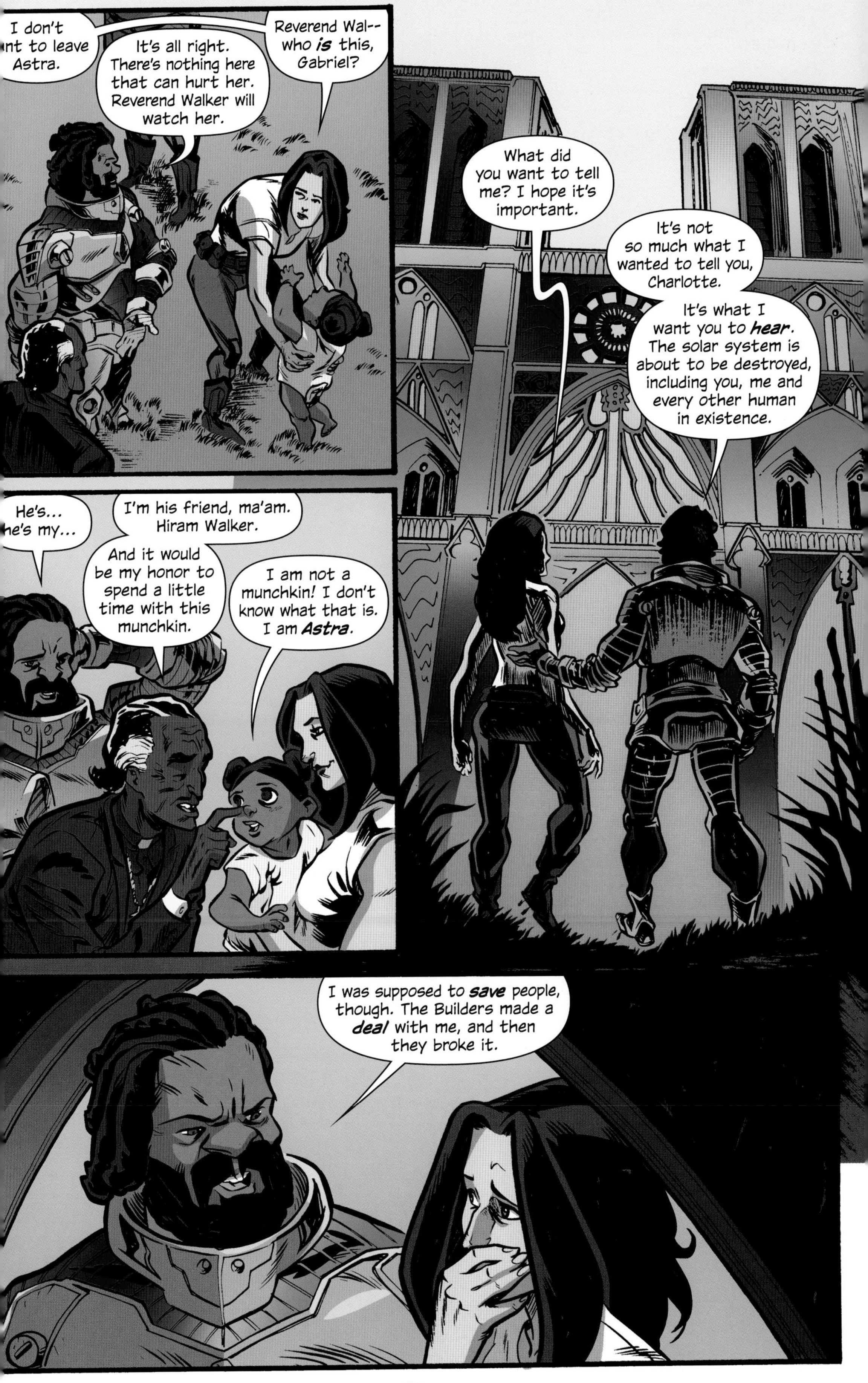

I don't
nt to leave
Astra.
It's all right.
There's nothing here
that can hurt her.
Reverend Walker will
watch her.
Reverend Wal--
who *is* this,
Gabriel?
What did
you want to tell
me? I hope it's
important.
It's not
so much what I
wanted to tell you,
Charlotte.
It's what I
want you to *hear*.
The solar system is
about to be destroyed,
including you, me and
every other human
in existence.
He's...
he's my...
I'm his friend, ma'am.
Hiram Walker.
And it would
be my honor to
spend a little
time with this
munchkin.
I am not a
munchkin! I don't
know what that is.
I am *Astra*.
I was supposed to *save* people,
though. The Builders made a
deal with me, and then
they broke it.

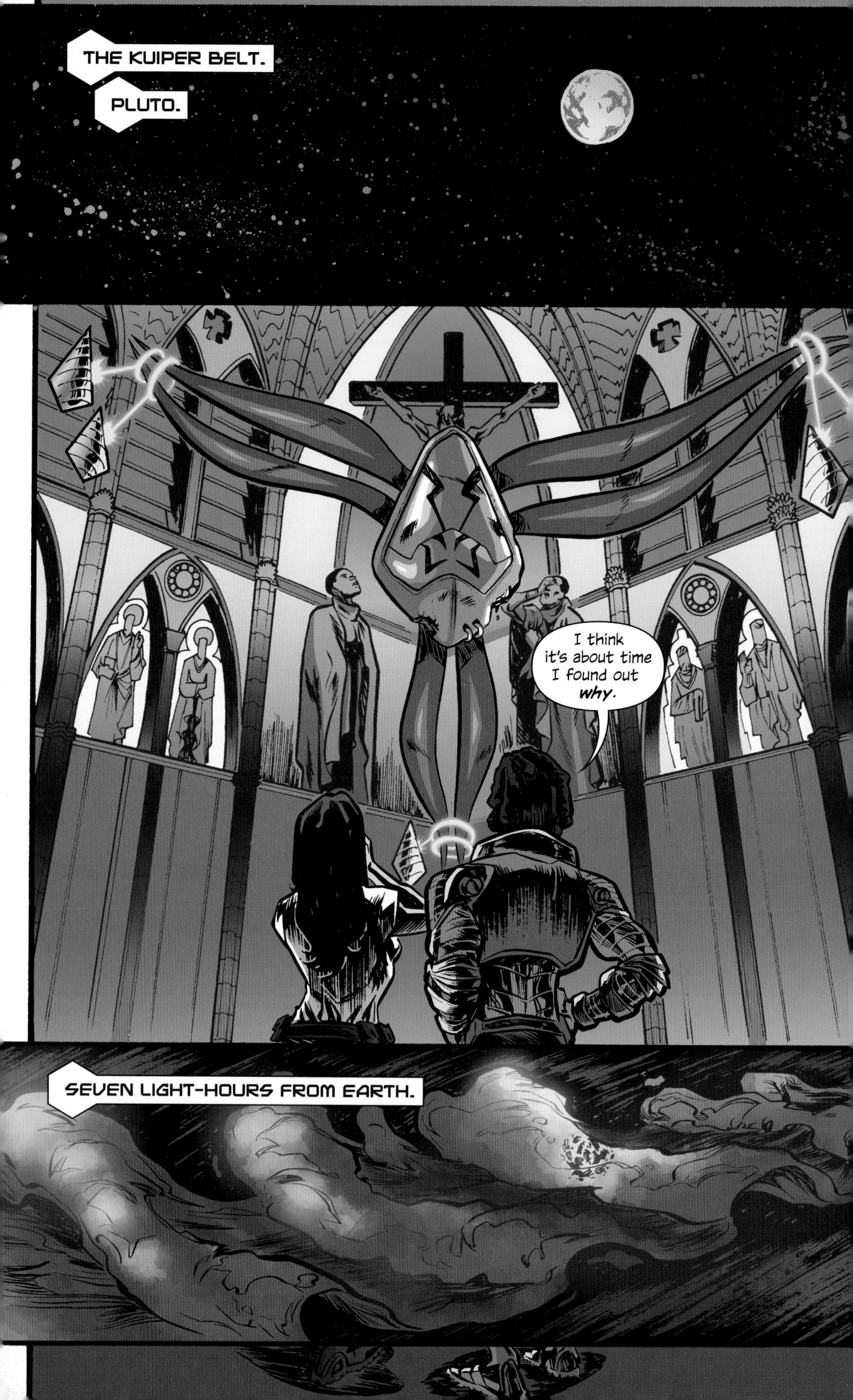
THE KUIPER BELT.
PLUTO.
I think it's about time I found out *why*.
SEVEN LIGHT-HOURS FROM EARTH.

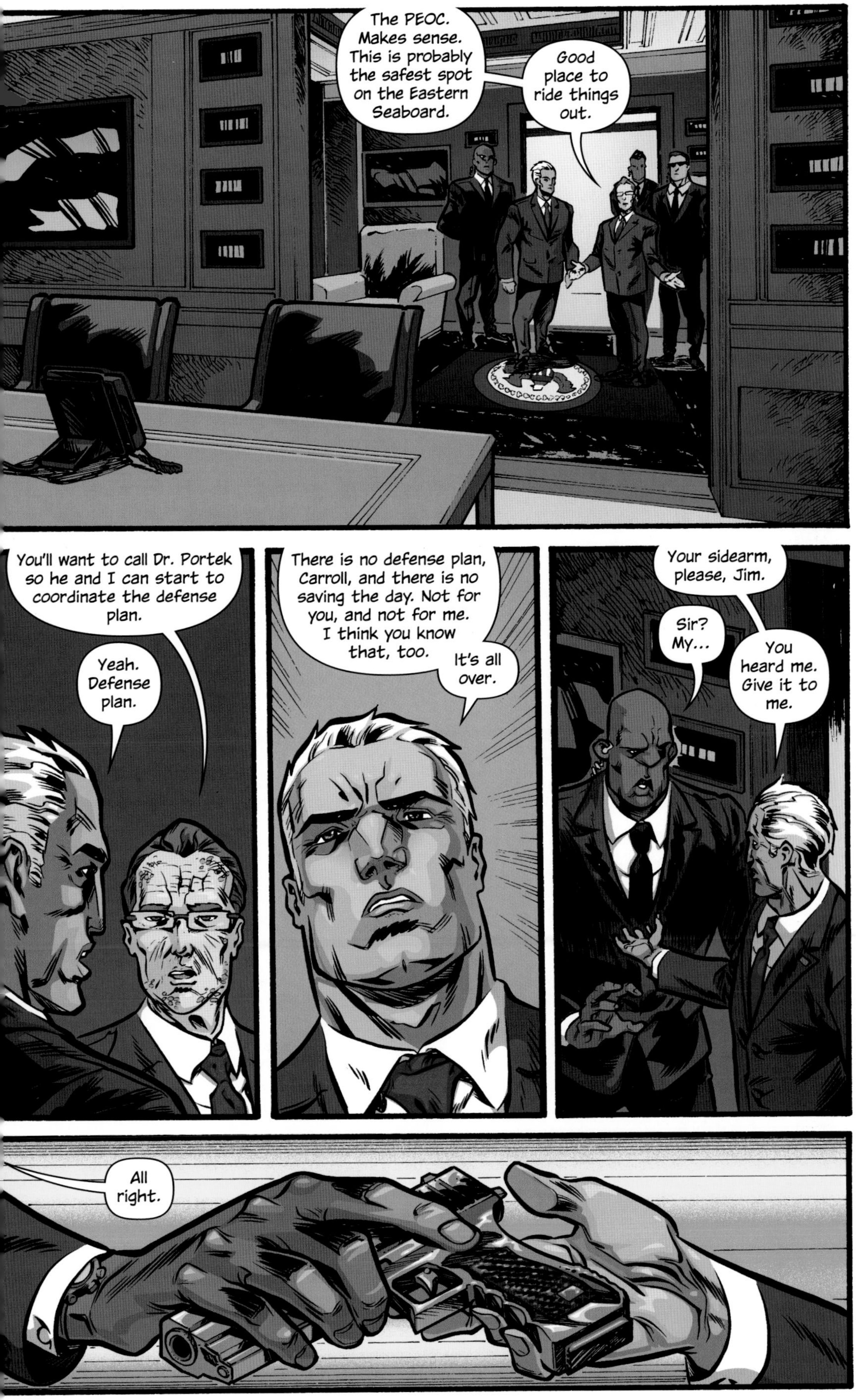
The PEOC. Makes sense. This is probably the safest spot on the Eastern Seaboard.
Good place to ride things out.
You'll want to call Dr. Portek so he and I can start to coordinate the defense plan.
Yeah. Defense plan.
There is no defense plan, Carroll, and there is no saving the day. Not for you, and not for me. I think you know that, too.
It's all over.
Your sidearm, please, Jim.
Sir? My...
You heard me. Give it to me.
All right.

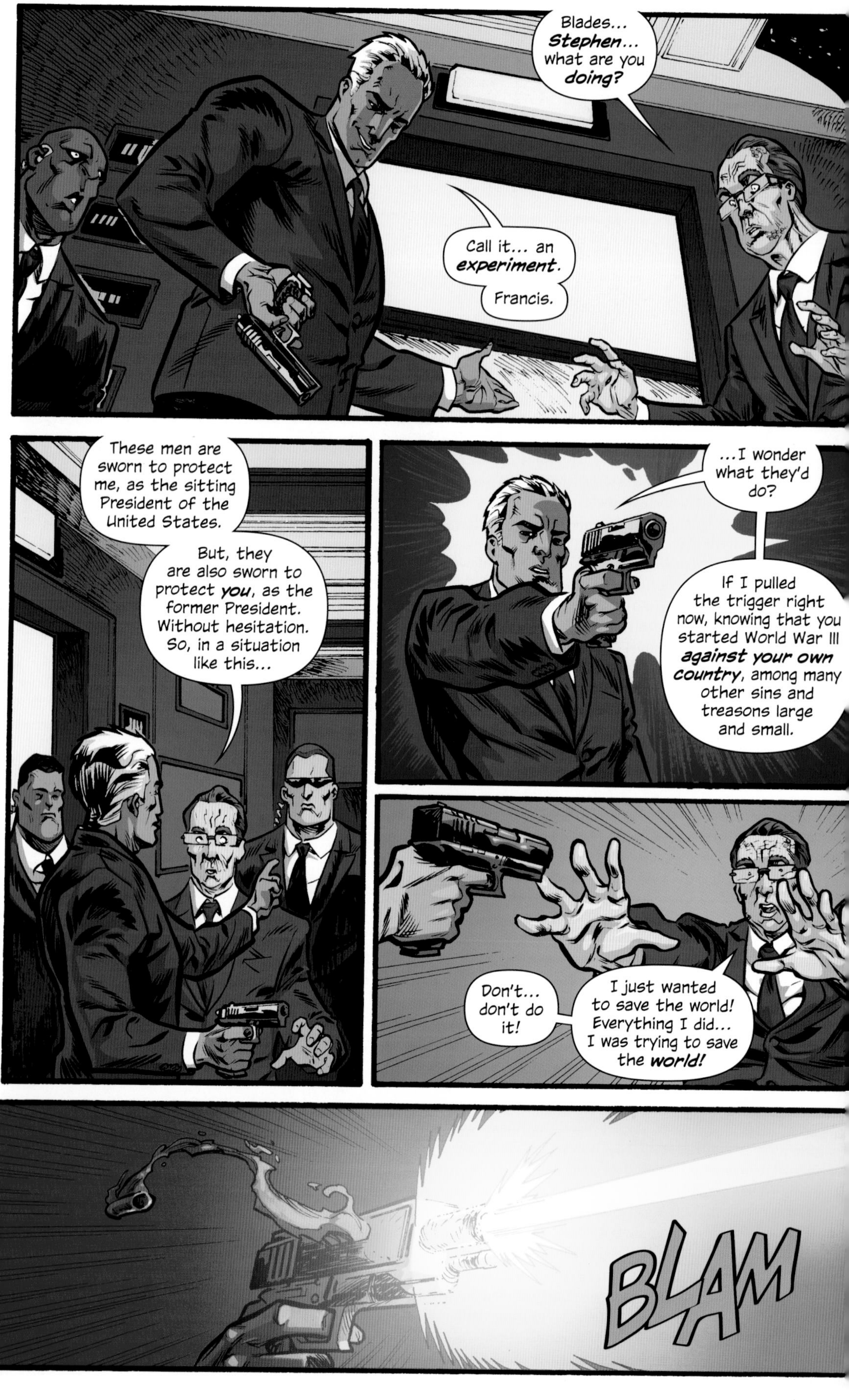

Blades... Stephen... what are you doing?
Call it... an experiment.
Francis.
These men are sworn to protect me, as the sitting President of the United States.
But, they are also sworn to protect you, as the former President. Without hesitation. So, in a situation like this...
...I wonder what they'd do?
If I pulled the trigger right now, knowing that you started World War III against your own country, among many other sins and treasons large and small.
Don't... don't do it!
I just wanted to save the world! Everything I did... I was trying to save the world!
BLAM

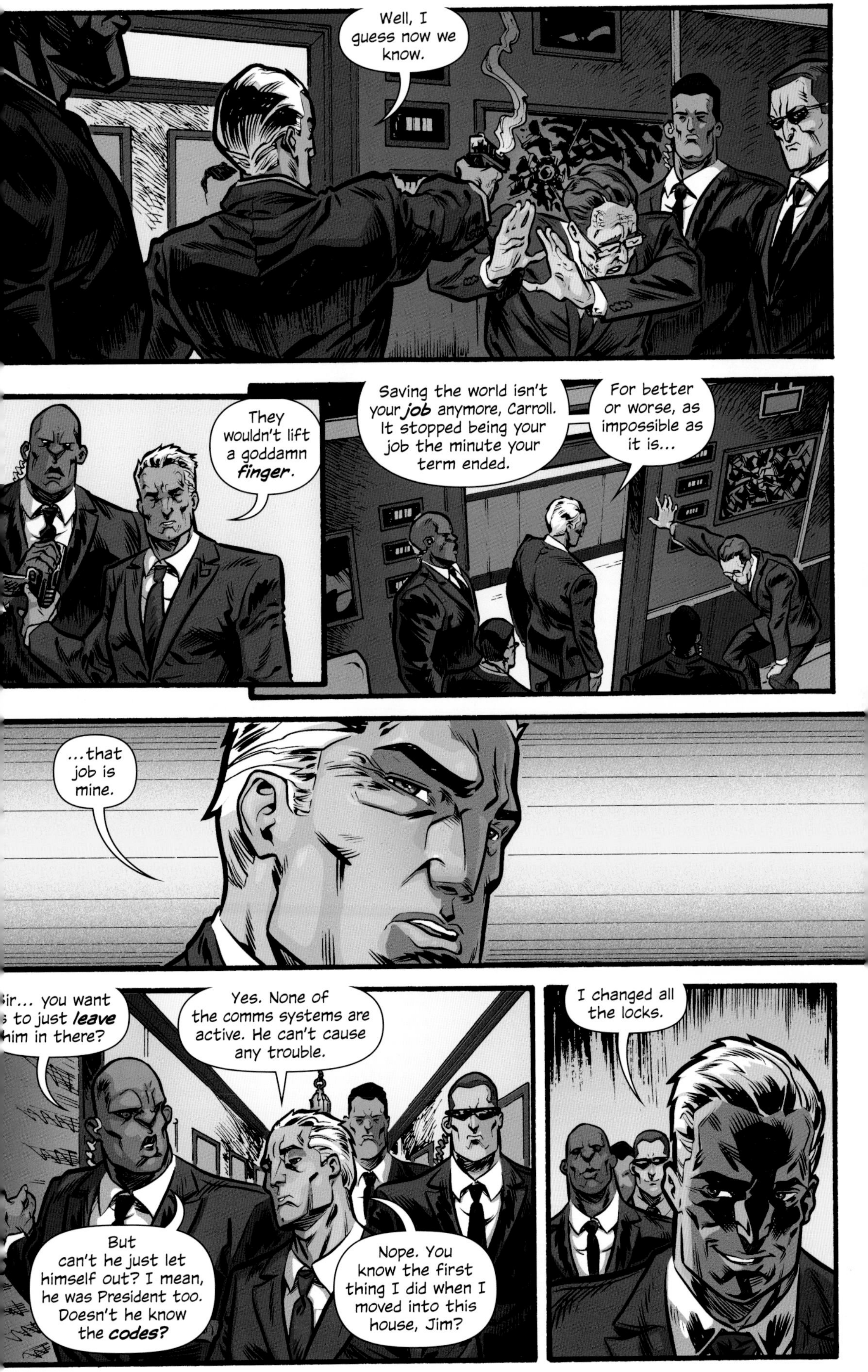
Well, I guess now we know.
They wouldn't lift a goddamn finger.
Saving the world isn't your job anymore, Carroll. It stopped being your job the minute your term ended.
For better or worse, as impossible as it is...
...that job is mine.
ir... you want to just leave him in there?
Yes. None of the comms systems are active. He can't cause any trouble.
But can't he just let himself out? I mean, he was President too. Doesn't he know the codes?
Nope. You know the first thing I did when I moved into this house, Jim?
I changed all the locks.

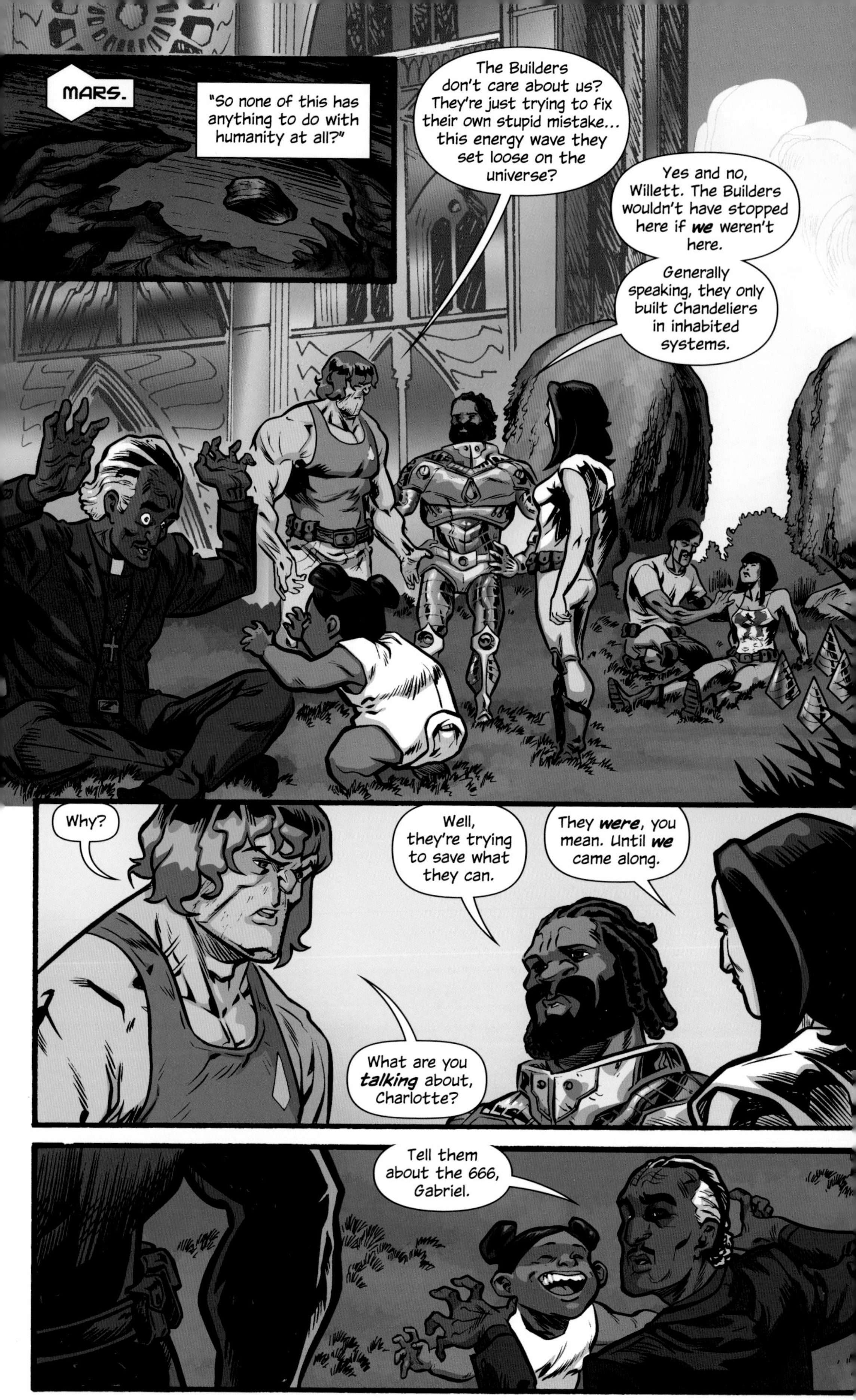
MARS.
"So none of this has anything to do with humanity at all?"
The Builders don't care about us? They're just trying to fix their own stupid mistake... this energy wave they set loose on the universe?
Yes and no, Willett. The Builders wouldn't have stopped here if *we* weren't here.
Generally speaking, they only built Chandeliers in inhabited systems.
Why?
Well, they're trying to save what they can.
They *were*, you mean. Until *we* came along.
What are you *talking* about, Charlotte?
Tell them about the 666, Gabriel.

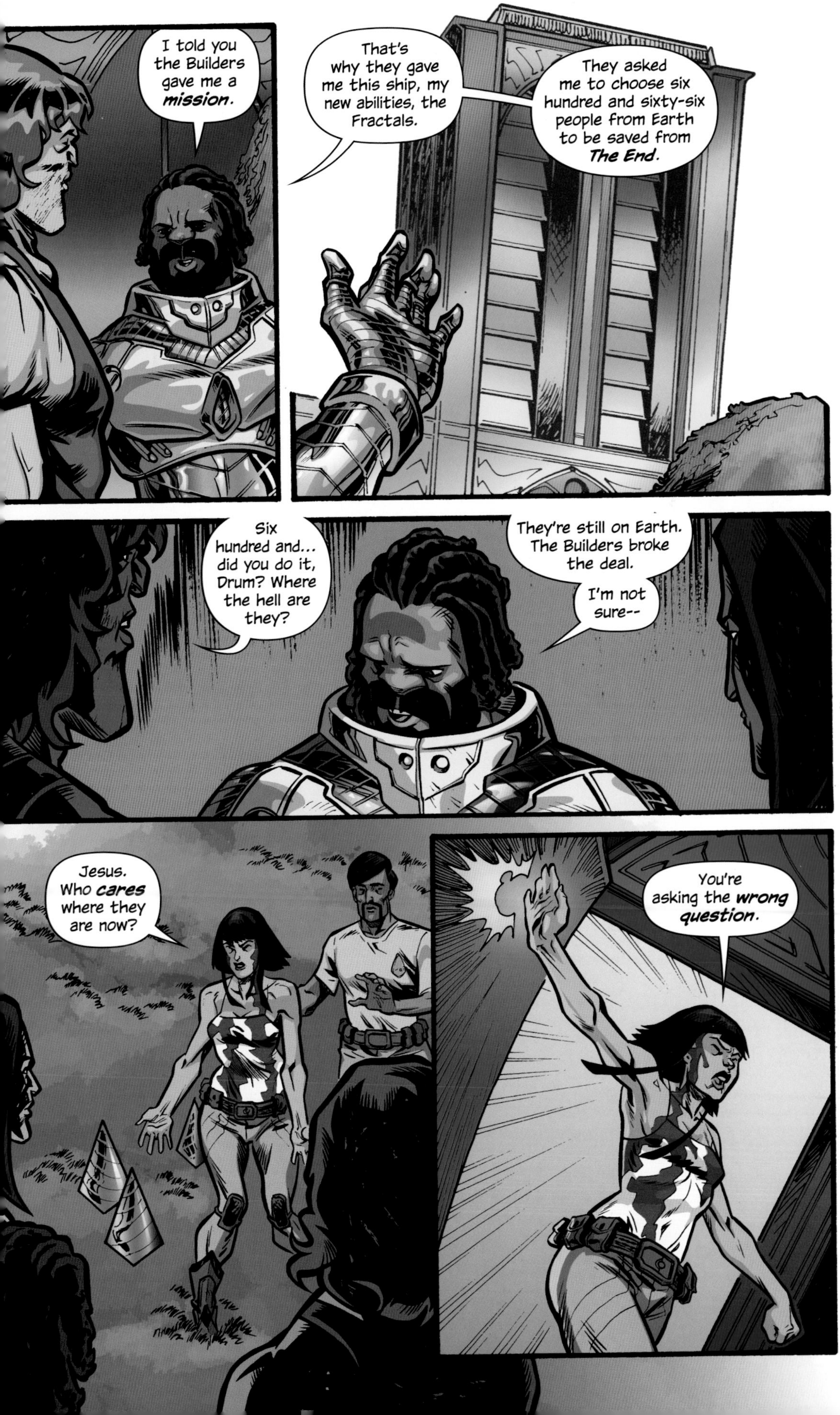
I told you the Builders gave me a *mission*.
That's why they gave me this ship, my new abilities, the Fractals.
They asked me to choose six hundred and sixty-six people from Earth to be saved from *The End*.
Six hundred and... did you do it, Drum? Where the hell are they?
They're still on Earth. The Builders broke the deal.
I'm not sure--
Jesus. Who *cares* where they are now?
You're asking the *wrong question*.

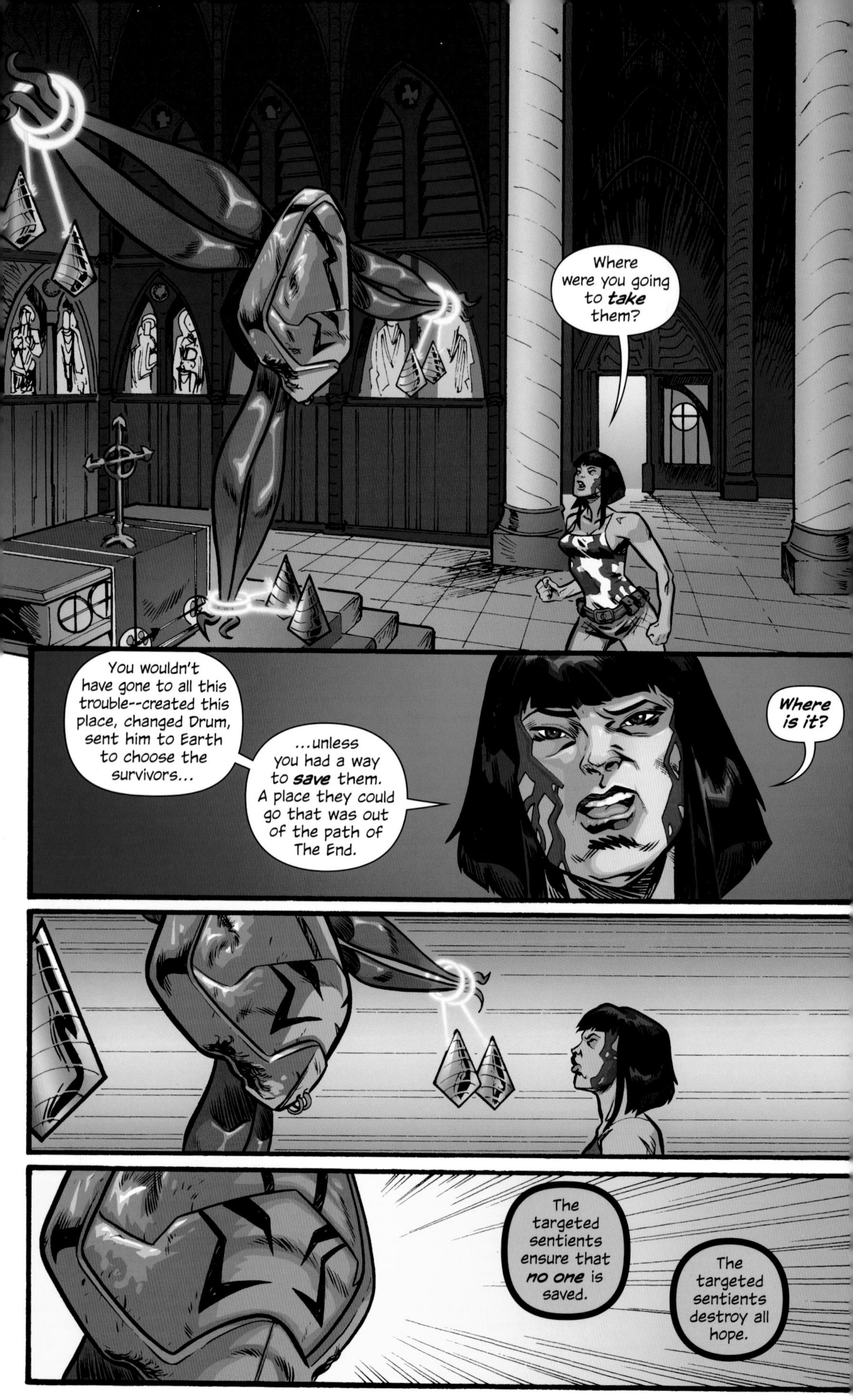
Where were you going to *take* them?
You wouldn't have gone to all this trouble--created this place, changed Drum, sent him to Earth to choose the survivors...
...unless you had a way to *save* them. A place they could go that was out of the path of The End.
Where is it?
The targeted sentients ensure that *no one* is saved.
The targeted sentients destroy all hope.

The targeted sentients? **Us?**

We didn't turn on the fucking energy wave that's eating the galaxy, you goddamn **squid**.

Kyoko's right. If the Builders wanted you to save people, they must have a refuge. They didn't tell you where you were supposed to take the 666?

No. I was supposed to bring them to a rendezvous point between Earth and Mars. That's all I know.

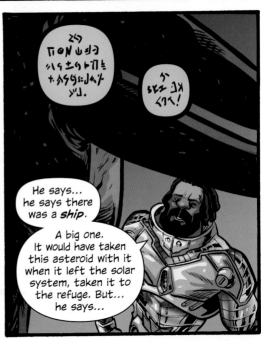

He says... he says there was a **ship**.

A big one. It would have taken this asteroid with it when it left the solar system, taken it to the refuge. But... he says...

...you **destroyed** it?

I... I didn't **know that!** I thought they were trying to **cut and run!**

The targeted sentients destroy all hope.

[87]

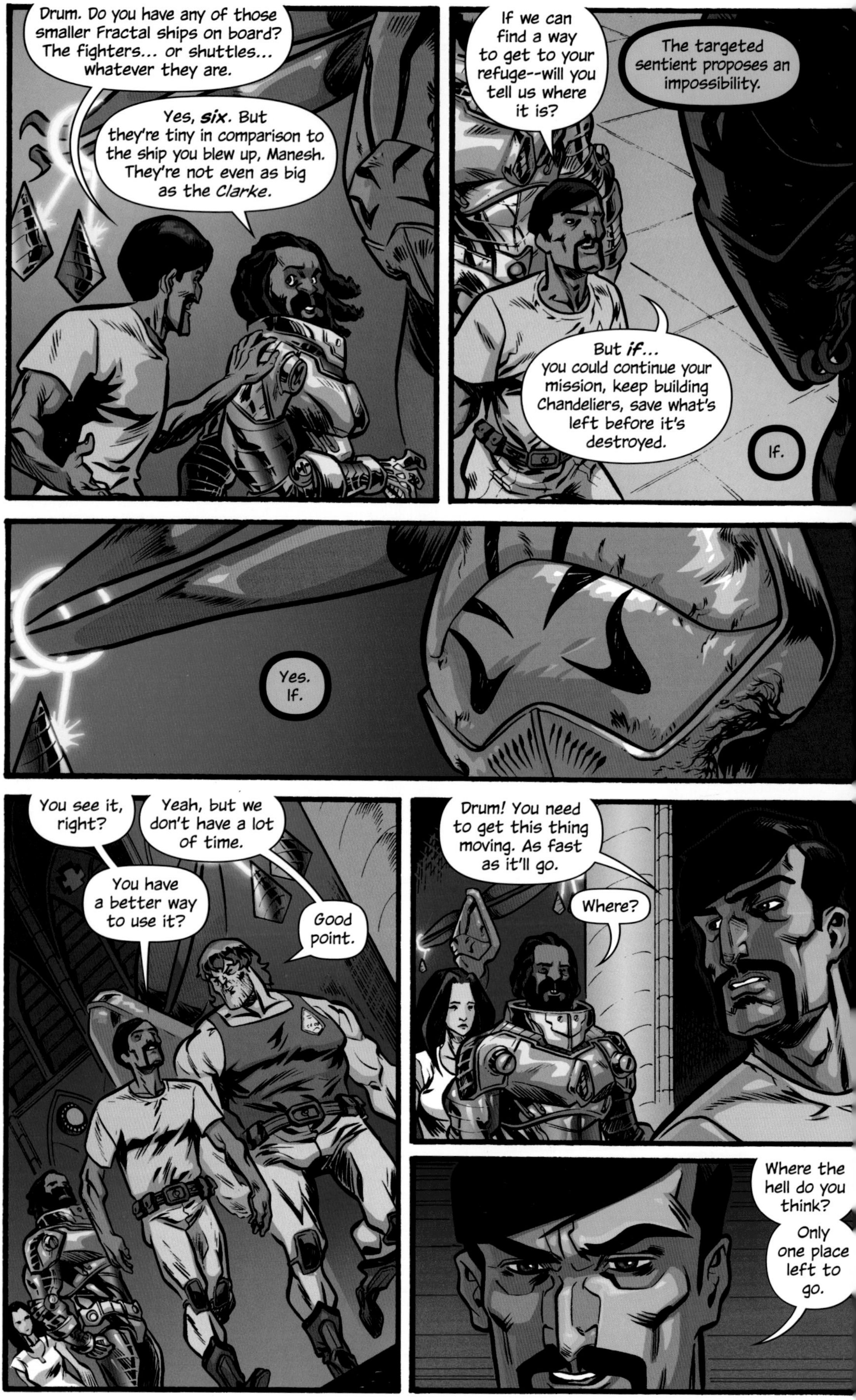
Drum. Do you have any of those smaller Fractal ships on board? The fighters... or shuttles... whatever they are.
Yes, *six*. But they're tiny in comparison to the ship you blew up, Manesh. They're not even as big as the *Clarke*.
If we can find a way to get to your refuge--will you tell us where it is?
The targeted sentient proposes an impossibility.
But *if*... you could continue your mission, keep building Chandeliers, save what's left before it's destroyed.
If.
Yes. If.
You see it, right?
Yeah, but we don't have a lot of time.
You have a better way to use it?
Good point.
Drum! You need to get this thing moving. As fast as it'll go.
Where?
Where the hell do you think?
Only one place left to go.

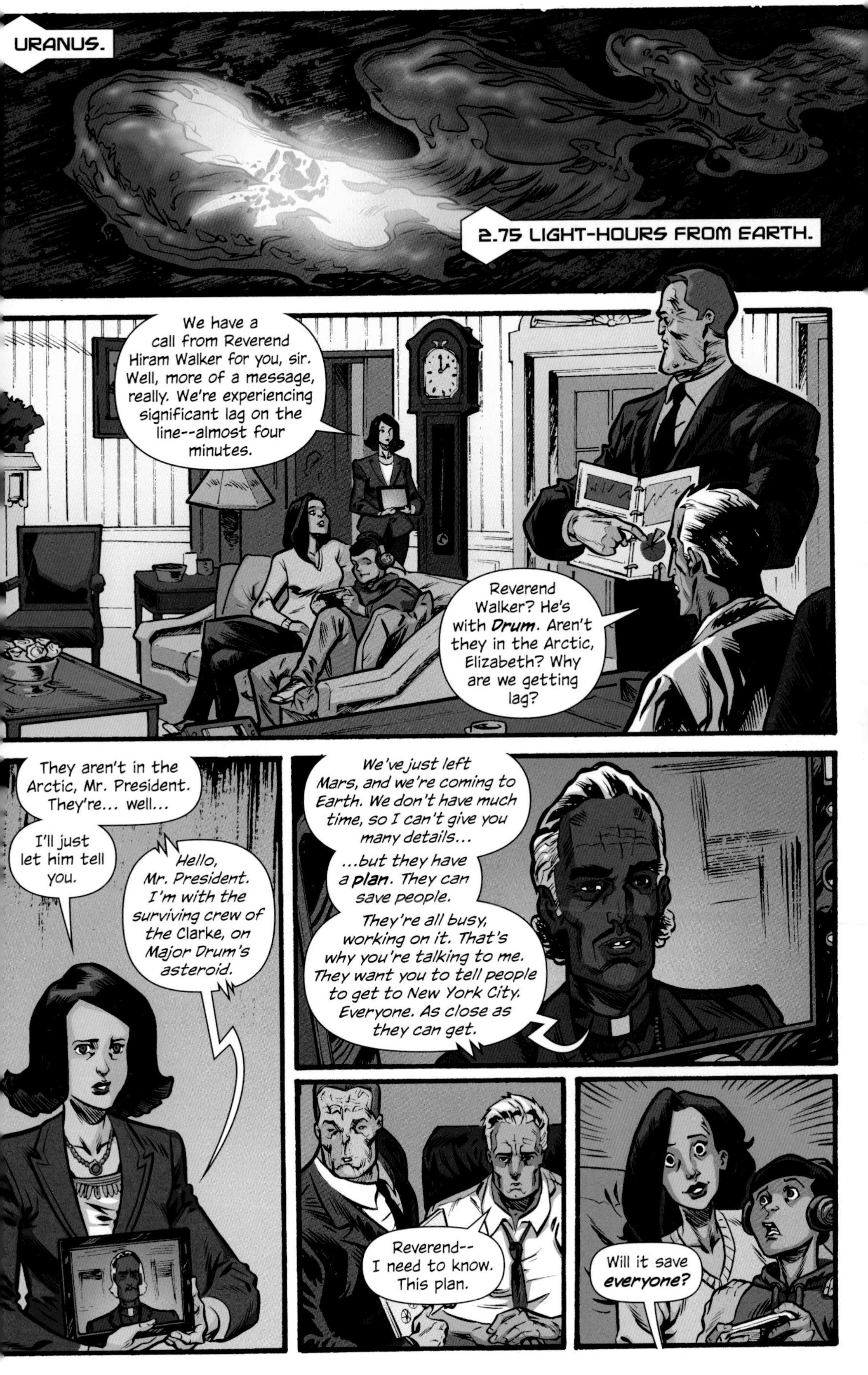
URANUS.
2.75 LIGHT-HOURS FROM EARTH.
We have a call from Reverend Hiram Walker for you, sir. Well, more of a message, really. We're experiencing significant lag on the line--almost four minutes.
Reverend Walker? He's with Drum. Aren't they in the Arctic, Elizabeth? Why are we getting lag?
They aren't in the Arctic, Mr. President. They're... well...
I'll just let him tell you.
Hello, Mr. President. I'm with the surviving crew of the Clarke, on Major Drum's asteroid.
We've just left Mars, and we're coming to Earth. We don't have much time, so I can't give you many details...
...but they have a plan. They can save people.
They're all busy, working on it. That's why you're talking to me. They want you to tell people to get to New York City. Everyone. As close as they can get.
Reverend-- I need to know. This plan.
Will it save everyone?

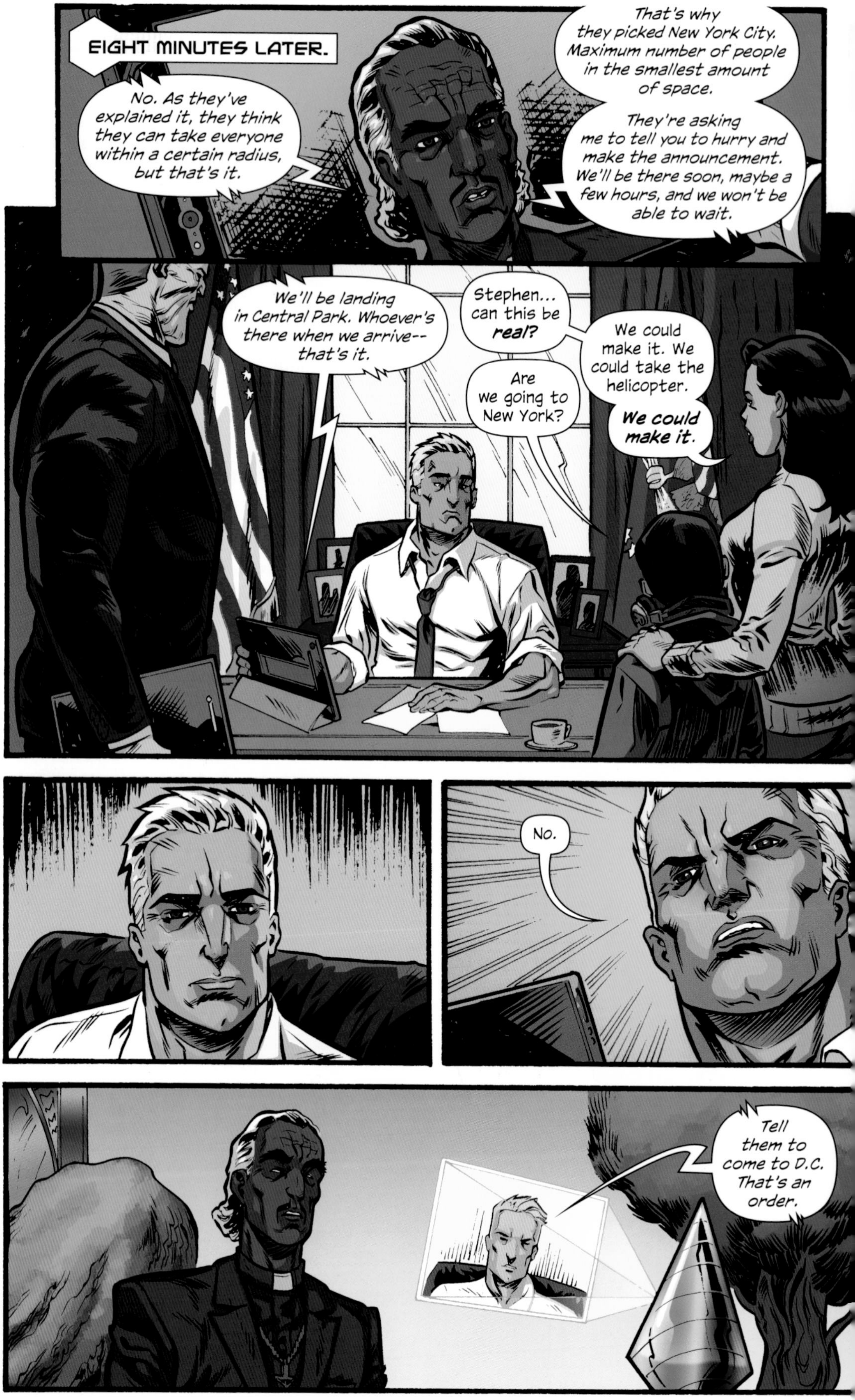
EIGHT MINUTES LATER.
No. As they've explained it, they think they can take everyone within a certain radius, but that's it.
That's why they picked New York City. Maximum number of people in the smallest amount of space.
They're asking me to tell you to hurry and make the announcement. We'll be there soon, maybe a few hours, and we won't be able to wait.
We'll be landing in Central Park. Whoever's there when we arrive--that's it.
Stephen... can this be *real?*
Are we going to New York?
We could make it. We could take the helicopter.
We could make it.
No.
Tell them to come to D.C. That's an order.

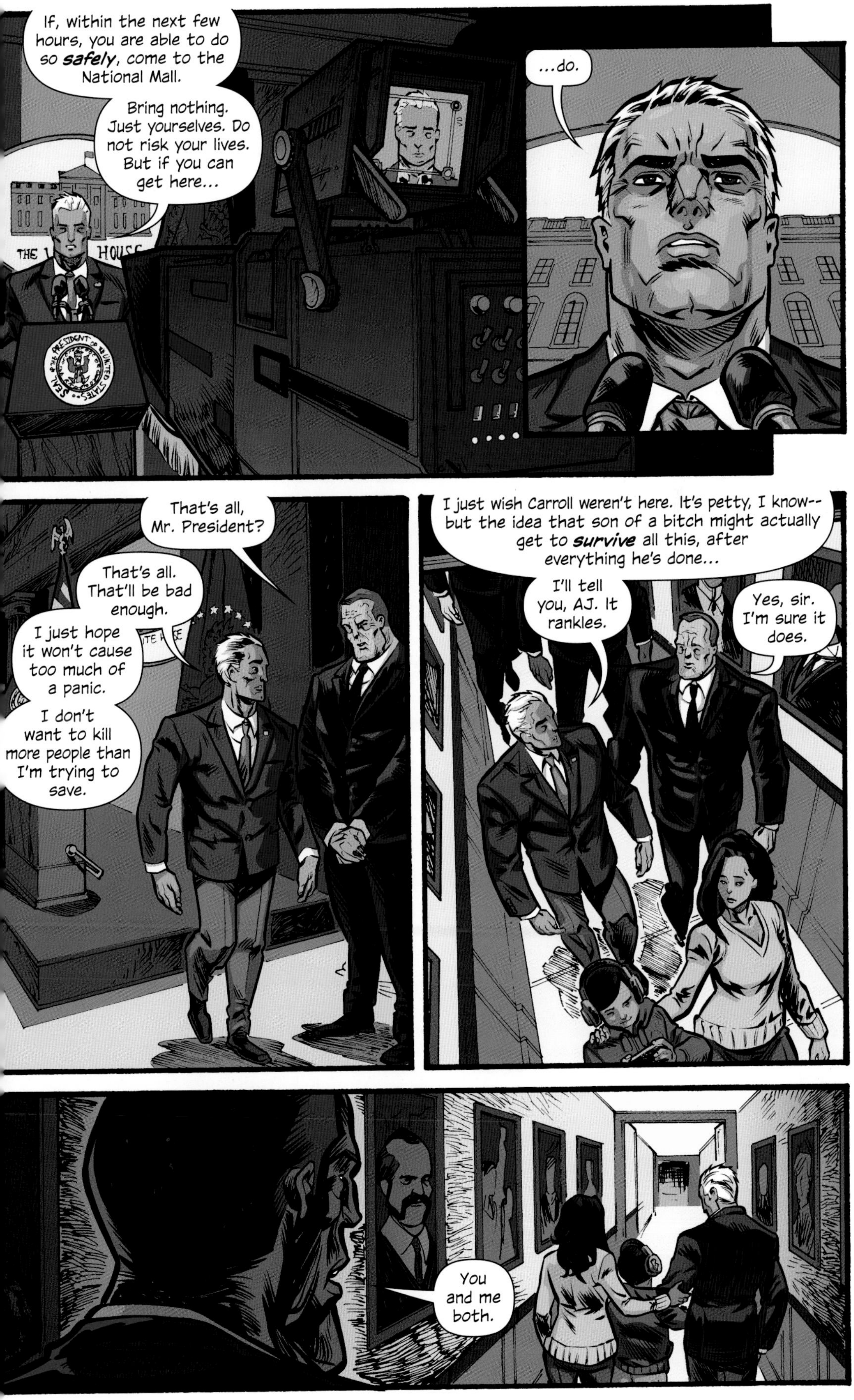
If, within the next few hours, you are able to do so *safely*, come to the National Mall.
Bring nothing. Just yourselves. Do not risk your lives. But if you can get here...
THE HOUSE
SEAL OF THE PRESIDENT OF THE UNITED STATES
...do.
That's all, Mr. President?
That's all. That'll be bad enough.
I just hope it won't cause too much of a panic.
I don't want to kill more people than I'm trying to save.
I just wish Carroll weren't here. It's petty, I know--but the idea that son of a bitch might actually get to *survive* all this, after everything he's done...
I'll tell you, AJ. It rankles.
Yes, sir. I'm sure it does.
You and me both.

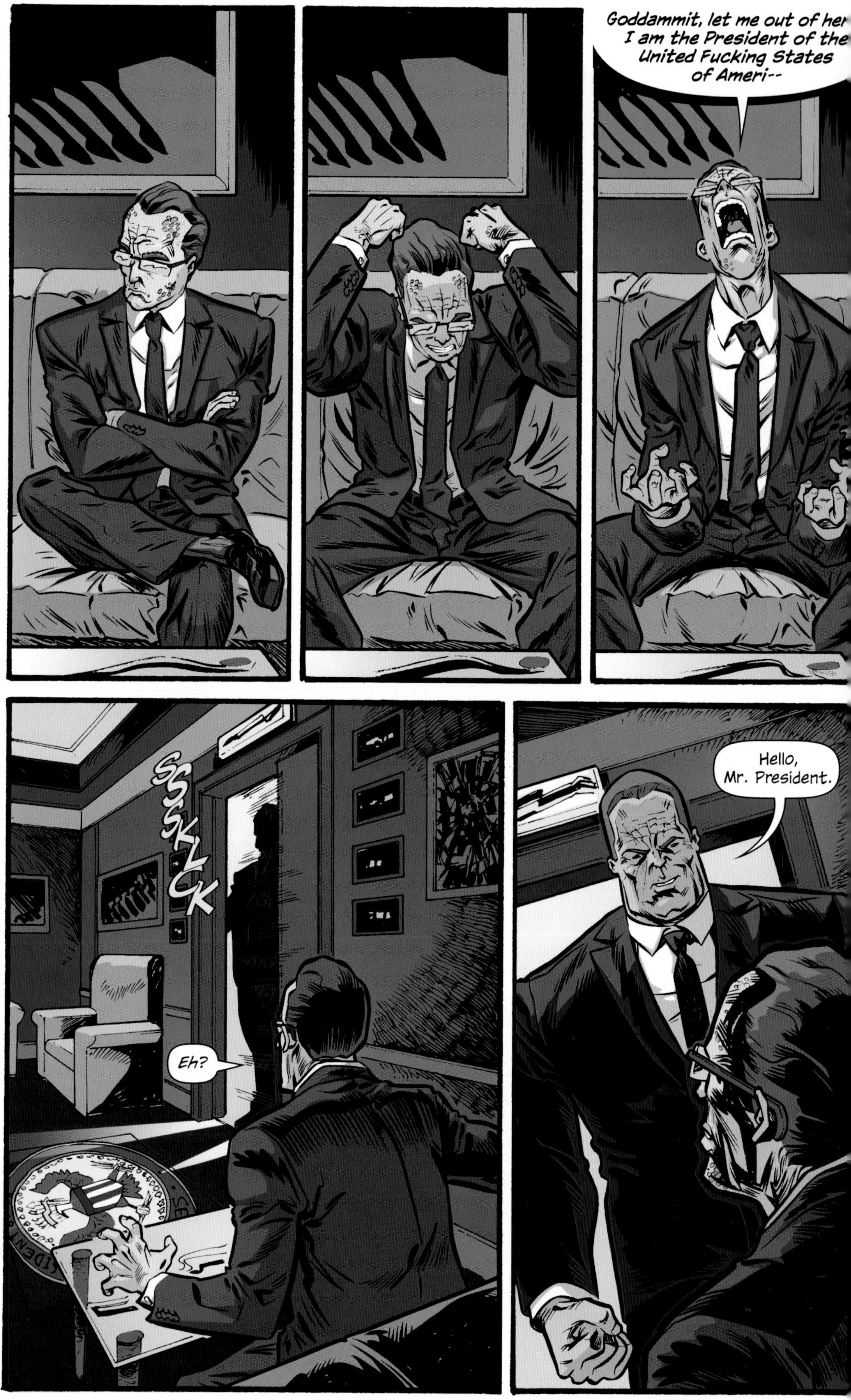
Goddammit, let me out of her
I am the President of the
United Fucking States
of Ameri--
SSSKLICK
Eh?
Hello,
Mr. President.

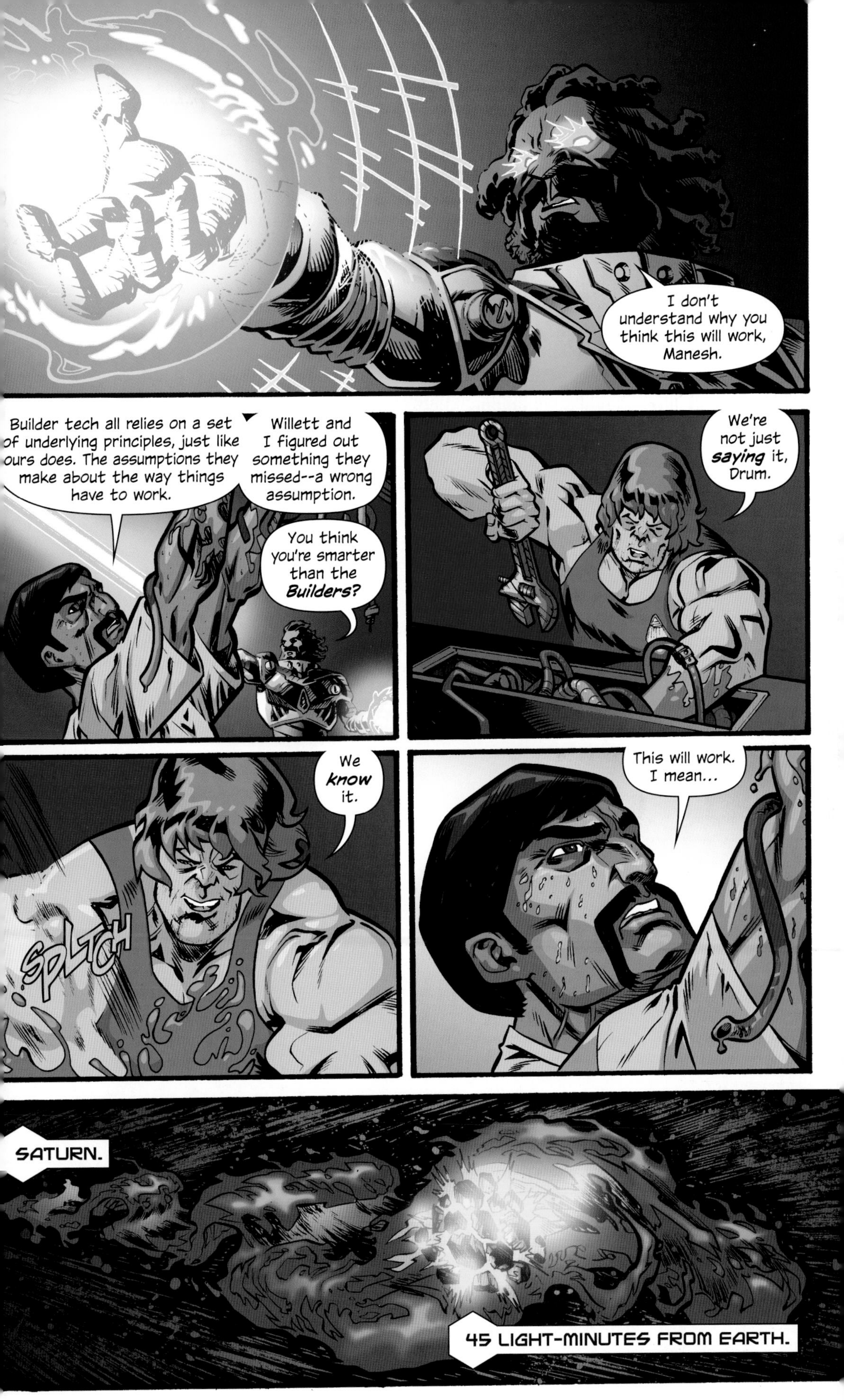

I don't understand why you think this will work, Manesh.
Builder tech all relies on a set of underlying principles, just like ours does. The assumptions they make about the way things have to work.
Willett and I figured out something they missed--a wrong assumption.
You think you're smarter than the **Builders?**
We're not just **saying** it, Drum.
We **know** it.
SPLTCH
This will work. I mean...
SATURN.
45 LIGHT-MINUTES FROM EARTH.

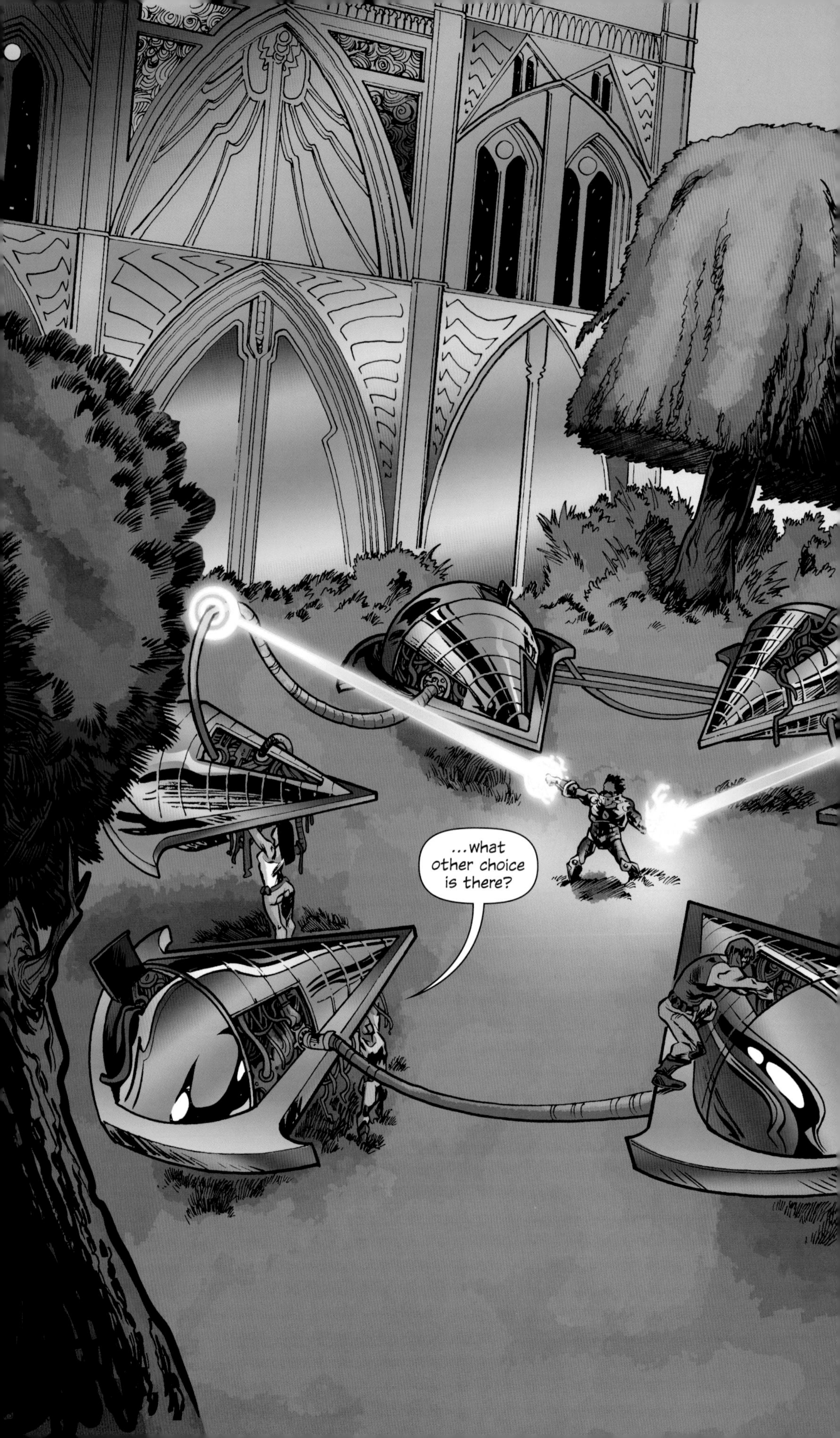
...what other choice is there?

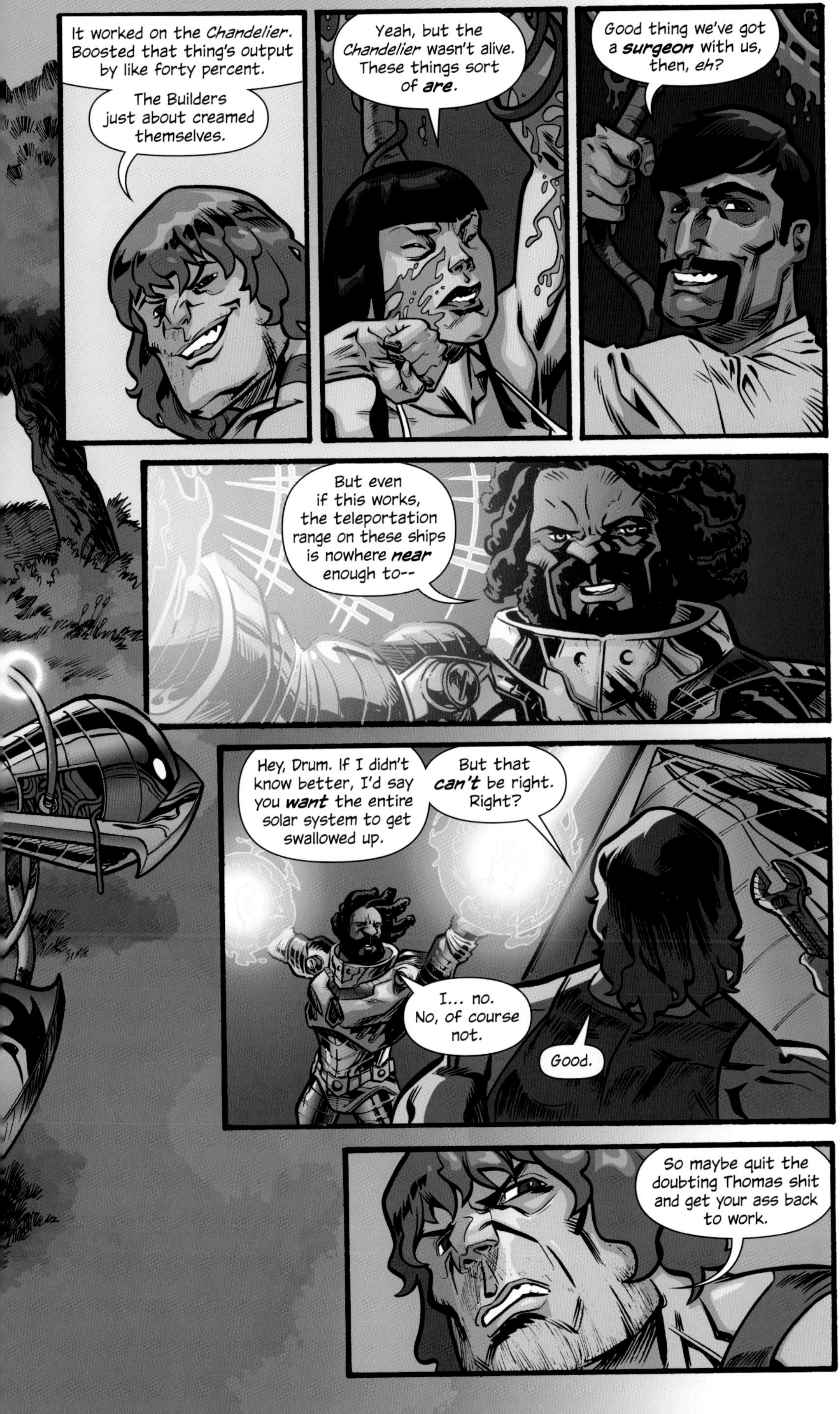
It worked on the Chandelier. Boosted that thing's output by like forty percent.
The Builders just about creamed themselves.
Yeah, but the Chandelier wasn't alive. These things sort of are.
Good thing we've got a surgeon with us, then, eh?
But even if this works, the teleportation range on these ships is nowhere near enough to--
Hey, Drum. If I didn't know better, I'd say you want the entire solar system to get swallowed up.
But that can't be right. Right?
I... no. No, of course not.
Good.
So maybe quit the doubting Thomas shit and get your ass back to work.

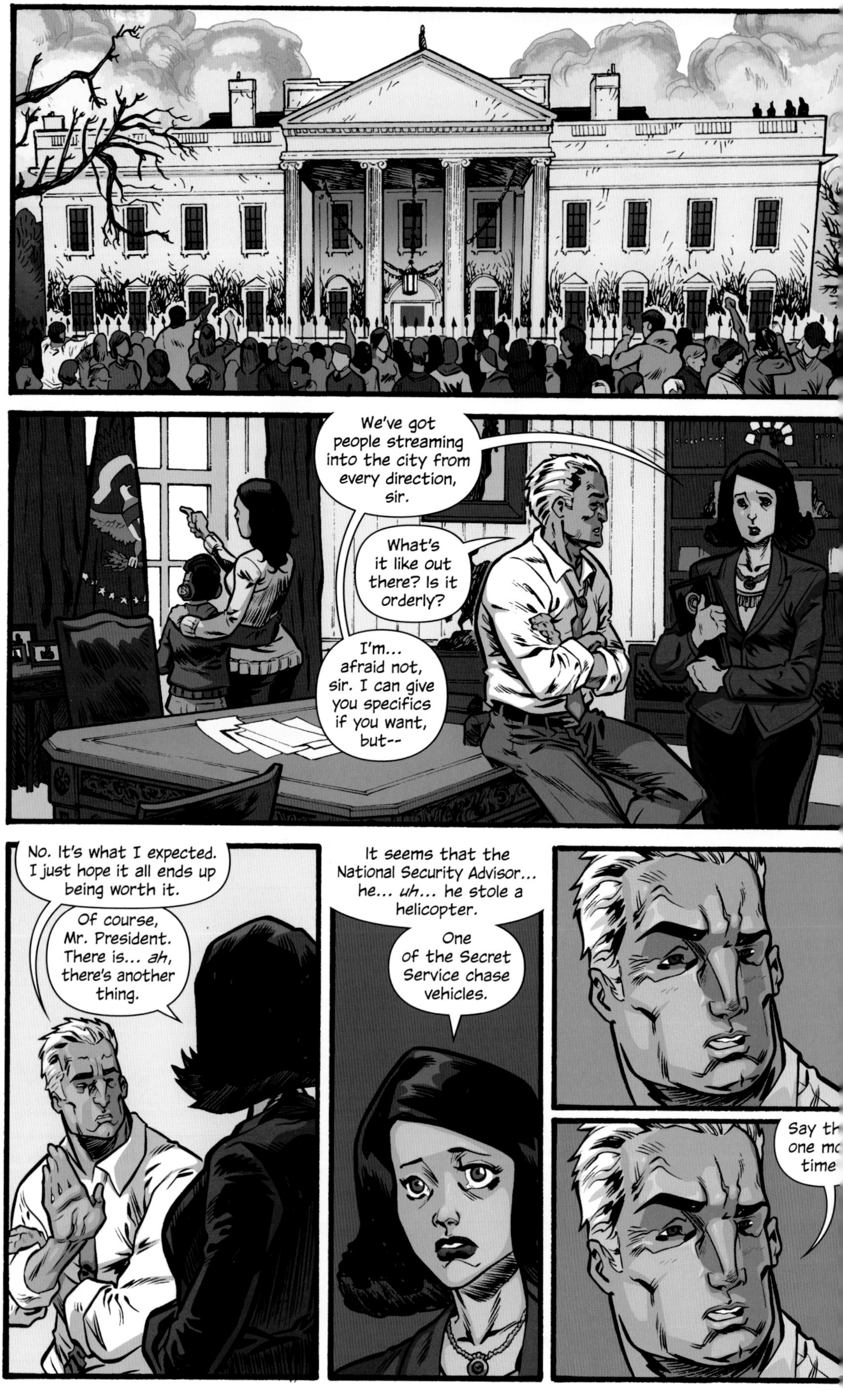
We've got people streaming into the city from every direction, sir.
What's it like out there? Is it orderly?
I'm... afraid not, sir. I can give you specifics if you want, but--
No. It's what I expected. I just hope it all ends up being worth it.
Of course, Mr. President. There is... *ah*, there's another thing.
It seems that the National Security Advisor... he... *uh*... he stole a helicopter.
One of the Secret Service chase vehicles.

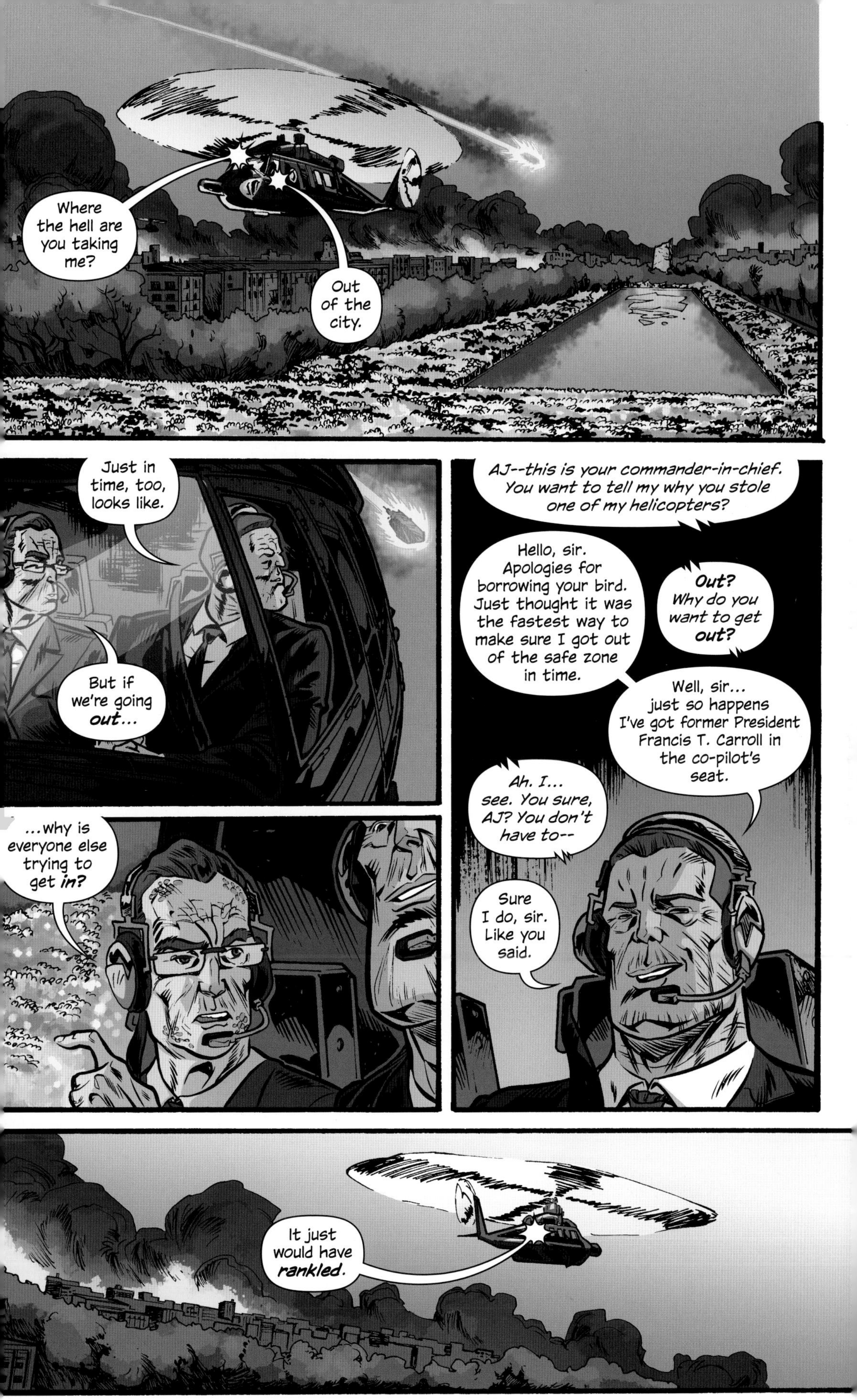
Where the hell are you taking me?
Out of the city.
Just in time, too, looks like.
But if we're going *out*...
...why is everyone else trying to get *in?*
AJ--this is your commander-in-chief. You want to tell my why you stole one of my helicopters?
Hello, sir. Apologies for borrowing your bird. Just thought it was the fastest way to make sure I got out of the safe zone in time.
Out? Why do you want to get *out?*
Well, sir... just so happens I've got former President Francis T. Carroll in the co-pilot's seat.
Ah. I... see. You sure, AJ? You don't have to--
Sure I do, sir. Like you said.
It just would have *rankled*.

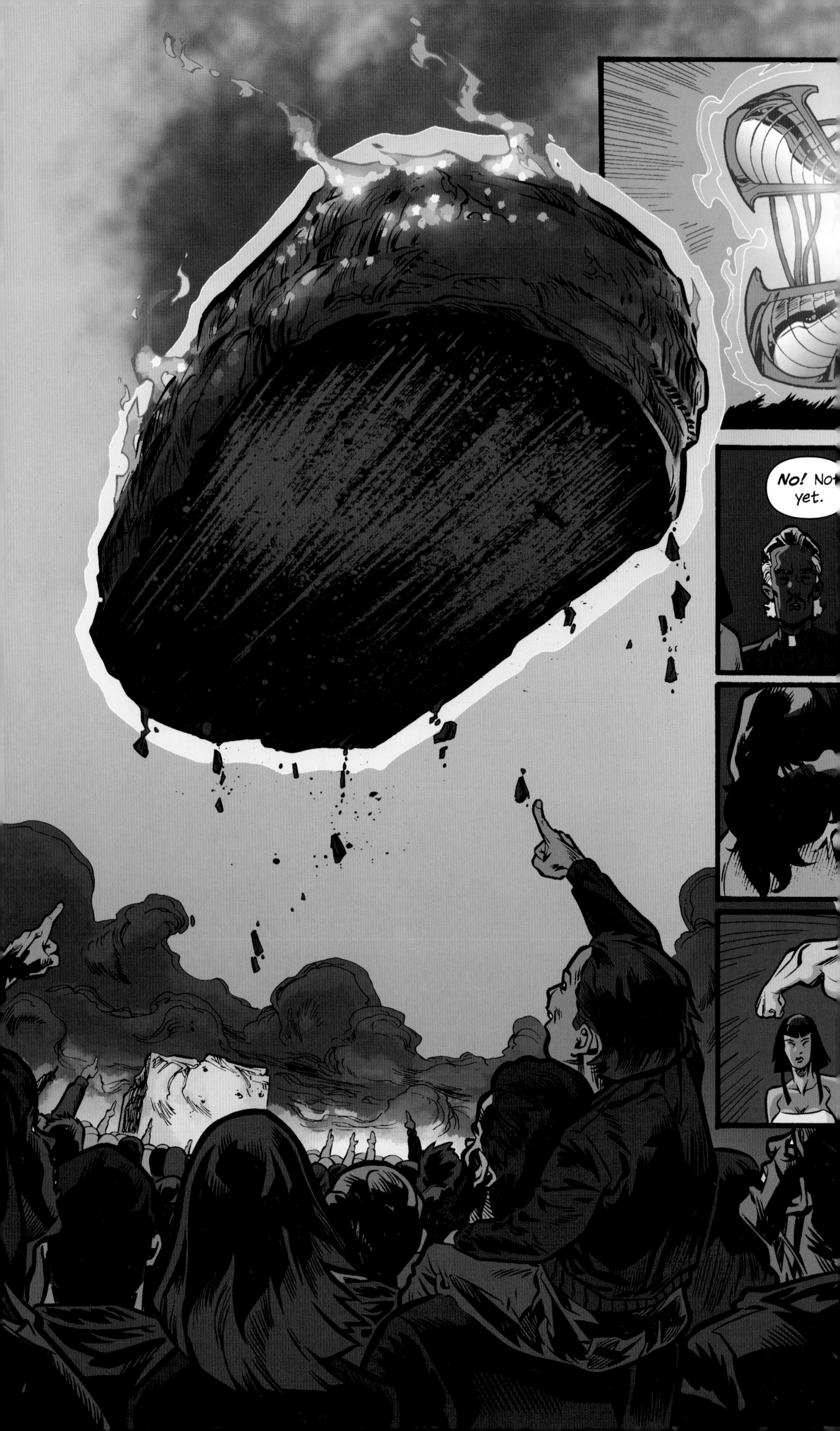
No! No
yet.

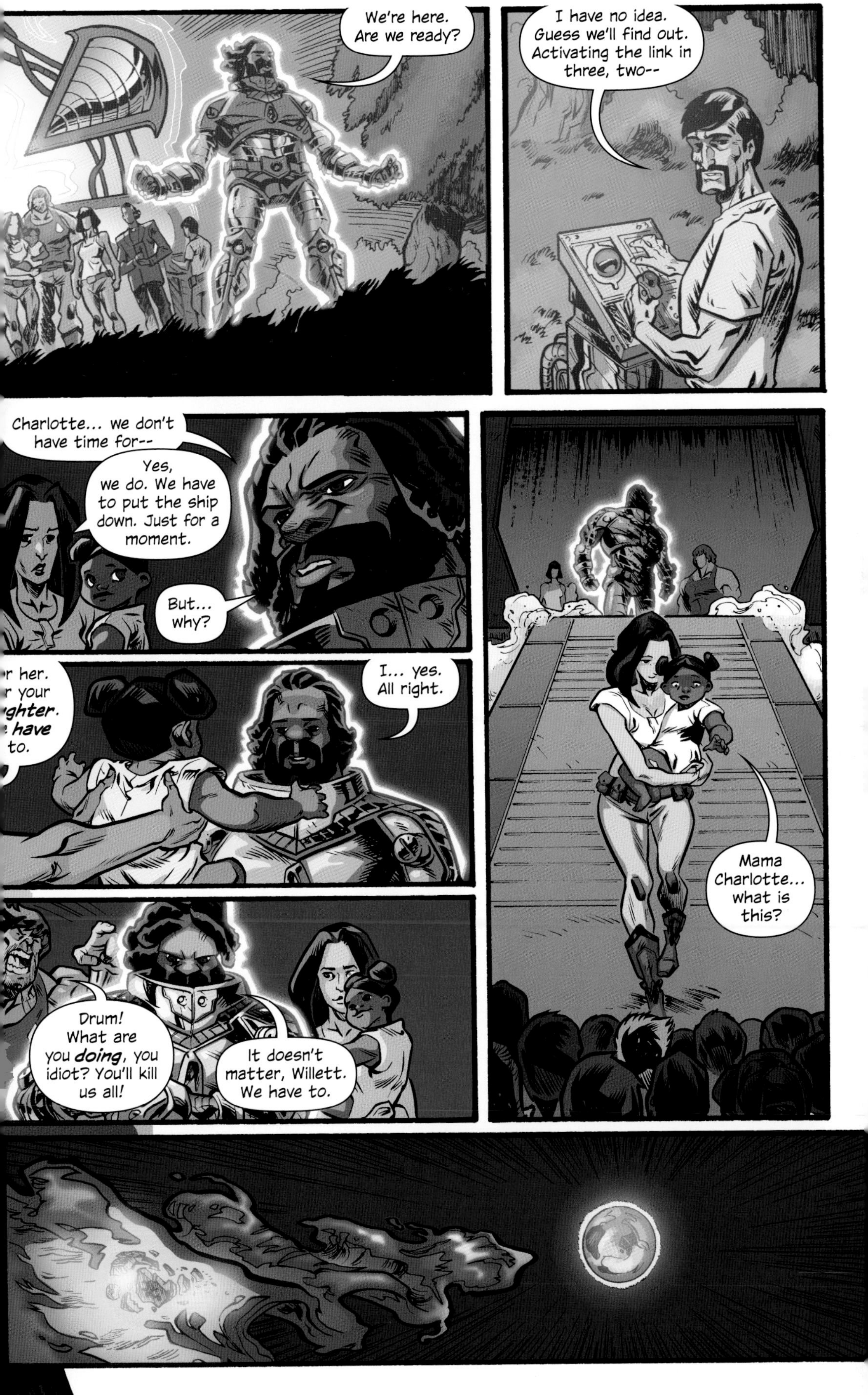
We're here. Are we ready?
I have no idea. Guess we'll find out. Activating the link in three, two--
Charlotte... we don't have time for--
Yes, we do. We have to put the ship down. Just for a moment.
But... why?
r her. r your ghter. have to.
I... yes. All right.
Drum! What are you *doing*, you idiot? You'll kill us all!
It doesn't matter, Willett. We have to.
Mama Charlotte... what is this?

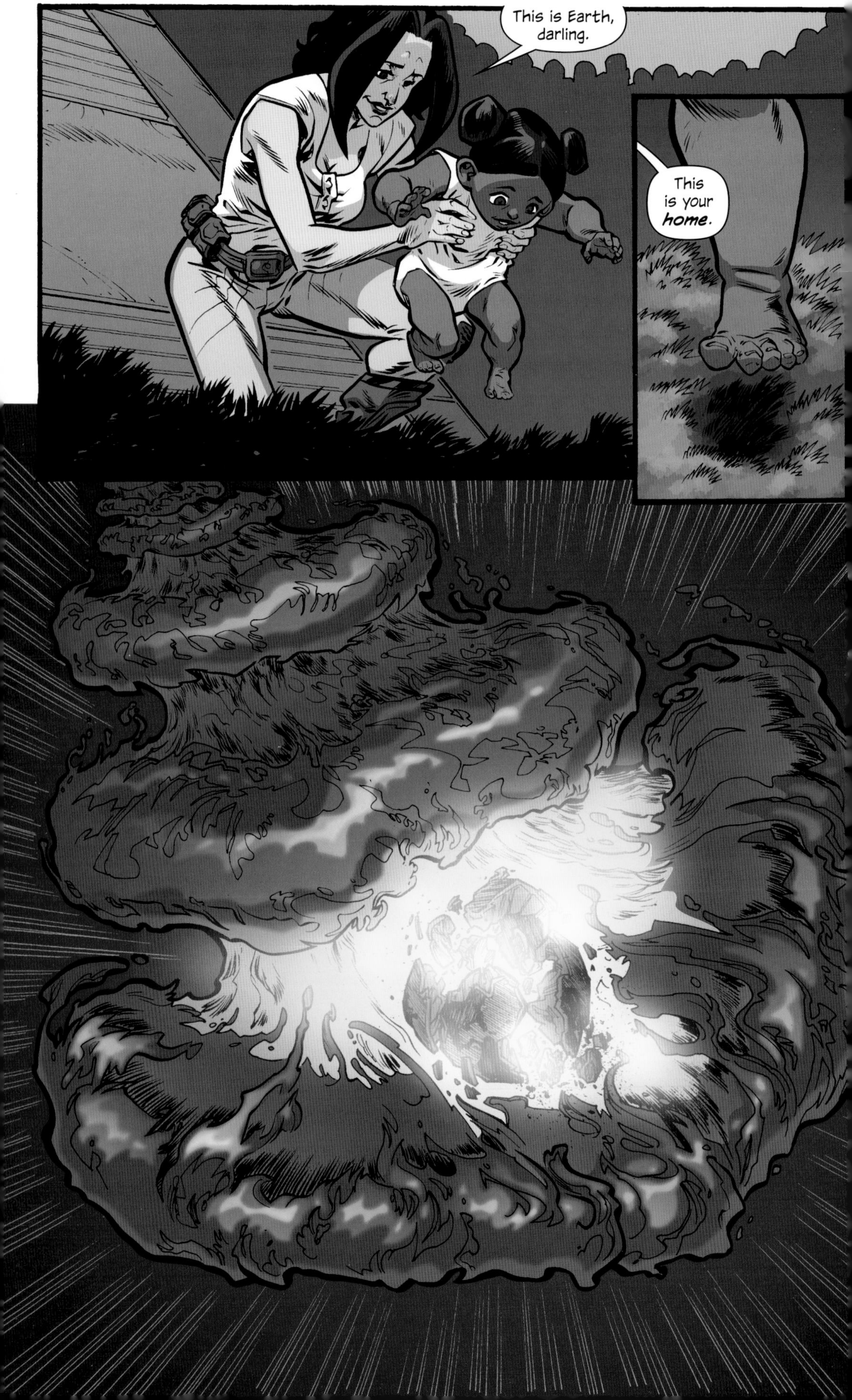
This is Earth, darling.
This is your *home*.

LETTER 44

CHAPTER V

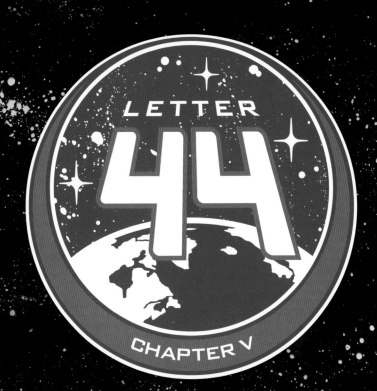

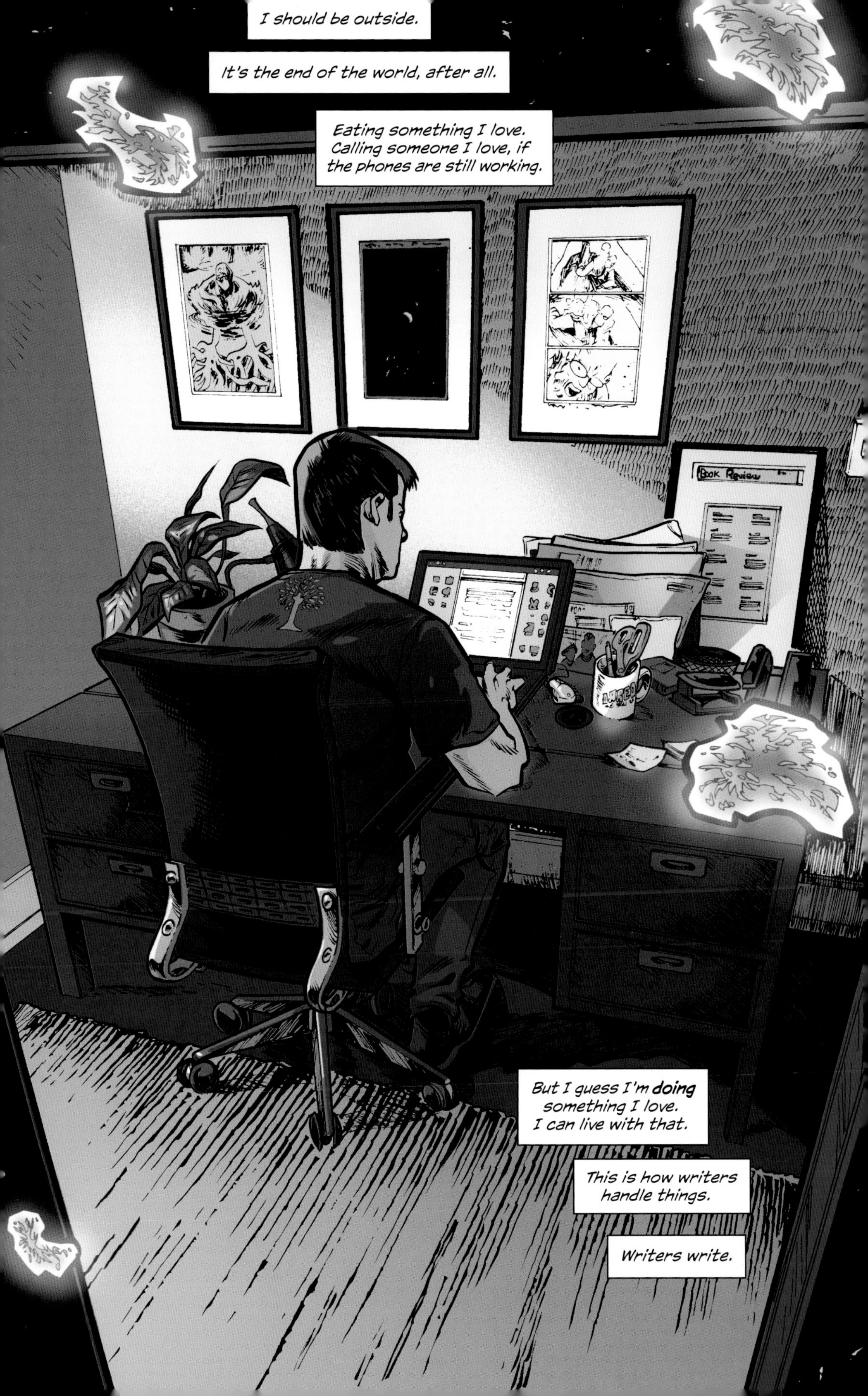
I should be outside.
It's the end of the world, after all.
Eating something I love. Calling someone I love, if the phones are still working.
BOOK Review
But I guess I'm **doing** something I love. I can live with that.
This is how writers handle things.
Writers write.

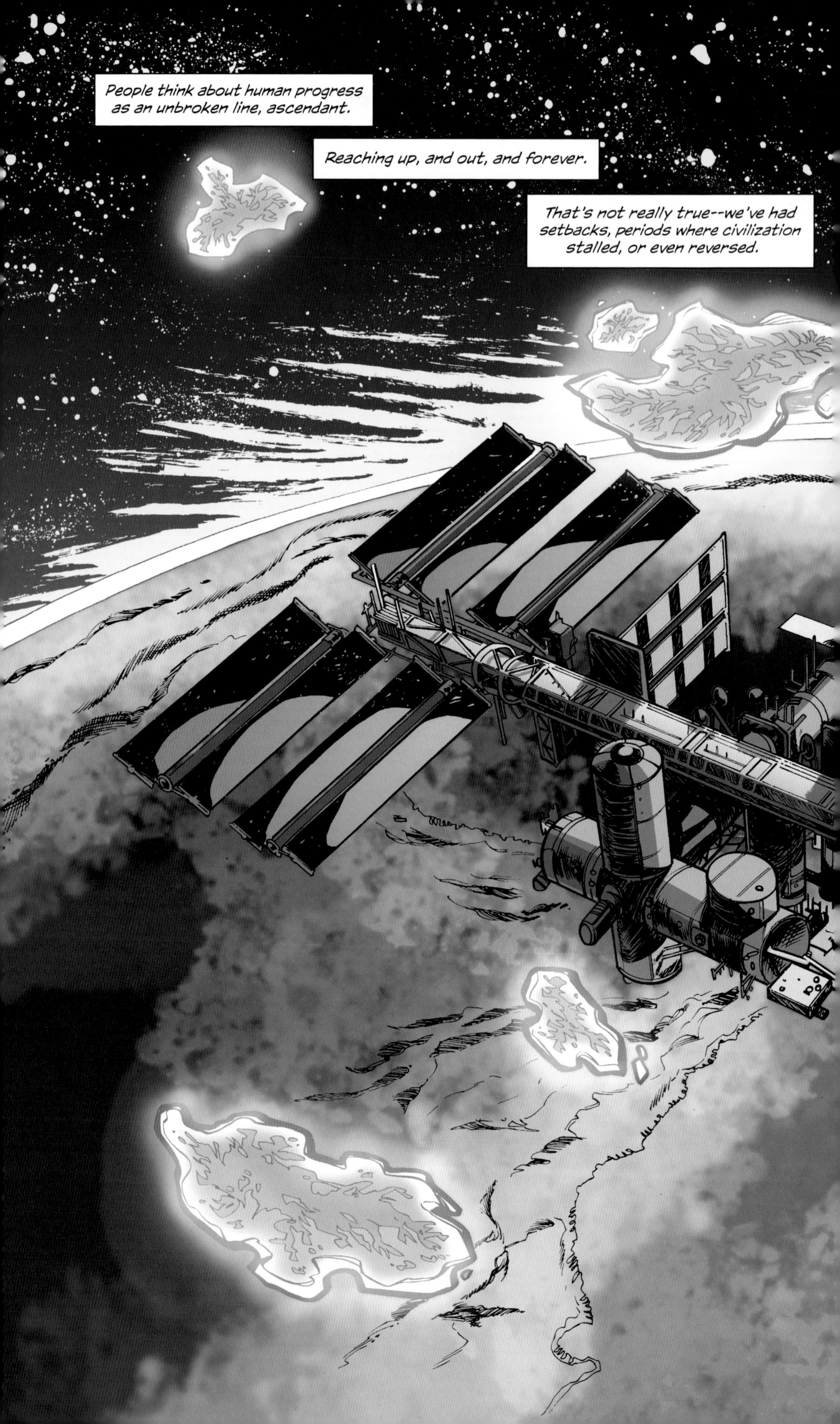
People think about human progress as an unbroken line, ascendant.
Reaching up, and out, and forever.
That's not really true--we've had setbacks, periods where civilization stalled, or even reversed.

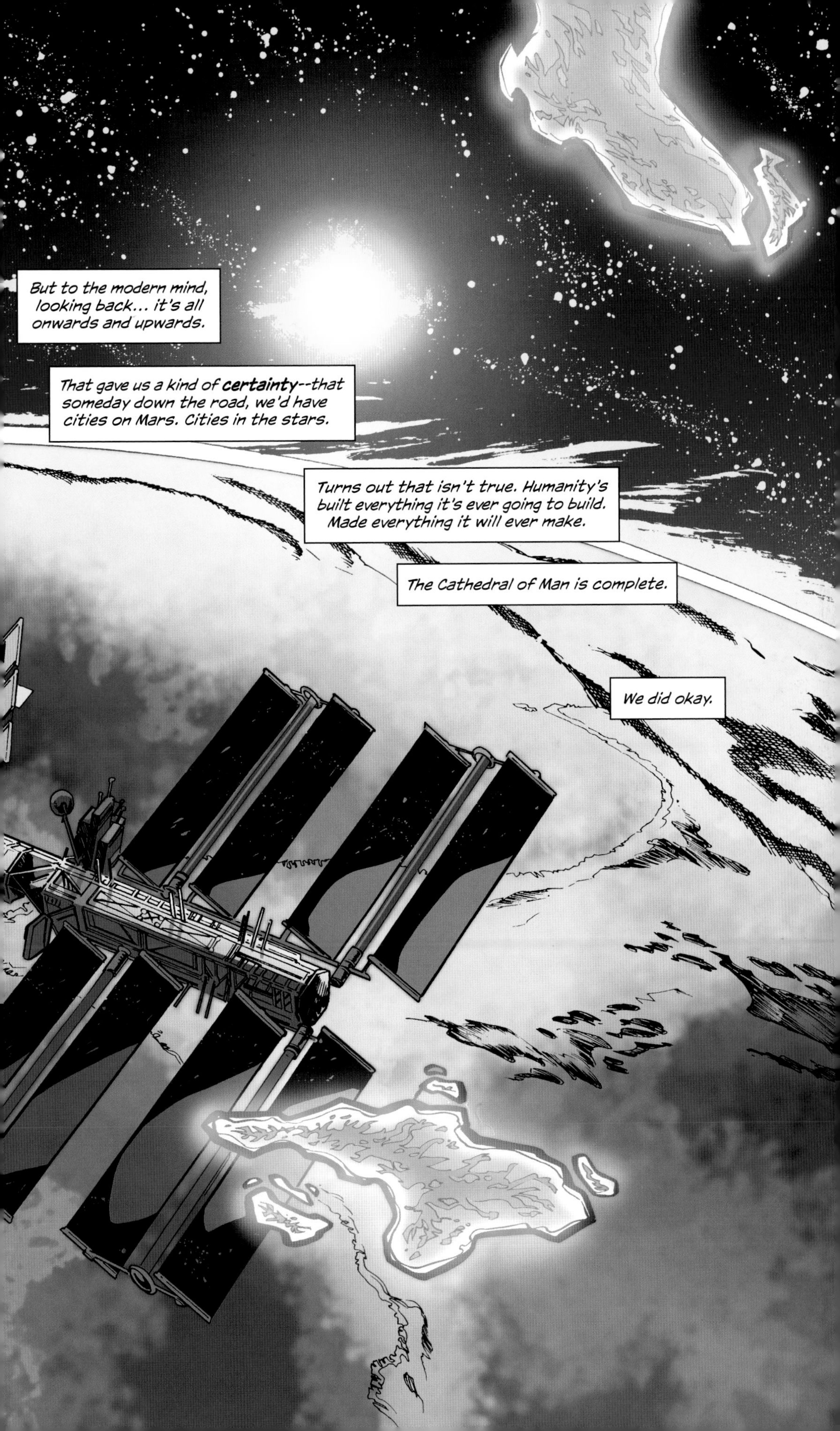
But to the modern mind, looking back... it's all onwards and upwards.
That gave us a kind of **certainty**--that someday down the road, we'd have cities on Mars. Cities in the stars.
Turns out that isn't true. Humanity's built everything it's ever going to build. Made everything it will ever make.
The Cathedral of Man is complete.
We did okay.

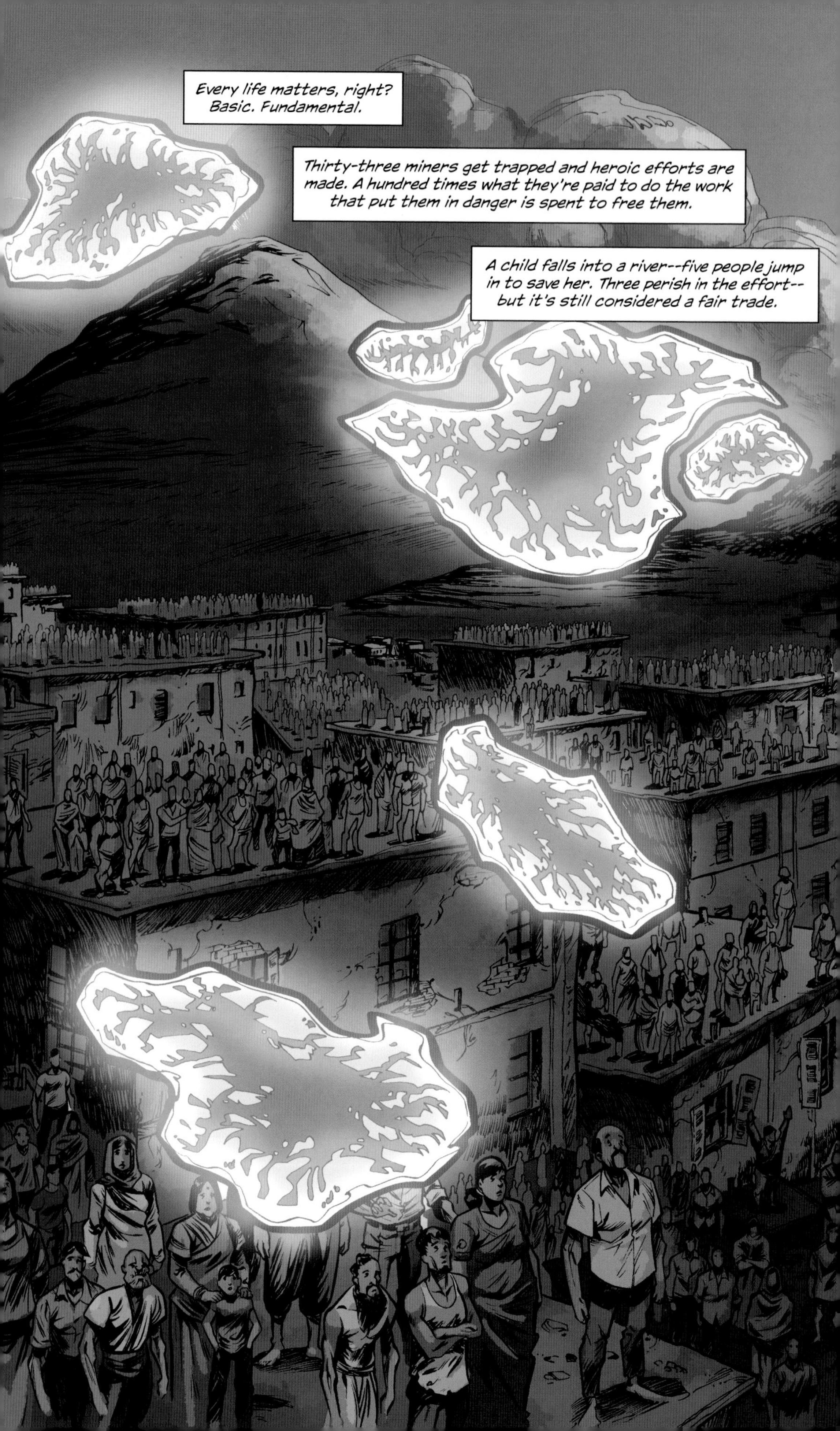
Every life matters, right? Basic. Fundamental.
Thirty-three miners get trapped and heroic efforts are made. A hundred times what they're paid to do the work that put them in danger is spent to free them.
A child falls into a river--five people jump in to save her. Three perish in the effort--but it's still considered a fair trade.

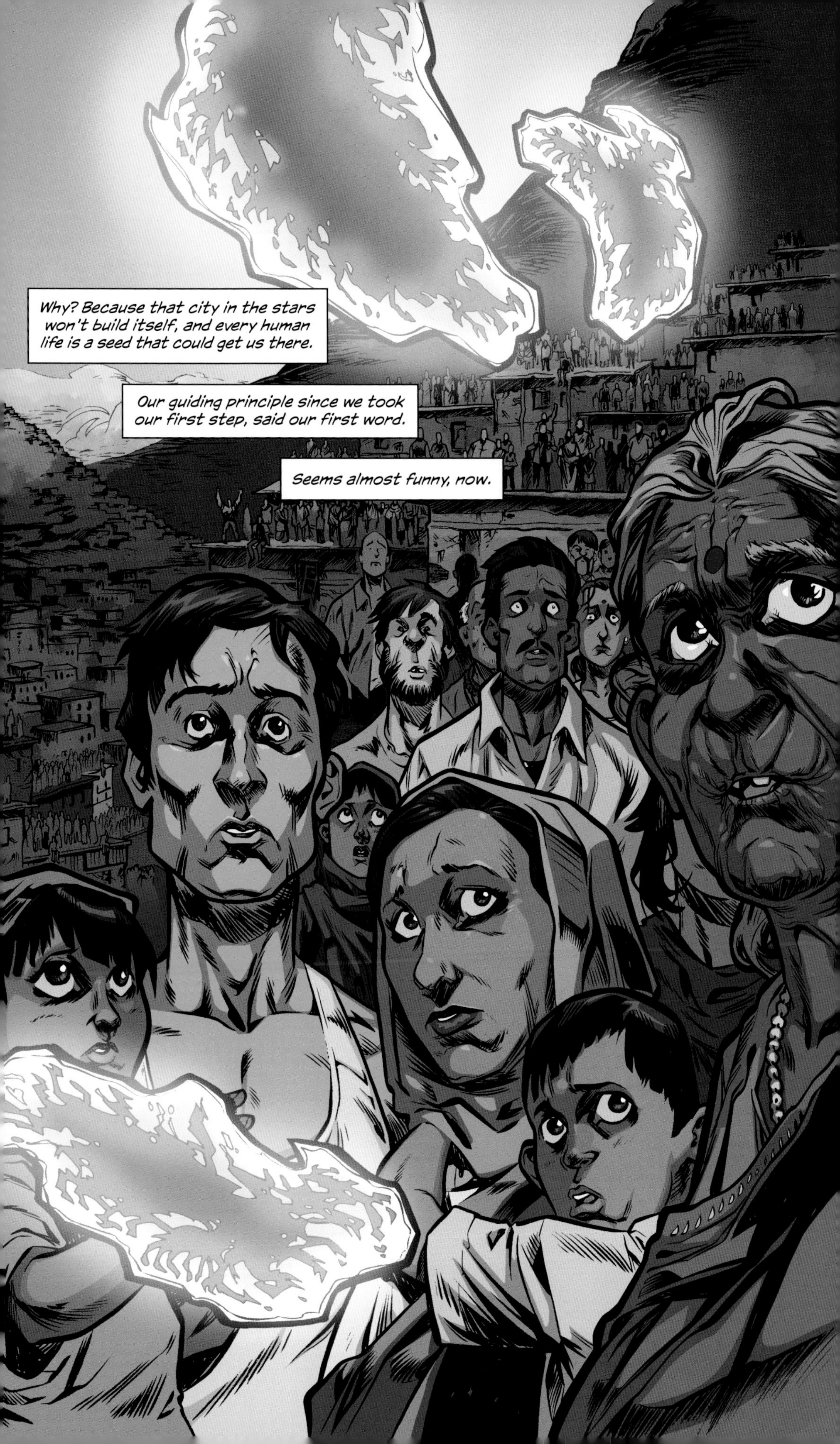
Why? Because that city in the stars won't build itself, and every human life is a seed that could get us there.
Our guiding principle since we took our first step, said our first word.
Seems almost funny, now.

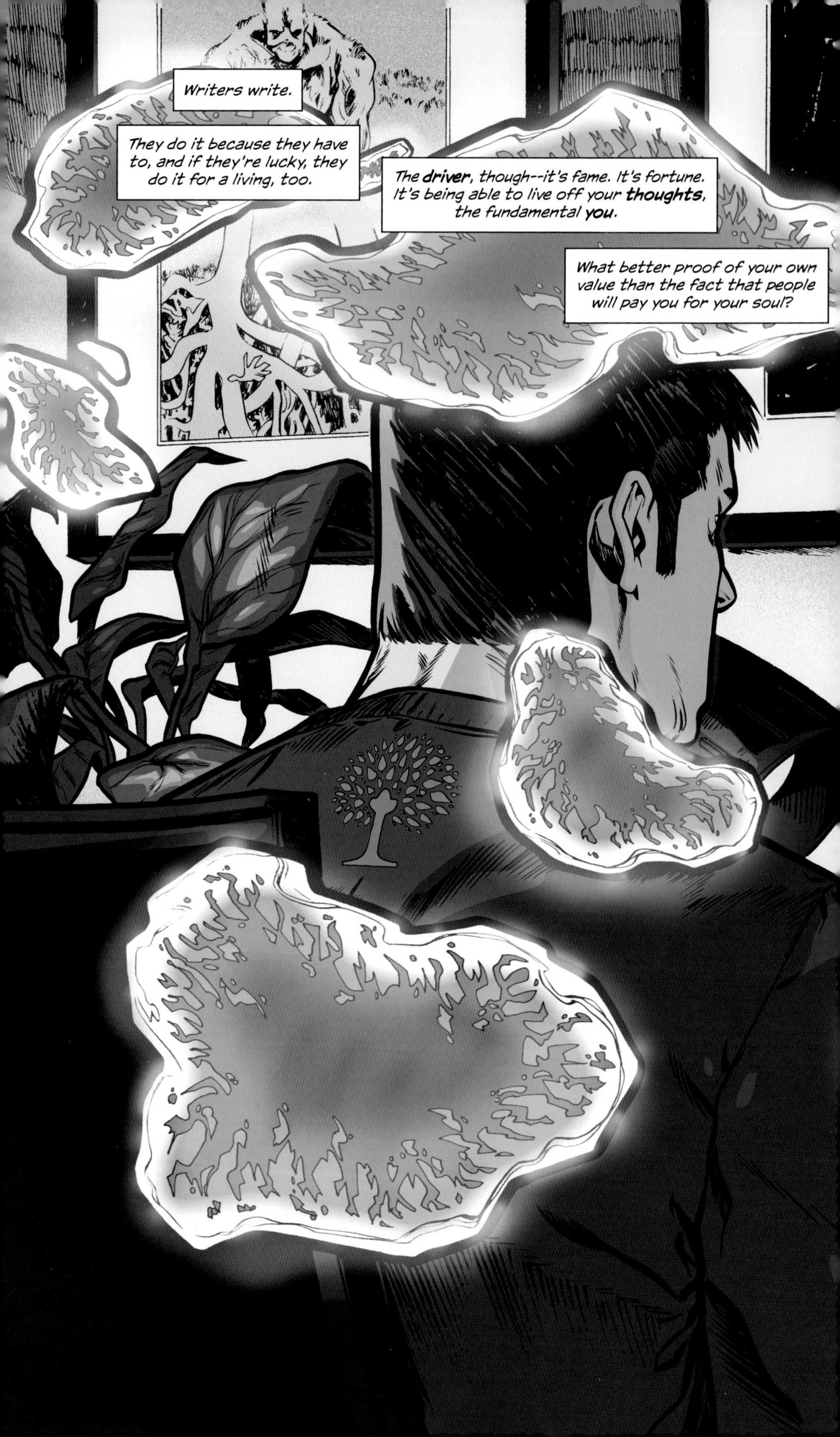
Writers write.
They do it because they have to, and if they're lucky, they do it for a living, too.
The driver, though--it's fame. It's fortune. It's being able to live off your thoughts, the fundamental you.
What better proof of your own value than the fact that people will pay you for your soul?

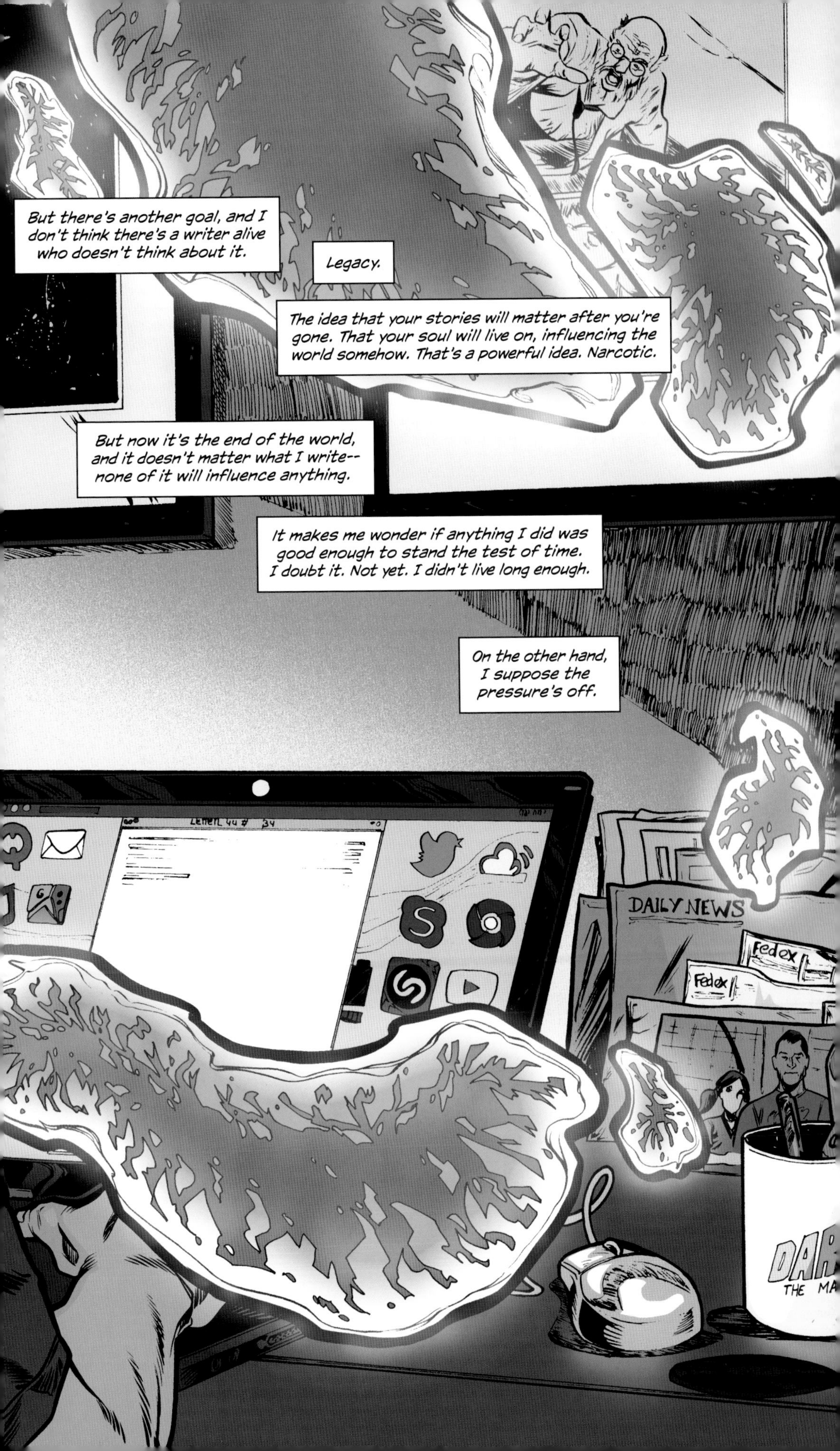
But there's another goal, and I don't think there's a writer alive who doesn't think about it.
Legacy.
The idea that your stories will matter after you're gone. That your soul will live on, influencing the world somehow. That's a powerful idea. Narcotic.
But now it's the end of the world, and it doesn't matter what I write-- none of it will influence anything.
It makes me wonder if anything I did was good enough to stand the test of time. I doubt it. Not yet. I didn't live long enough.
On the other hand, I suppose the pressure's off.
DAILY NEWS
Fedex
Fedex

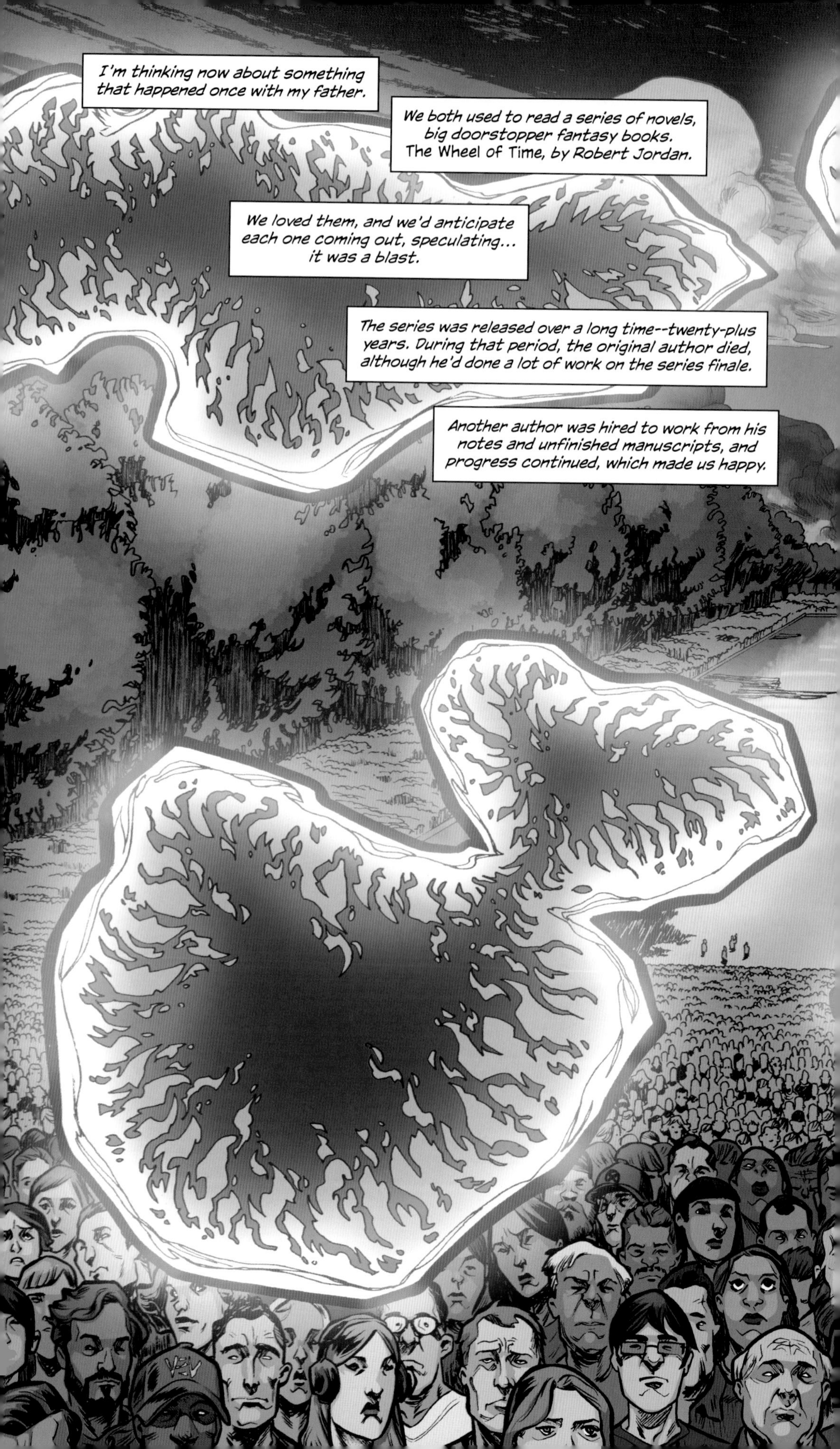
I'm thinking now about something that happened once with my father.
We both used to read a series of novels, big doorstopper fantasy books. The Wheel of Time, by Robert Jordan.
We loved them, and we'd anticipate each one coming out, speculating... it was a blast.
The series was released over a long time--twenty-plus years. During that period, the original author died, although he'd done a lot of work on the series finale.
Another author was hired to work from his notes and unfinished manuscripts, and progress continued, which made us happy.

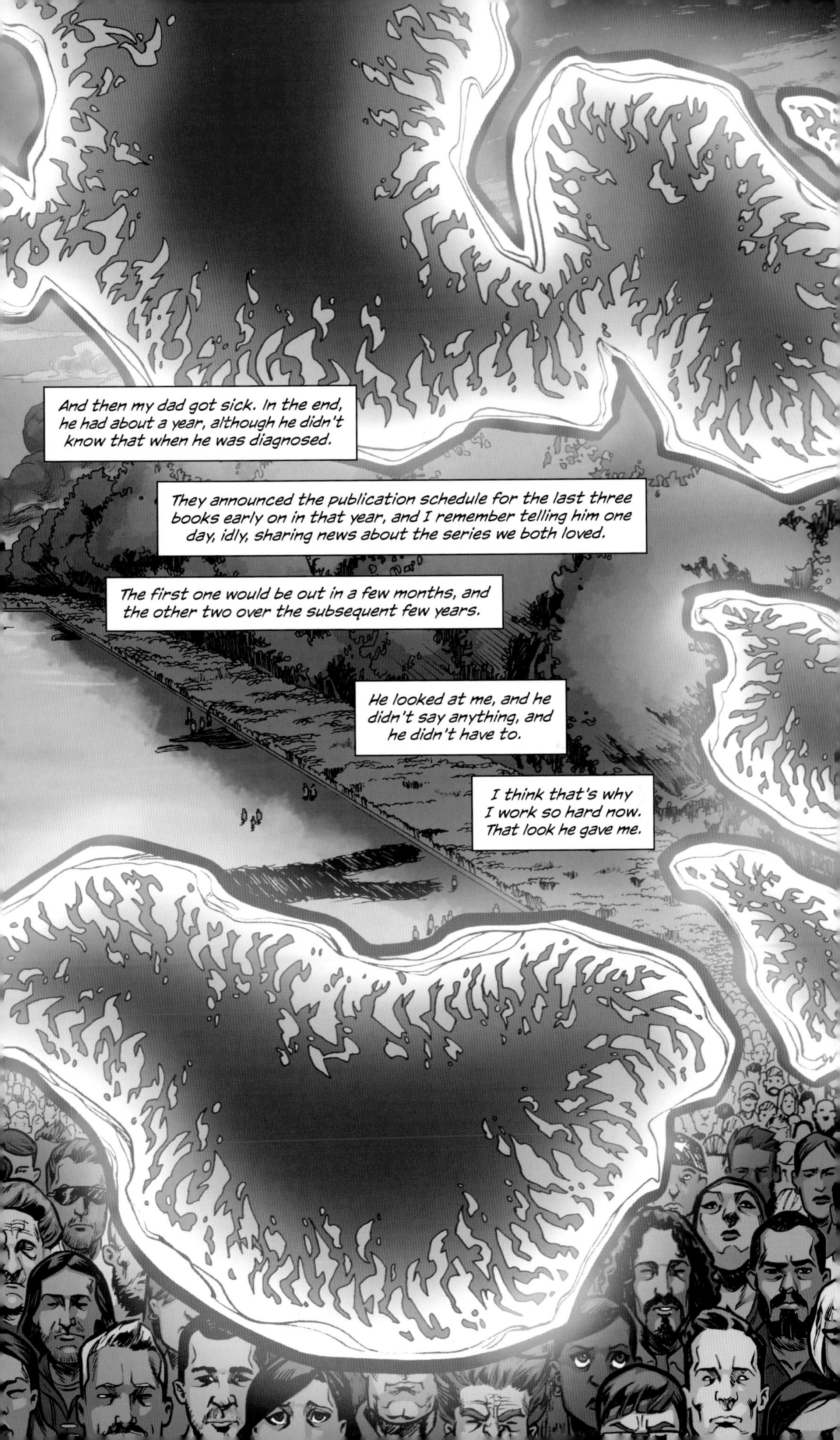
And then my dad got sick. In the end, he had about a year, although he didn't know that when he was diagnosed.
They announced the publication schedule for the last three books early on in that year, and I remember telling him one day, idly, sharing news about the series we both loved.
The first one would be out in a few months, and the other two over the subsequent few years.
He looked at me, and he didn't say anything, and he didn't have to.
I think that's why I work so hard now. That look he gave me.

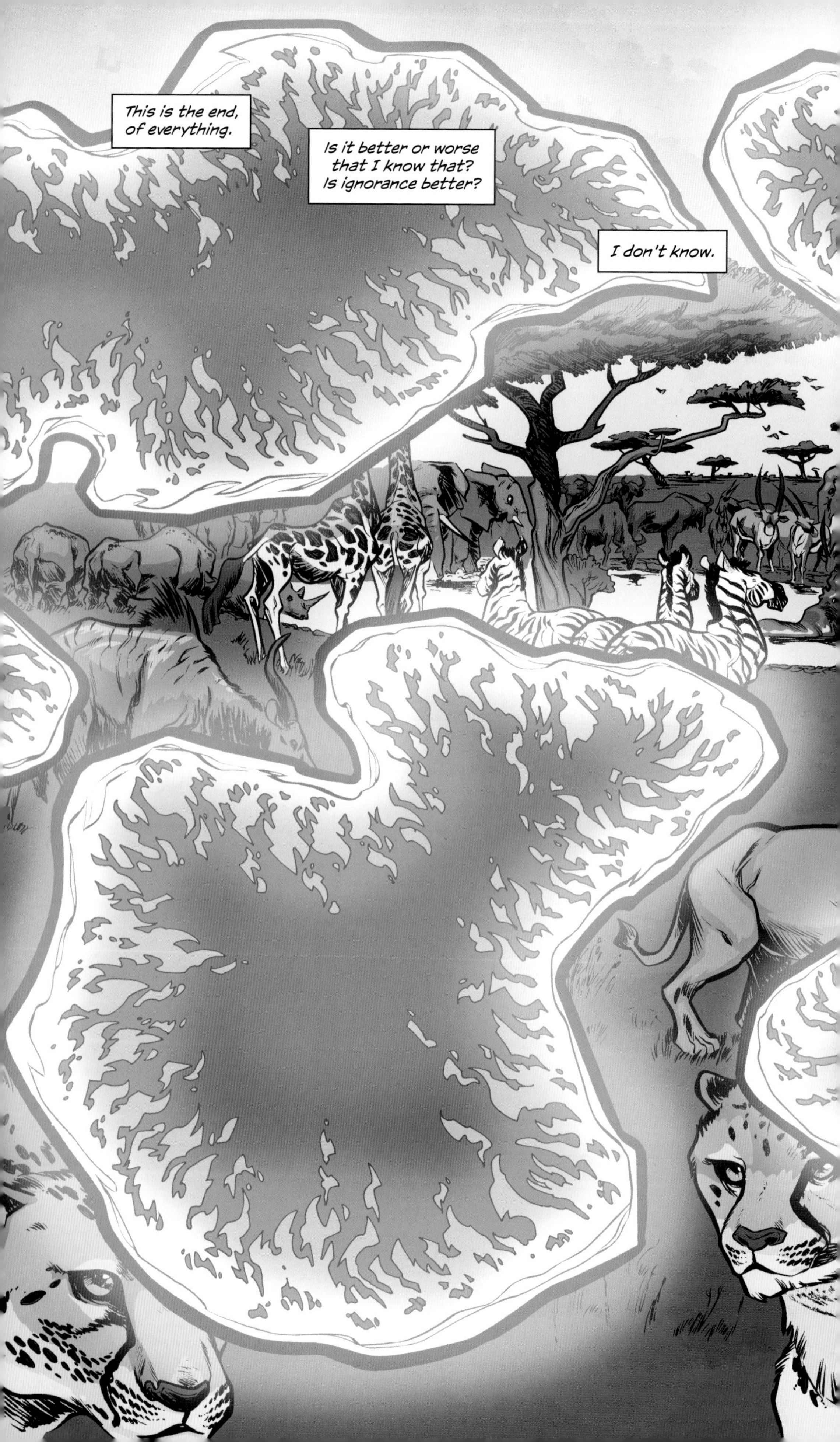
This is the end, of everything.
Is it better or worse that I know that? Is ignorance better?
I don't know.

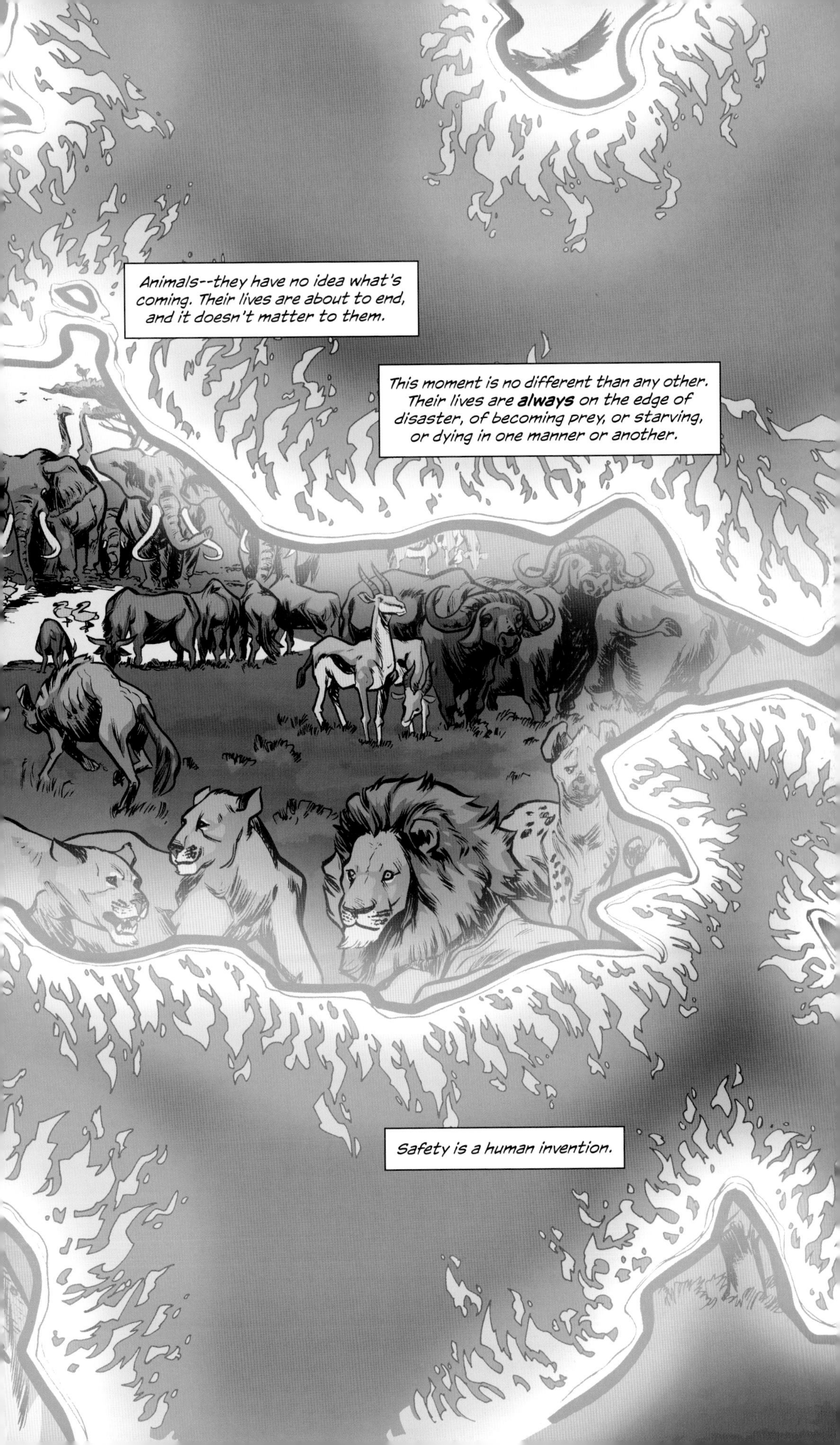
Animals--they have no idea what's coming. Their lives are about to end, and it doesn't matter to them.
This moment is no different than any other. Their lives are **always** on the edge of disaster, of becoming prey, or starving, or dying in one manner or another.
Safety is a human invention.

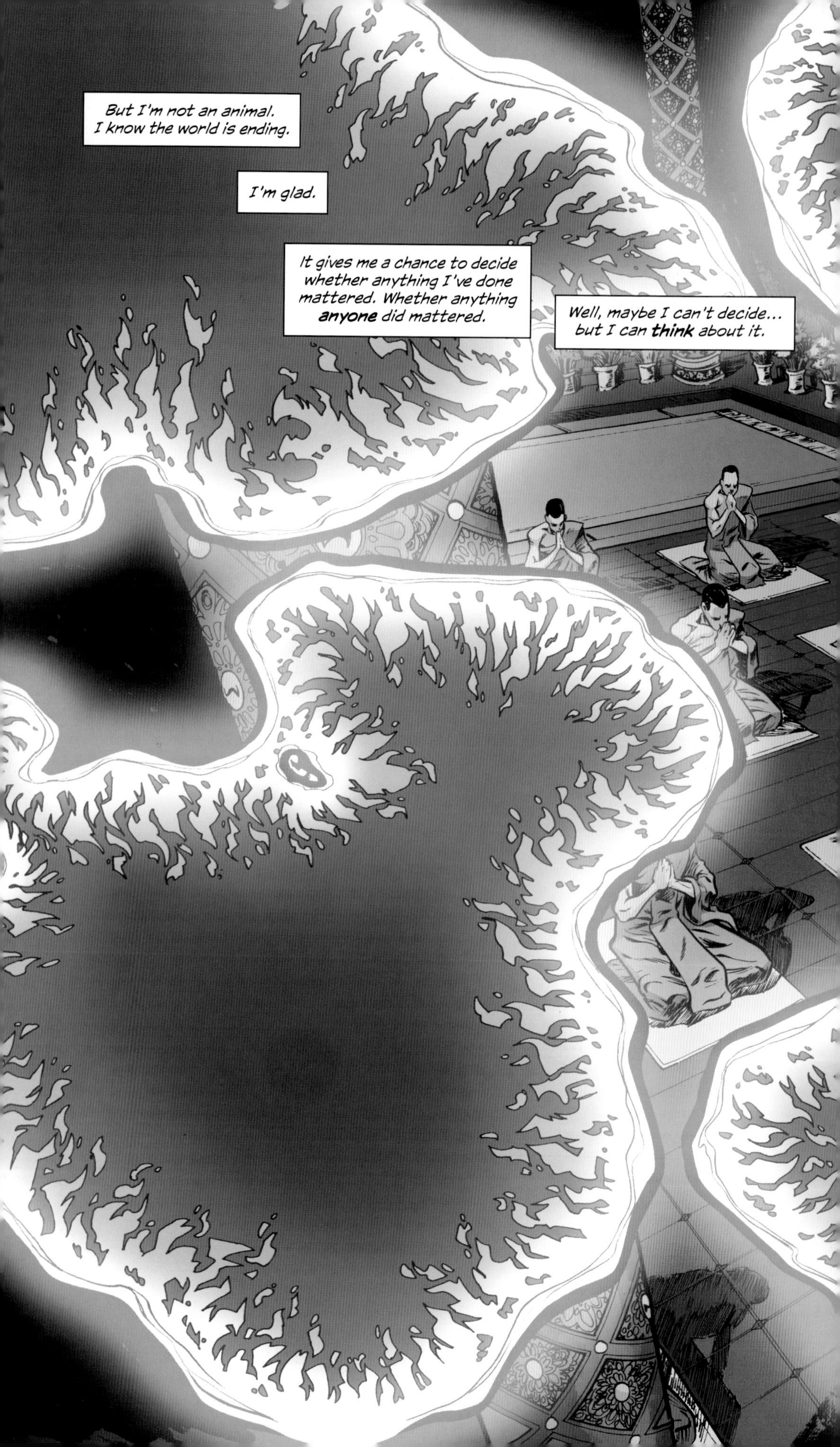
But I'm not an animal. I know the world is ending.
I'm glad.
It gives me a chance to decide whether anything I've done mattered. Whether anything **anyone** did mattered.
Well, maybe I can't decide... but I can **think** about it.

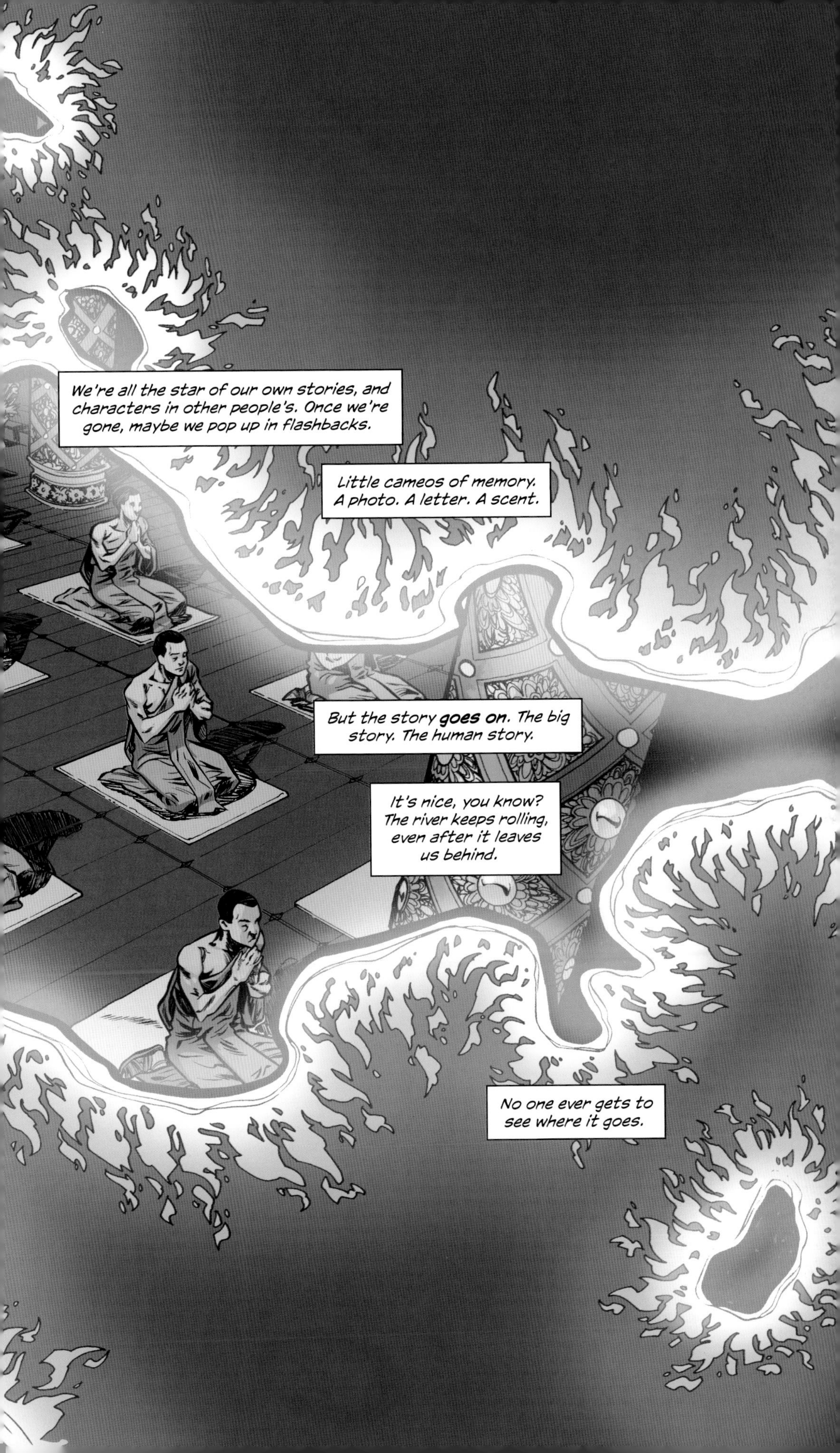
We're all the star of our own stories, and characters in other people's. Once we're gone, maybe we pop up in flashbacks.
Little cameos of memory. A photo. A letter. A scent.
But the story **goes on**. The big story. The human story.
It's nice, you know? The river keeps rolling, even after it leaves us behind.
No one ever gets to see where it goes.

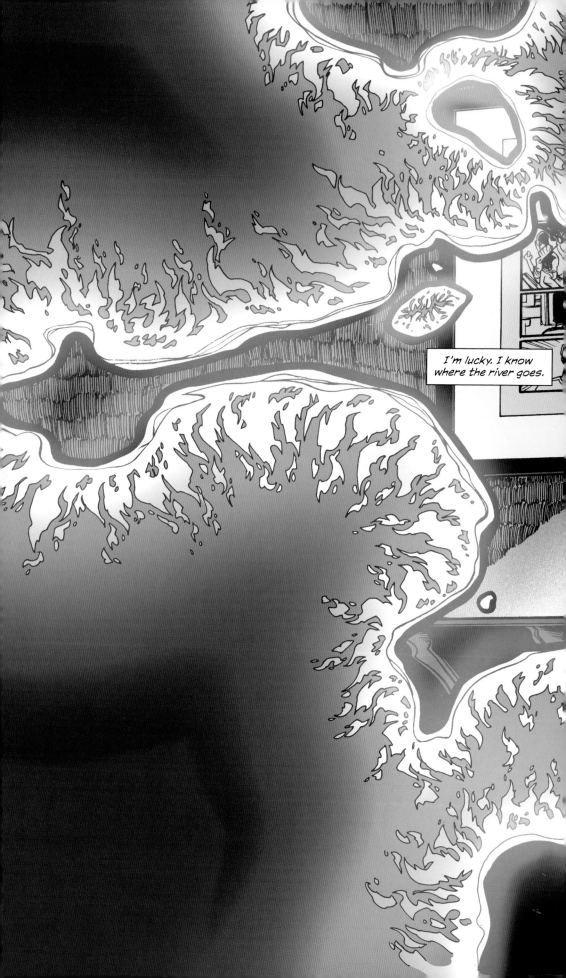

I'm lucky. I know where the river goes.

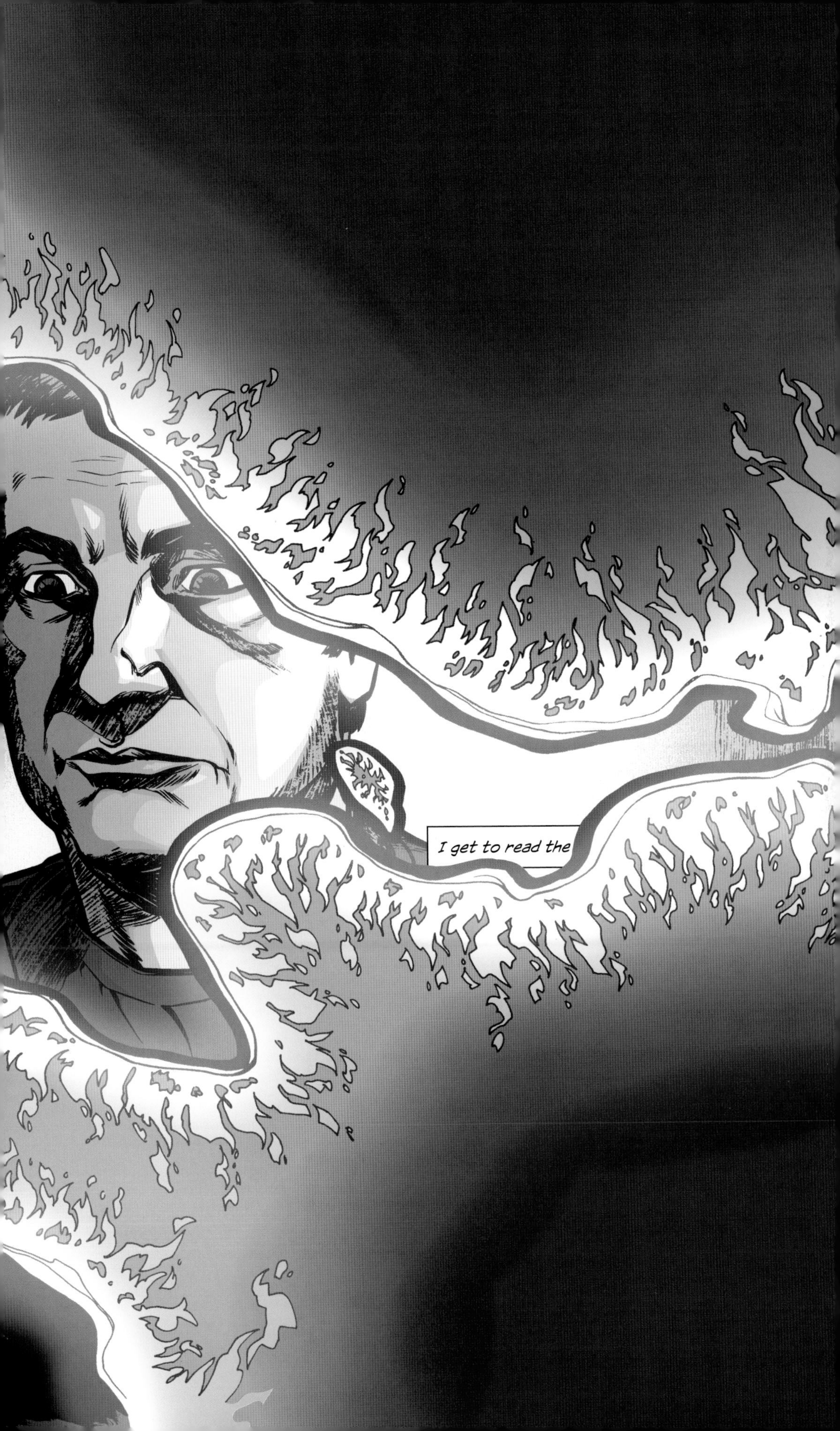
I get to read the

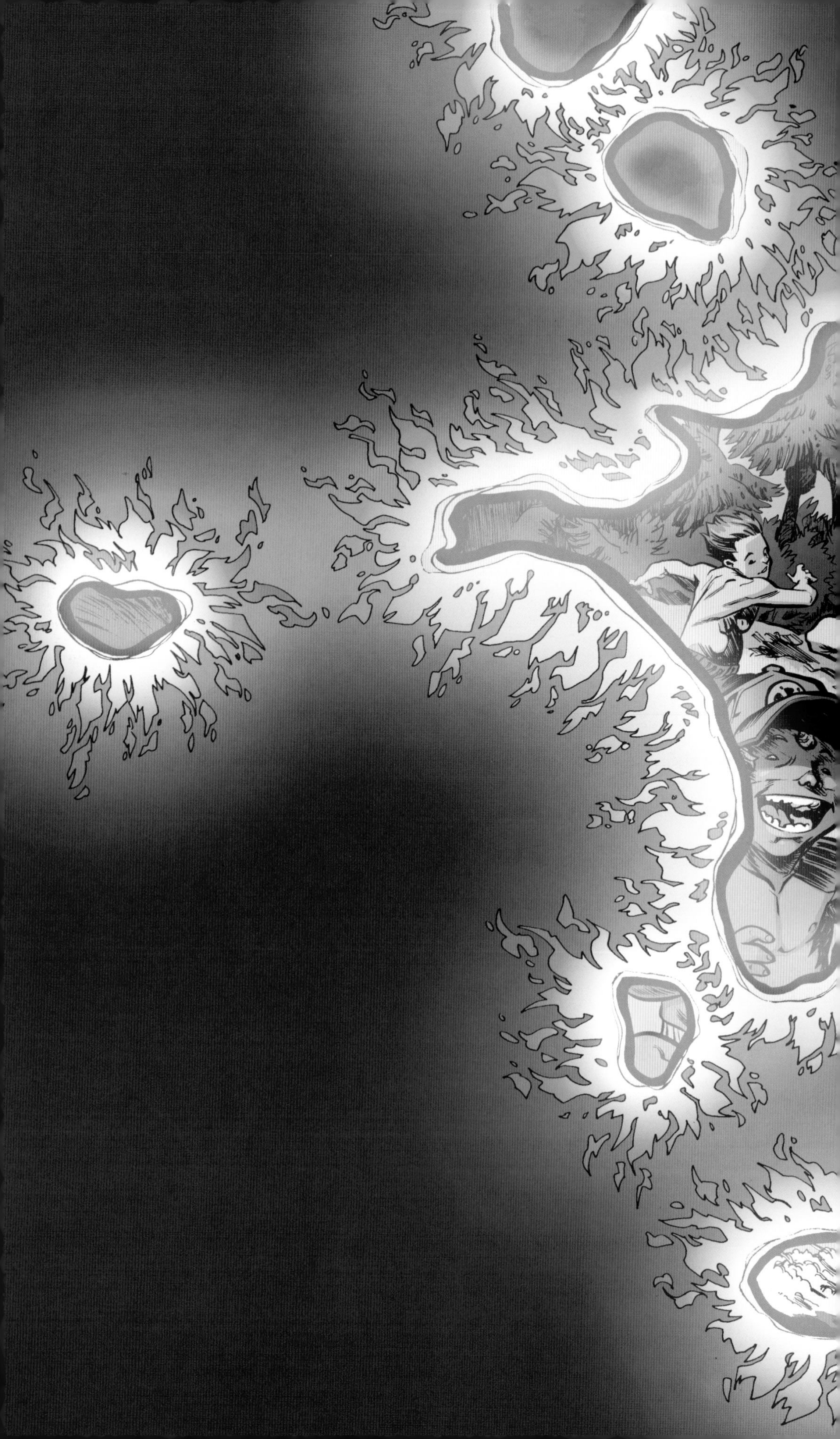

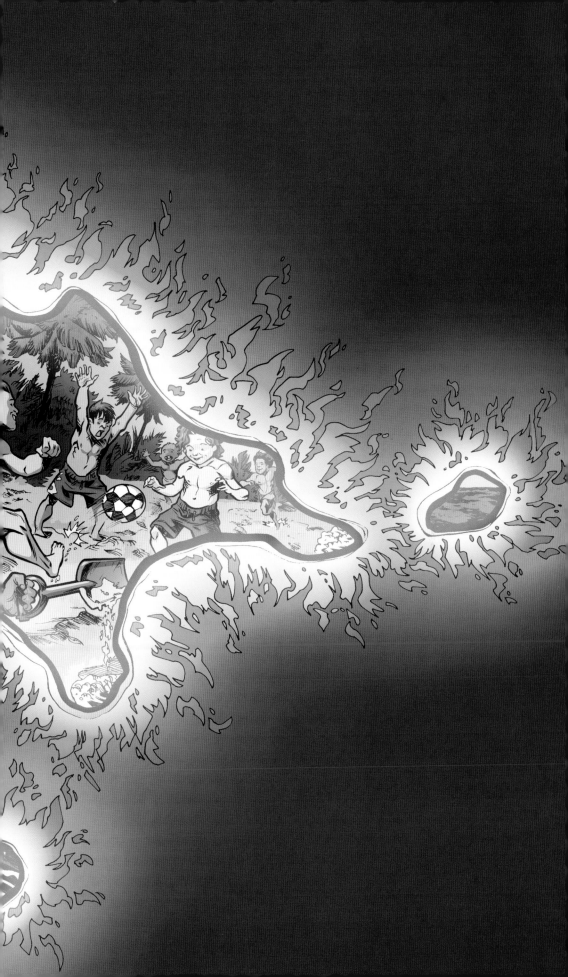

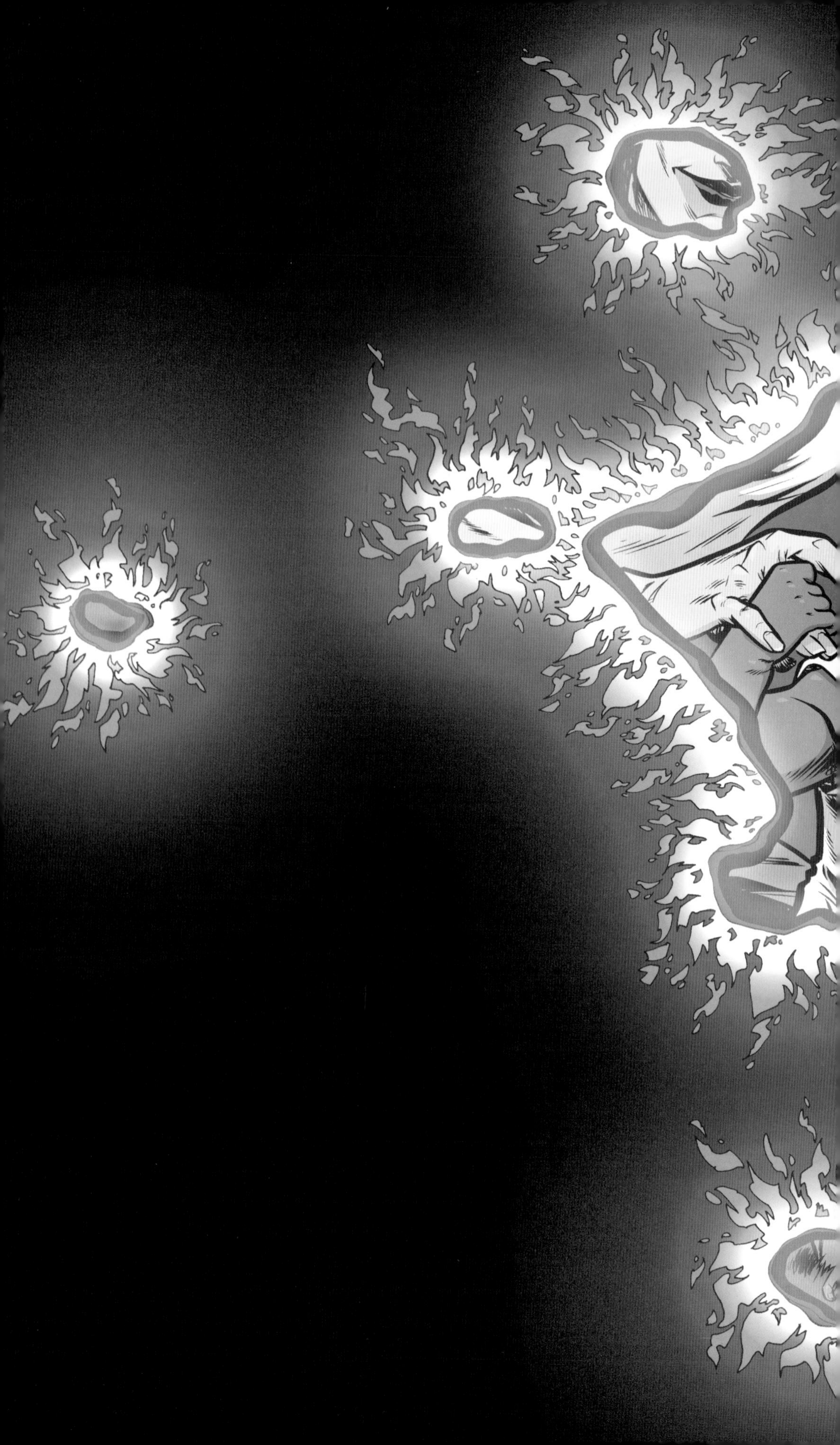

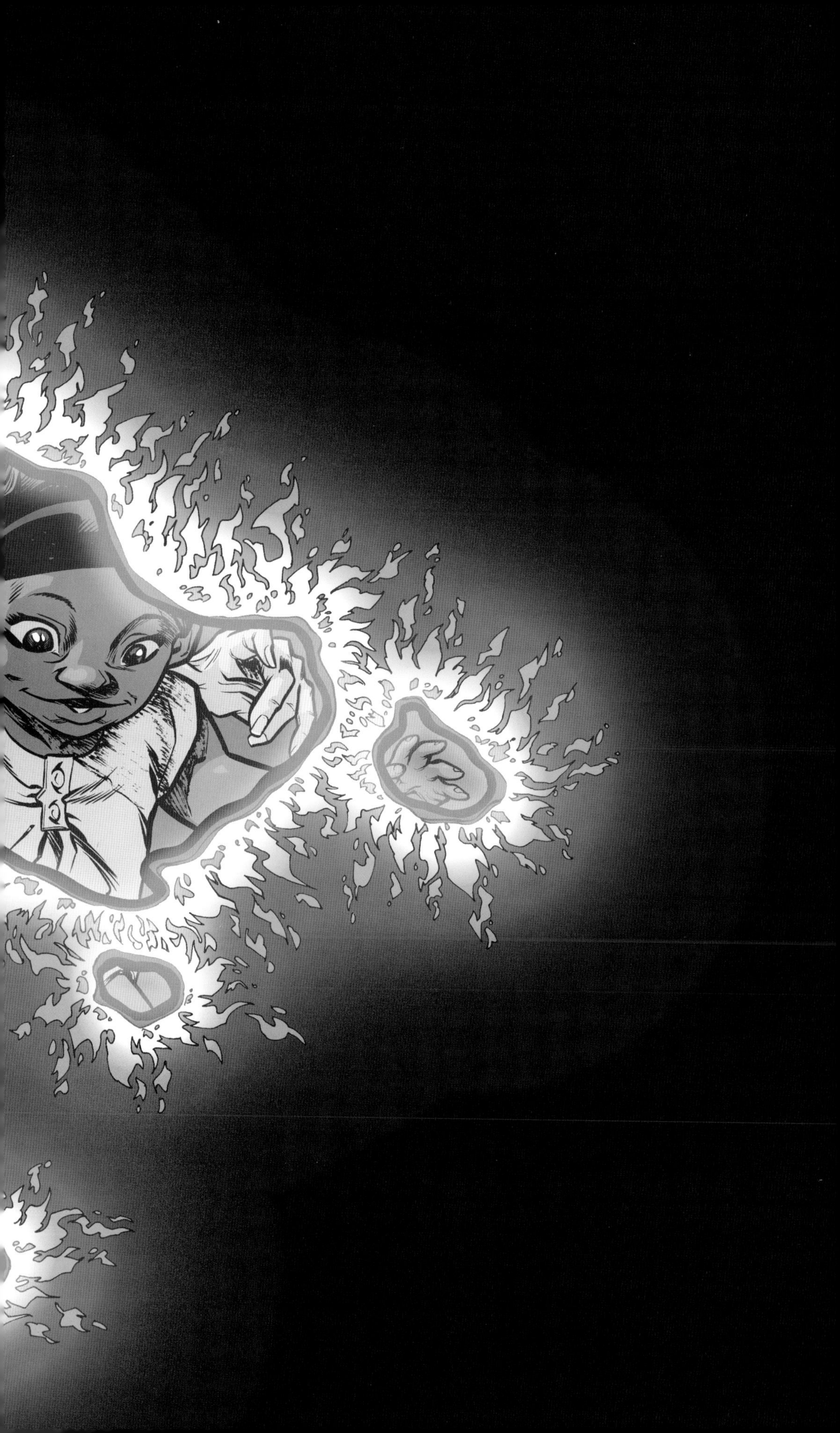

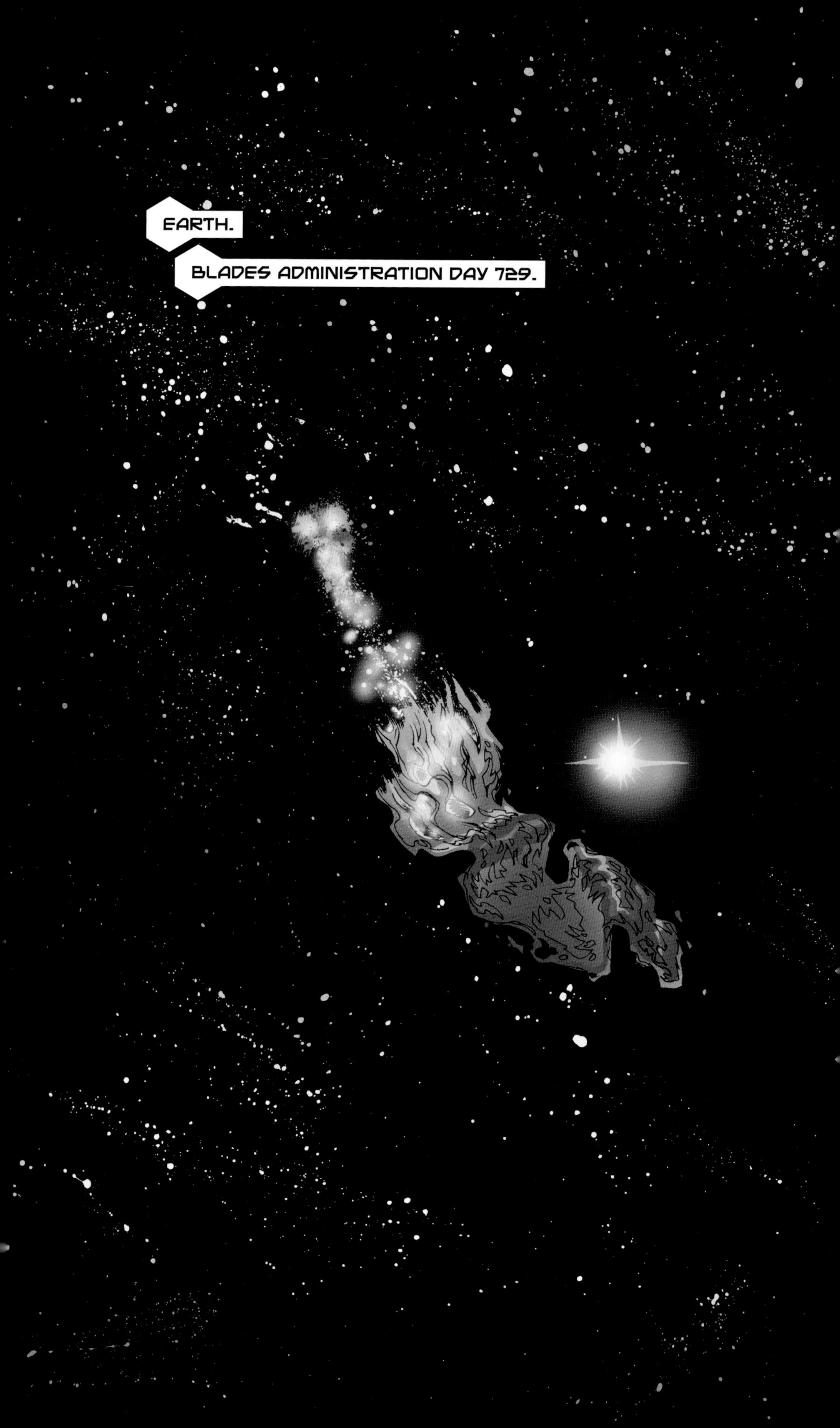
EARTH.
BLADES ADMINISTRATION DAY 729.

LETTER 44

CHAPTER VI

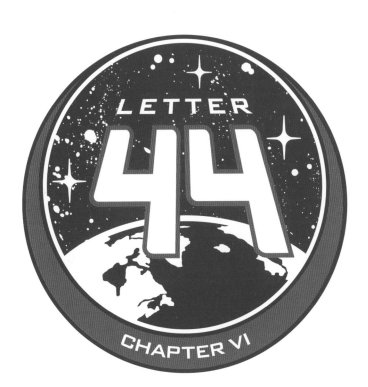

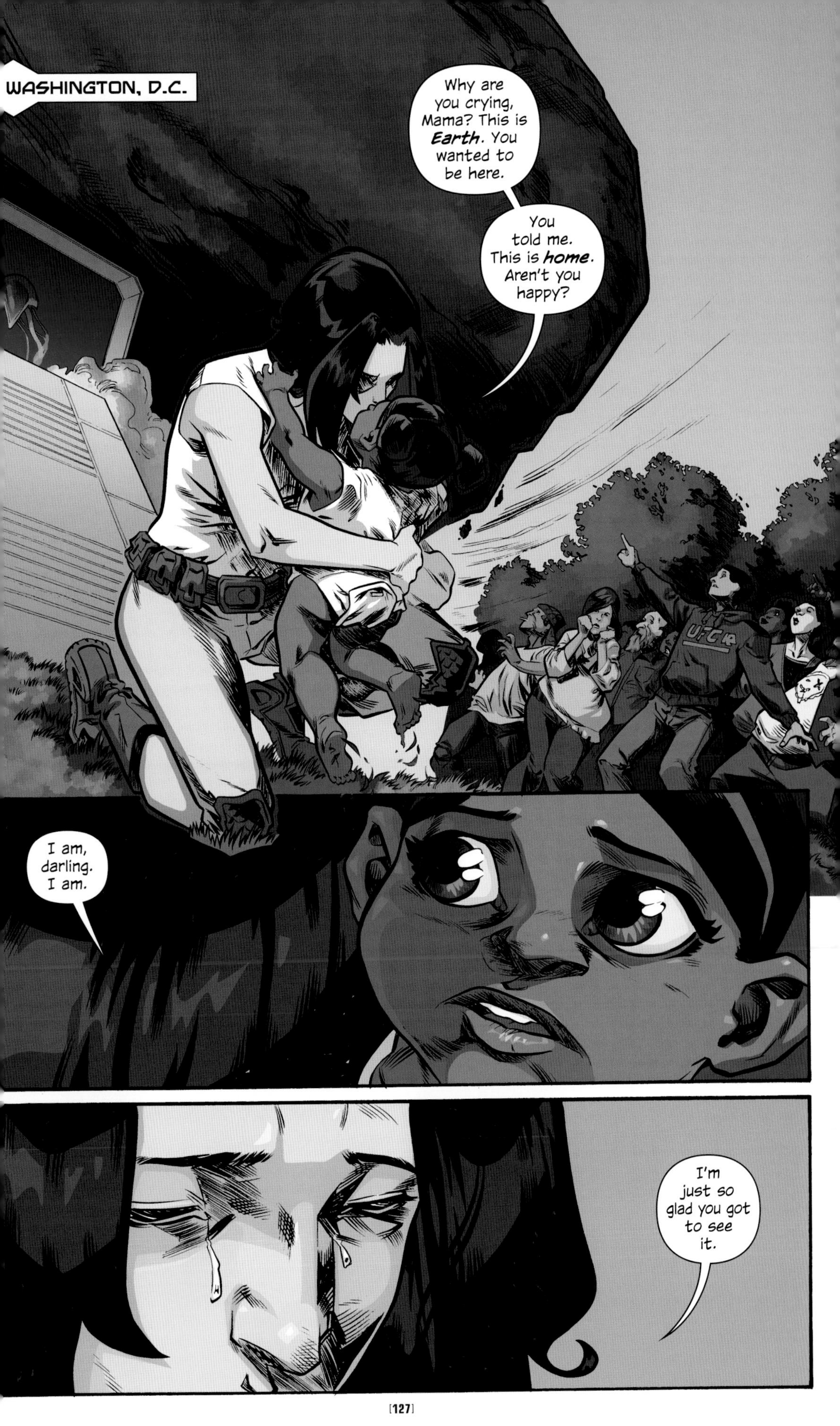

WASHINGTON, D.C.
Why are you crying, Mama? This is *Earth*. You wanted to be here.
You told me. This is *home*. Aren't you happy?
I am, darling. I am.
I'm just so glad you got to see it.

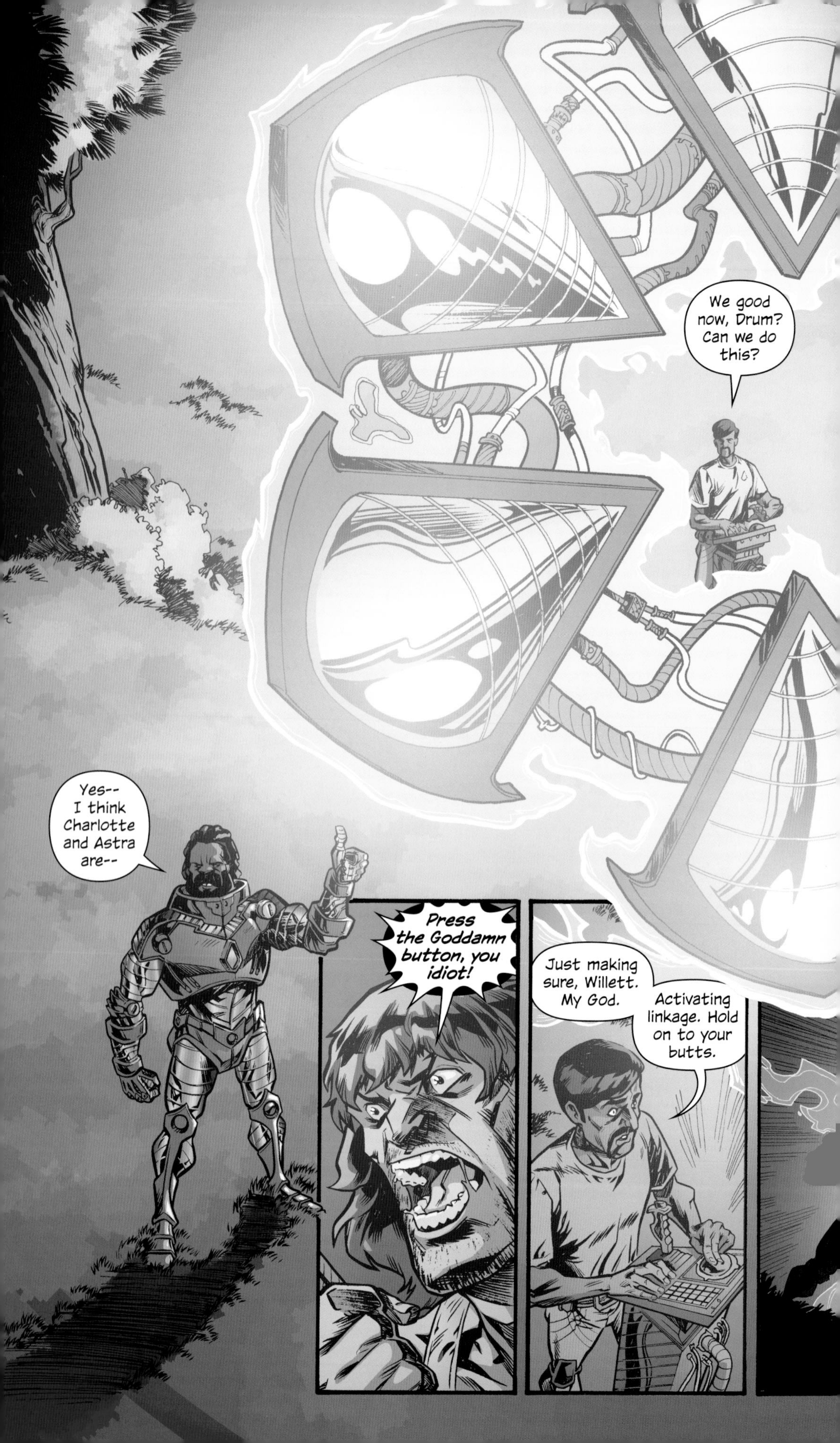
We good now, Drum? Can we do this?
Yes-- I think Charlotte and Astra are--
Press the Goddamn button, you idiot!
Just making sure, Willett. My God.
Activating linkage. Hold on to your butts.

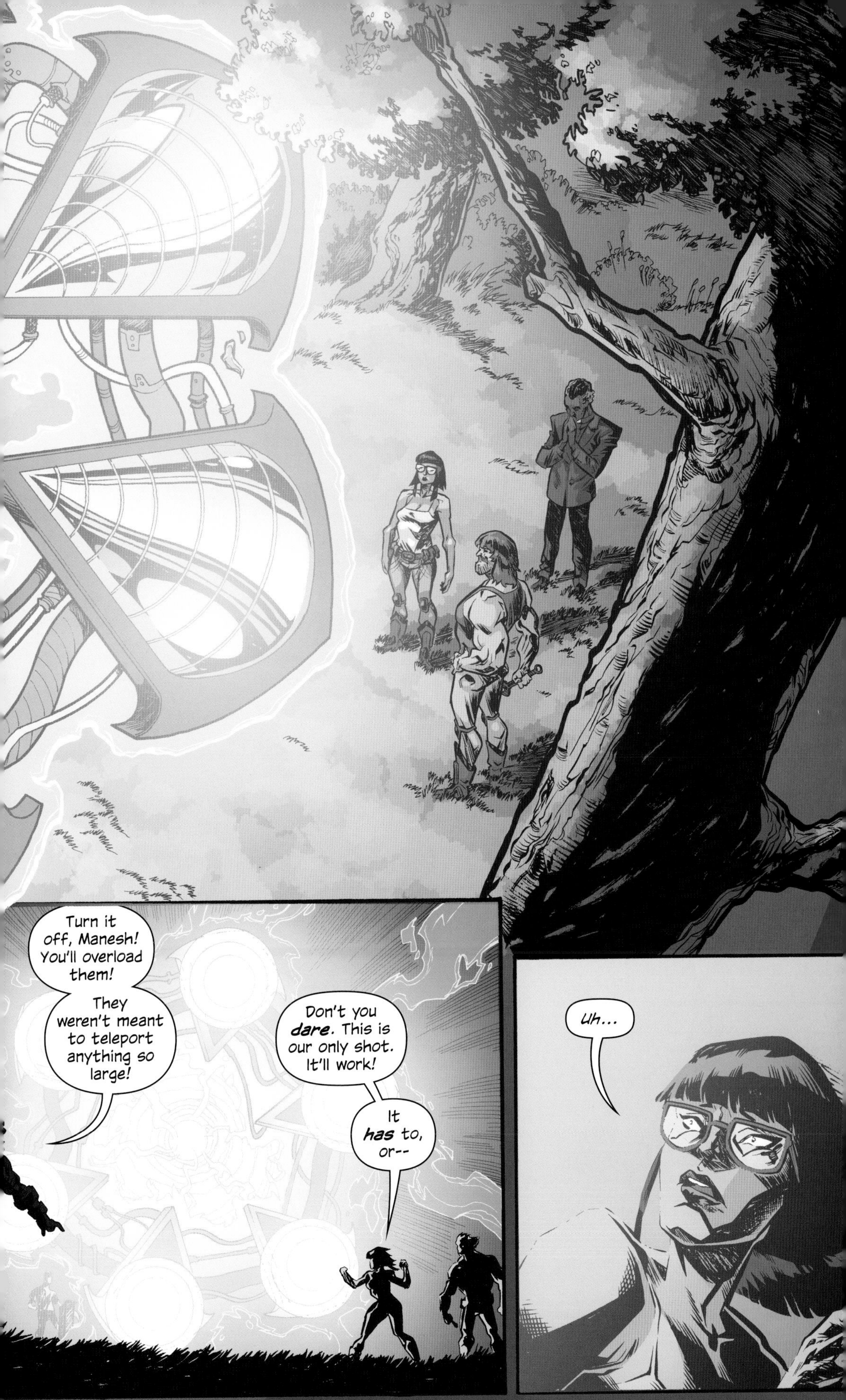
Turn it off, Manesh! You'll overload them!
They weren't meant to teleport anything so large!
Don't you *dare*. This is our only shot. It'll work!
It *has* to, or--
Uh...

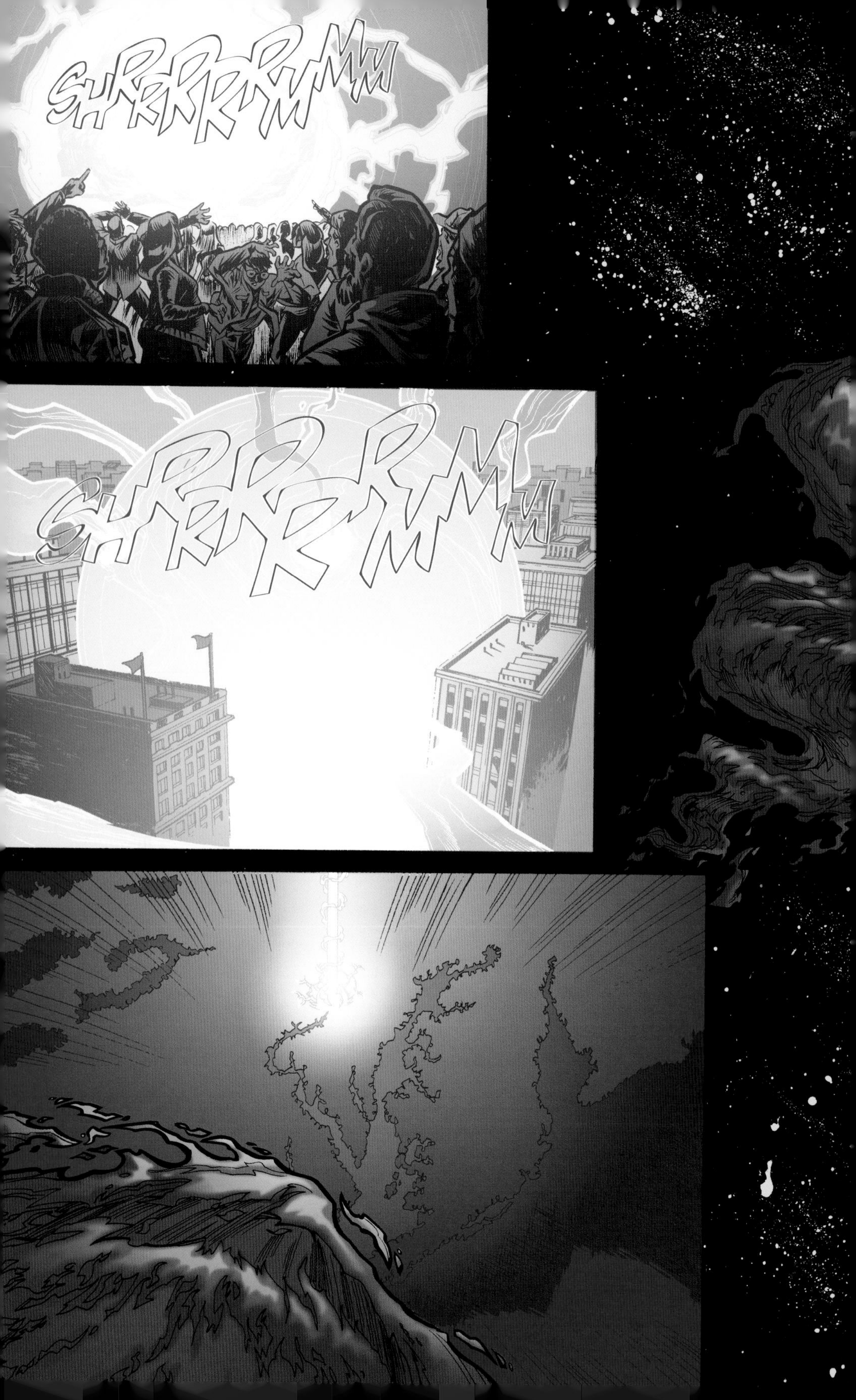
SHRRRRMMMM
SHRRRRMMMM

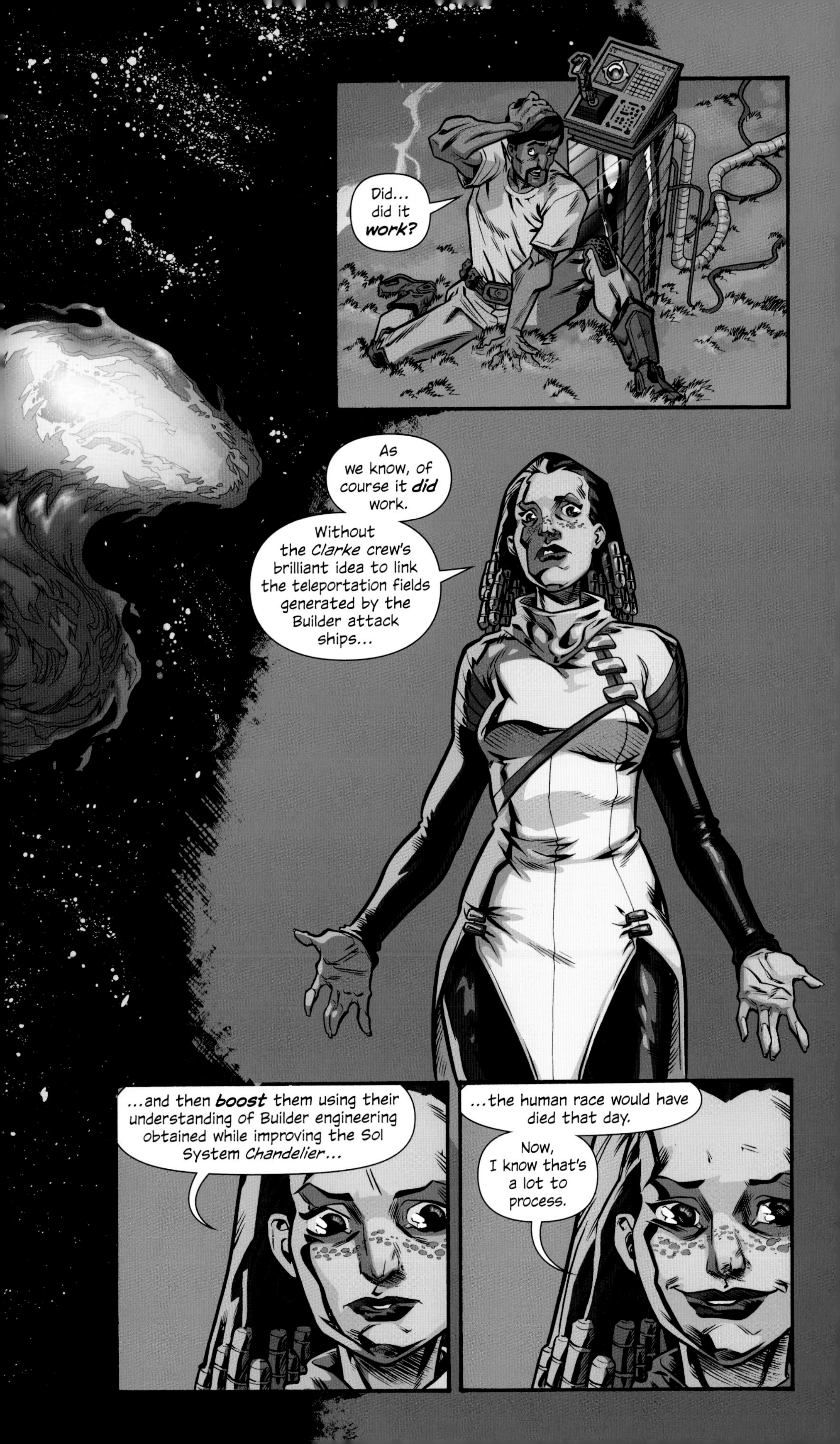
Did... did it *work?*
As we know, of course it *did* work.
Without the *Clarke* crew's brilliant idea to link the teleportation fields generated by the Builder attack ships...
...and then *boost* them using their understanding of Builder engineering obtained while improving the Sol System *Chandelier*...
...the human race would have died that day.
Now, I know that's a lot to process.

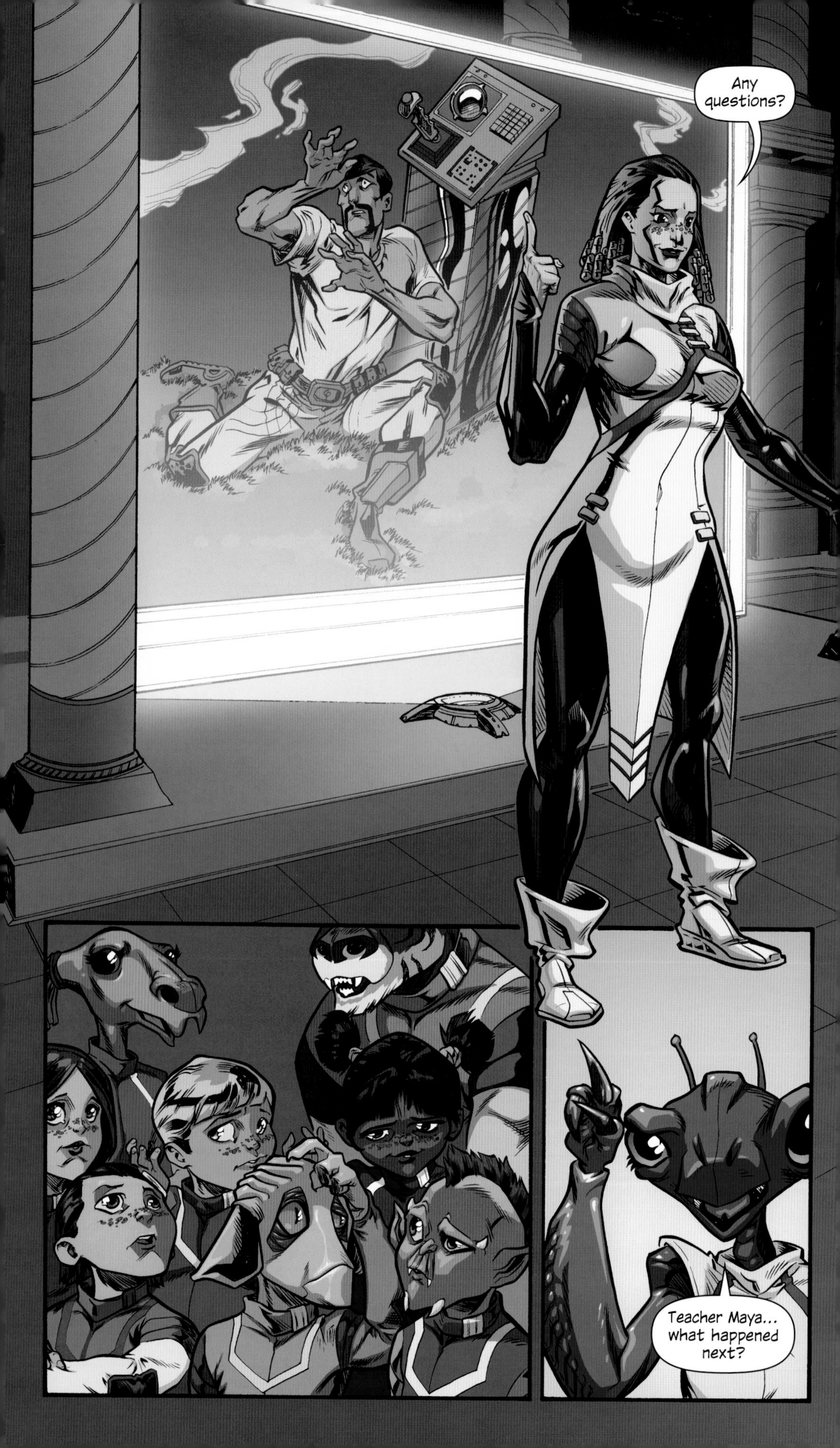
Any questions?
Teacher Maya... what happened next?

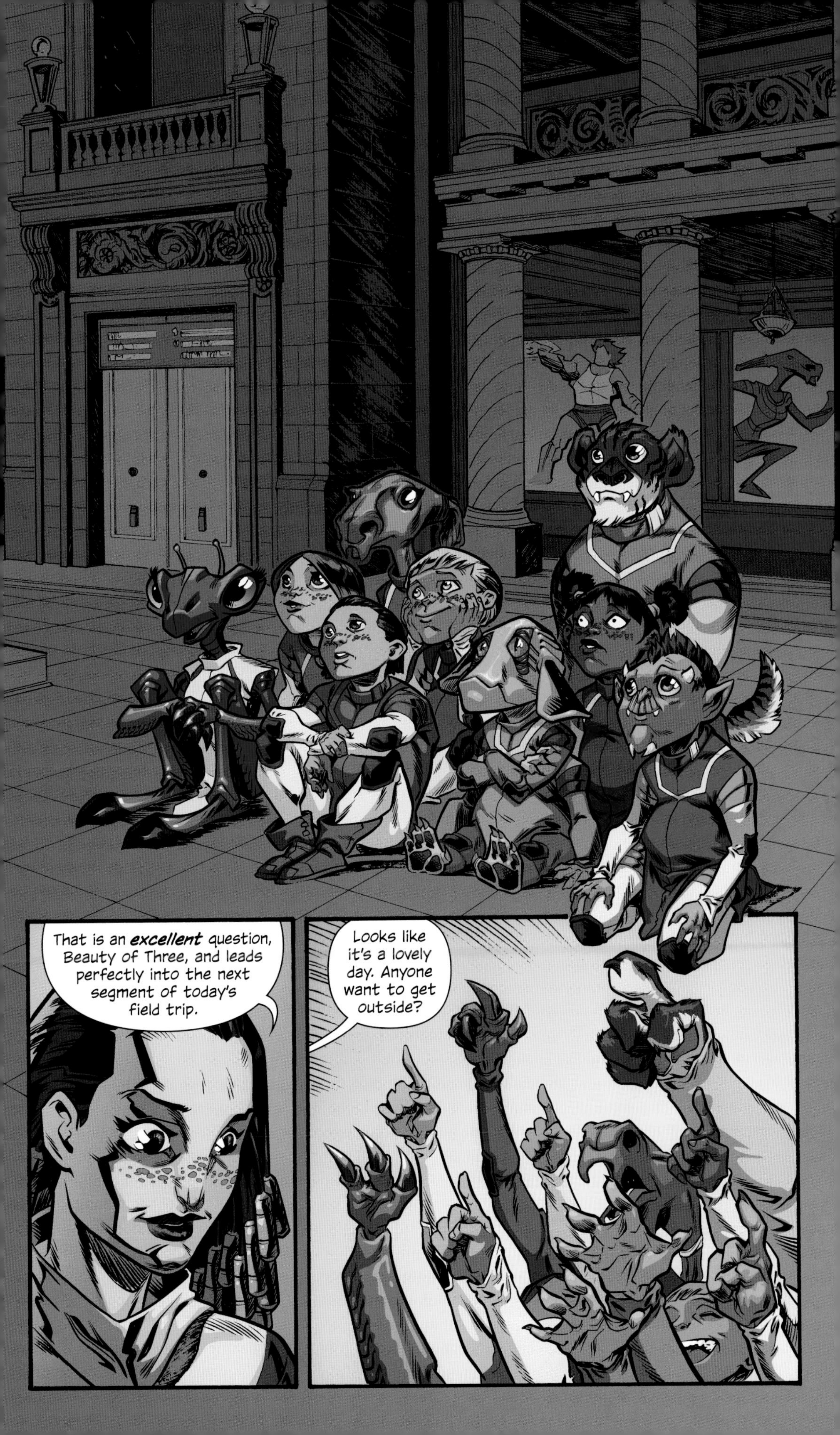
That is an ***excellent*** question, Beauty of Three, and leads perfectly into the next segment of today's field trip.
Looks like it's a lovely day. Anyone want to get outside?

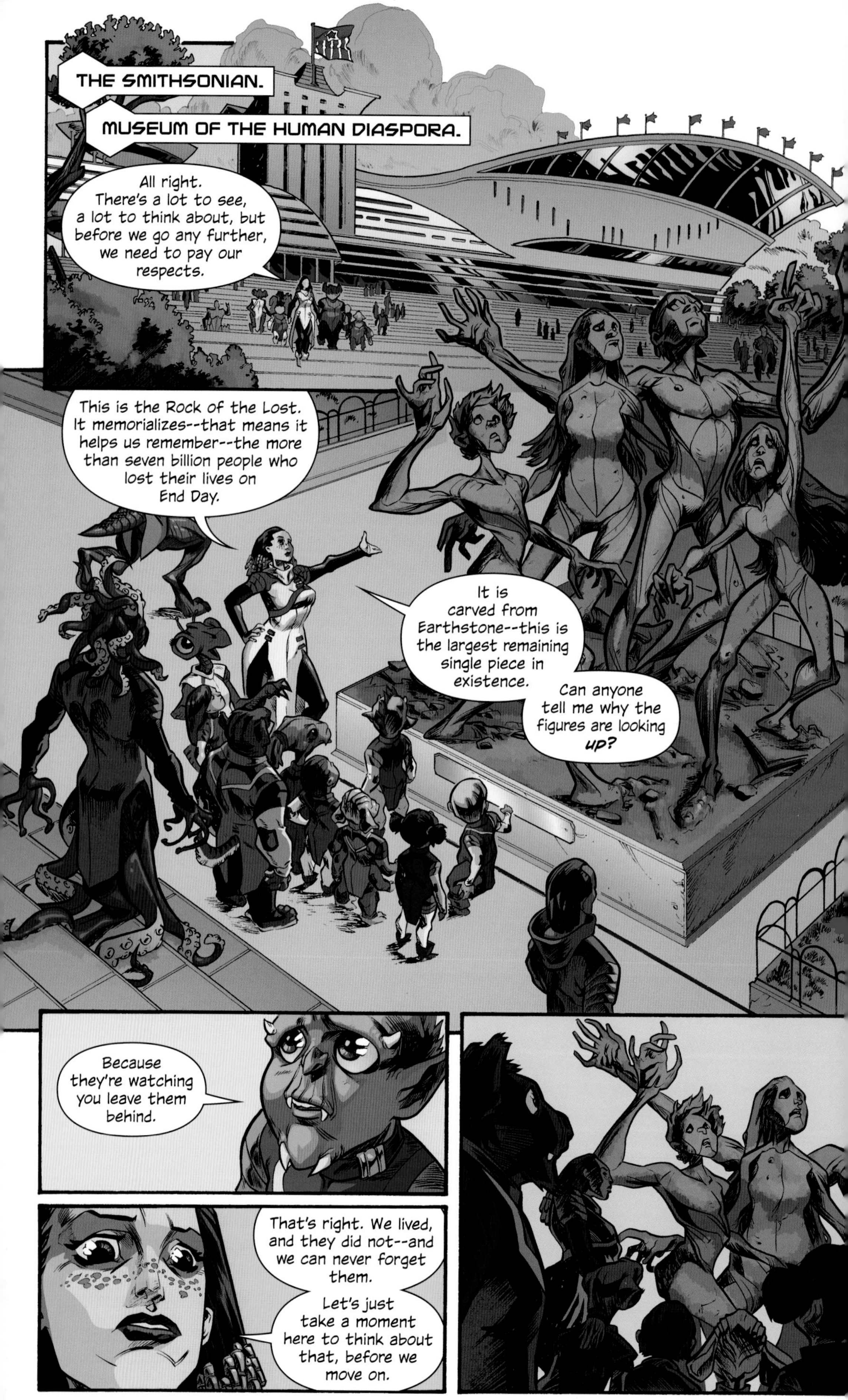
THE SMITHSONIAN.
MUSEUM OF THE HUMAN DIASPORA.
All right. There's a lot to see, a lot to think about, but before we go any further, we need to pay our respects.
This is the Rock of the Lost. It memorializes--that means it helps us remember--the more than seven billion people who lost their lives on End Day.
It is carved from Earthstone--this is the largest remaining single piece in existence.
Can anyone tell me why the figures are looking *up?*
Because they're watching you leave them behind.
That's right. We lived, and they did not--and we can never forget them.
Let's just take a moment here to think about that, before we move on.

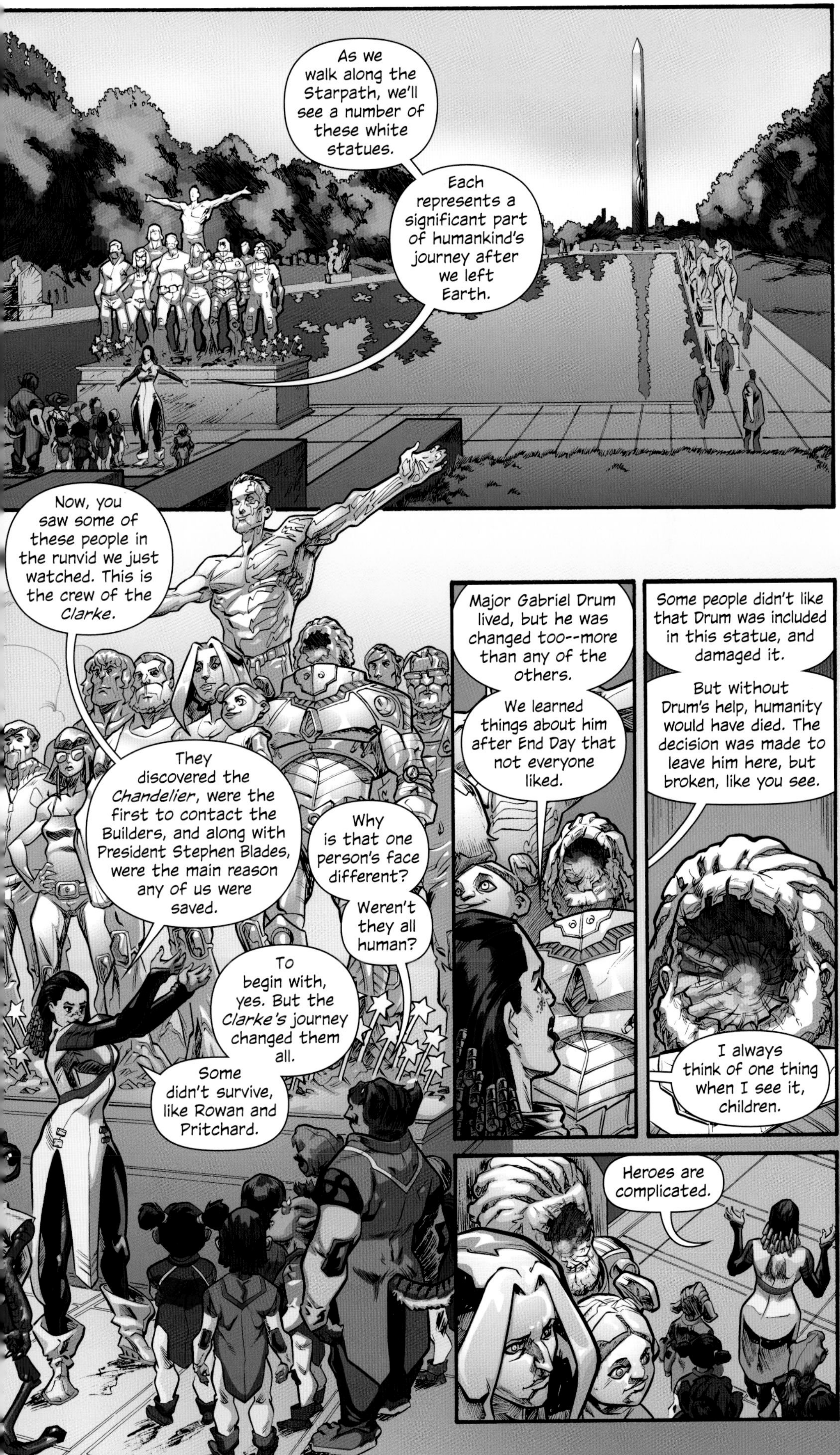
As we walk along the Starpath, we'll see a number of these white statues.
Each represents a significant part of humankind's journey after we left Earth.
Now, you saw some of these people in the runvid we just watched. This is the crew of the *Clarke*.
They discovered the *Chandelier*, were the first to contact the Builders, and along with President Stephen Blades, were the main reason any of us were saved.
Why is that one person's face different?
Weren't they all human?
To begin with, yes. But the *Clarke's* journey changed them all.
Some didn't survive, like Rowan and Pritchard.
Major Gabriel Drum lived, but he was changed too--more than any of the others.
We learned things about him after End Day that not everyone liked.
Some people didn't like that Drum was included in this statue, and damaged it.
But without Drum's help, humanity would have died. The decision was made to leave him here, but broken, like you see.
I always think of one thing when I see it, children.
Heroes are complicated.

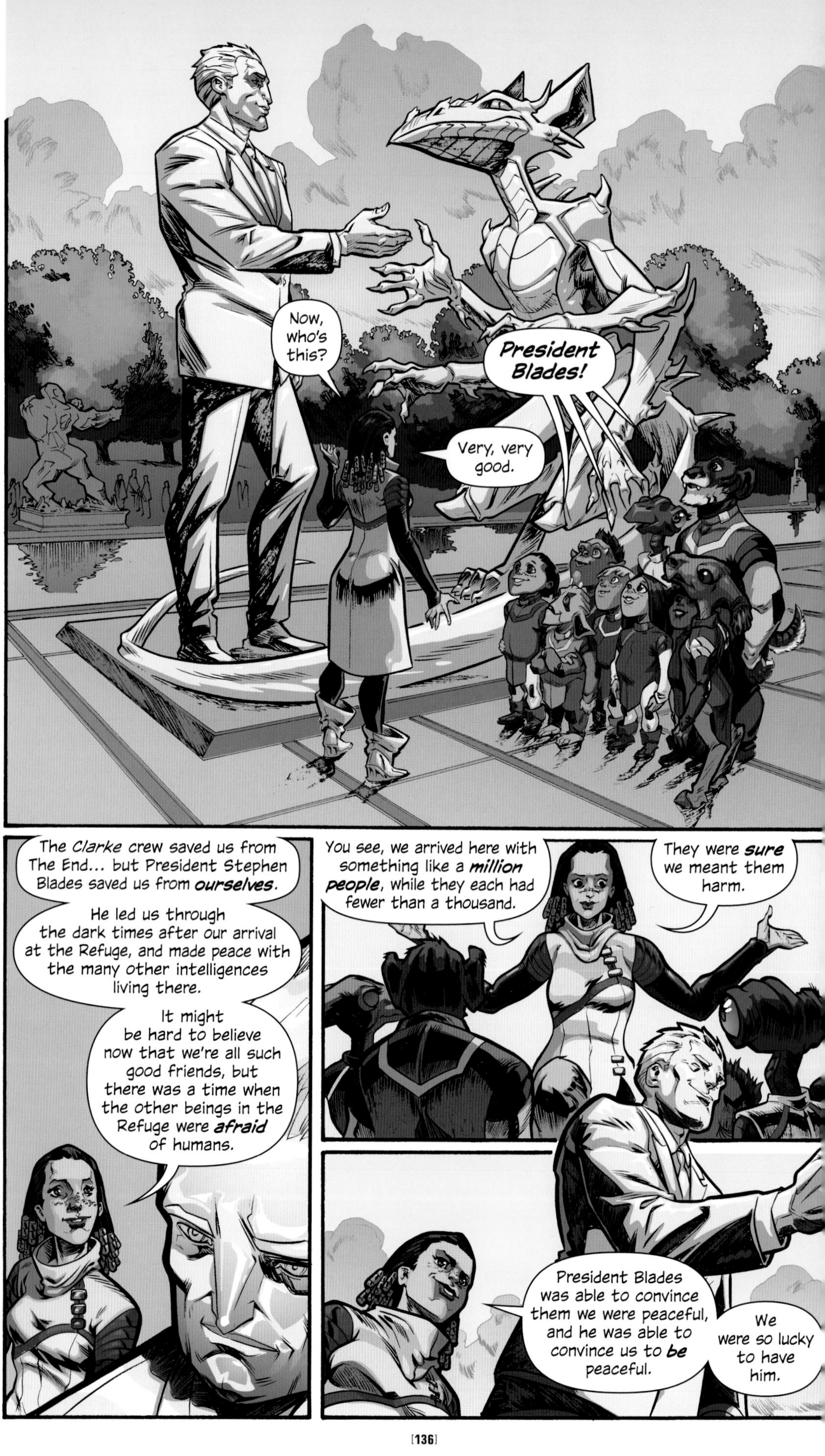
Now, who's this?
President Blades!
Very, very good.
The *Clarke* crew saved us from The End... but President Stephen Blades saved us from ***ourselves***.
He led us through the dark times after our arrival at the Refuge, and made peace with the many other intelligences living there.
It might be hard to believe now that we're all such good friends, but there was a time when the other beings in the Refuge were ***afraid*** of humans.
You see, we arrived here with something like a ***million people***, while they each had fewer than a thousand.
They were ***sure*** we meant them harm.
President Blades was able to convince them we were peaceful, and he was able to convince us to ***be*** peaceful.
We were so lucky to have him.

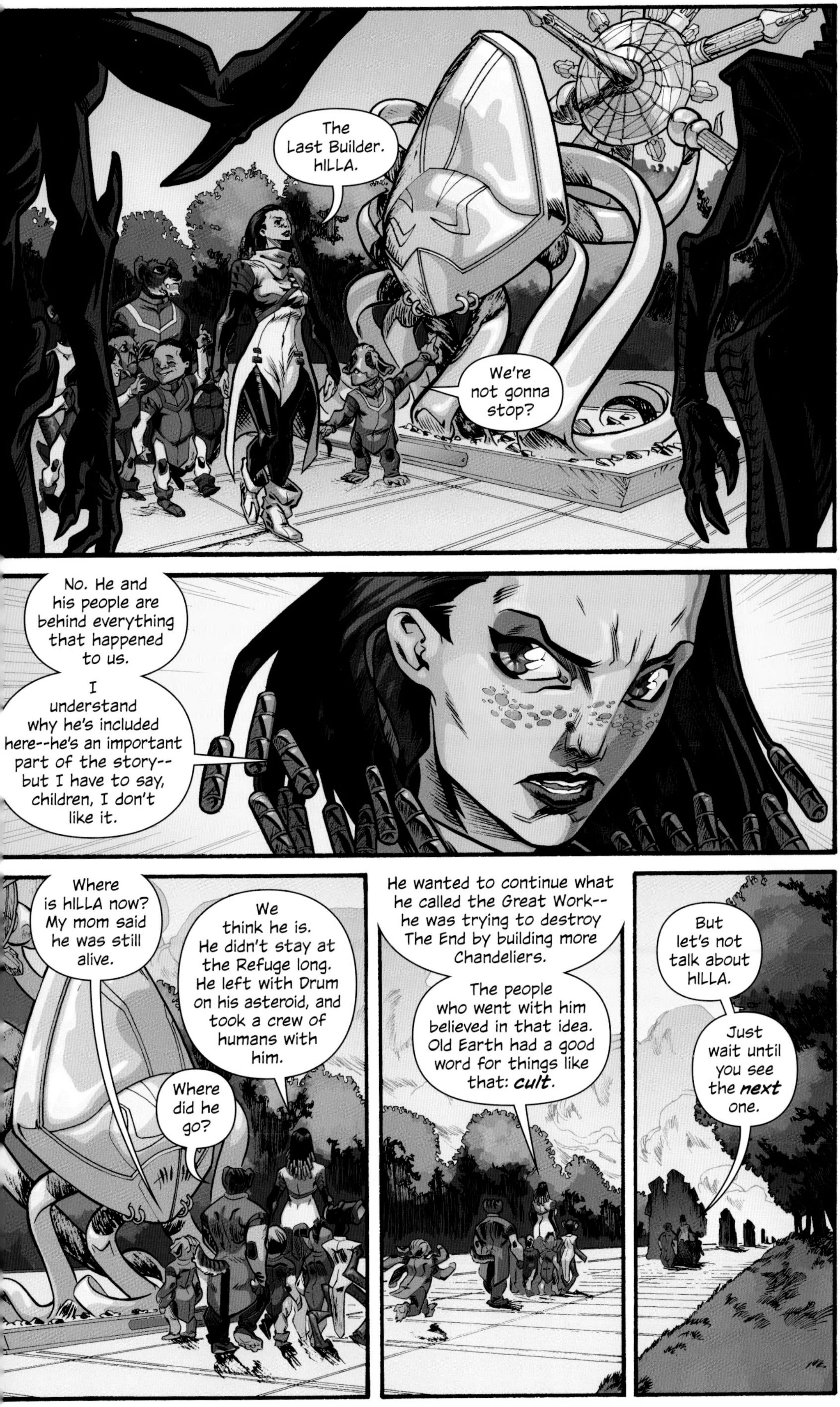
The Last Builder. hILLA.
We're not gonna stop?
No. He and his people are behind everything that happened to us.
I understand why he's included here--he's an important part of the story--but I have to say, children, I don't like it.
Where is hILLA now? My mom said he was still alive.
We think he is. He didn't stay at the Refuge long. He left with Drum on his asteroid, and took a crew of humans with him.
Where did he go?
He wanted to continue what he called the Great Work--he was trying to destroy The End by building more Chandeliers.
The people who went with him believed in that idea. Old Earth had a good word for things like that: ***cult***.
But let's not talk about hILLA.
Just wait until you see the ***next*** one.

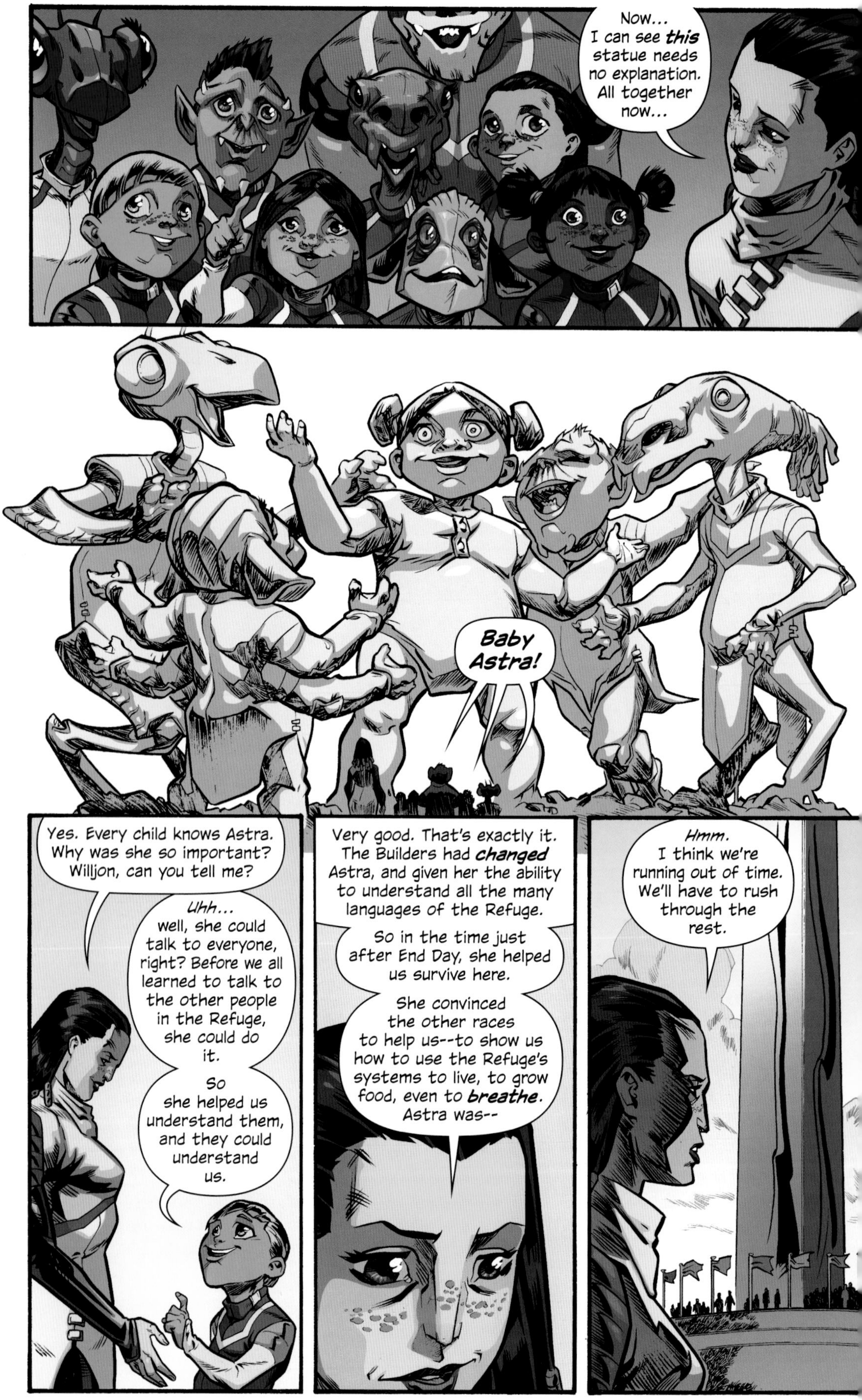
Now...
I can see *this* statue needs no explanation. All together now...
Baby Astra!
Yes. Every child knows Astra. Why was she so important? Willjon, can you tell me?
Uhh...
well, she could talk to everyone, right? Before we all learned to talk to the other people in the Refuge, she could do it.
So she helped us understand them, and they could understand us.
Very good. That's exactly it. The Builders had *changed* Astra, and given her the ability to understand all the many languages of the Refuge.
So in the time just after End Day, she helped us survive here.
She convinced the other races to help us--to show us how to use the Refuge's systems to live, to grow food, even to *breathe*. Astra was--
Hmm.
I think we're running out of time. We'll have to rush through the rest.

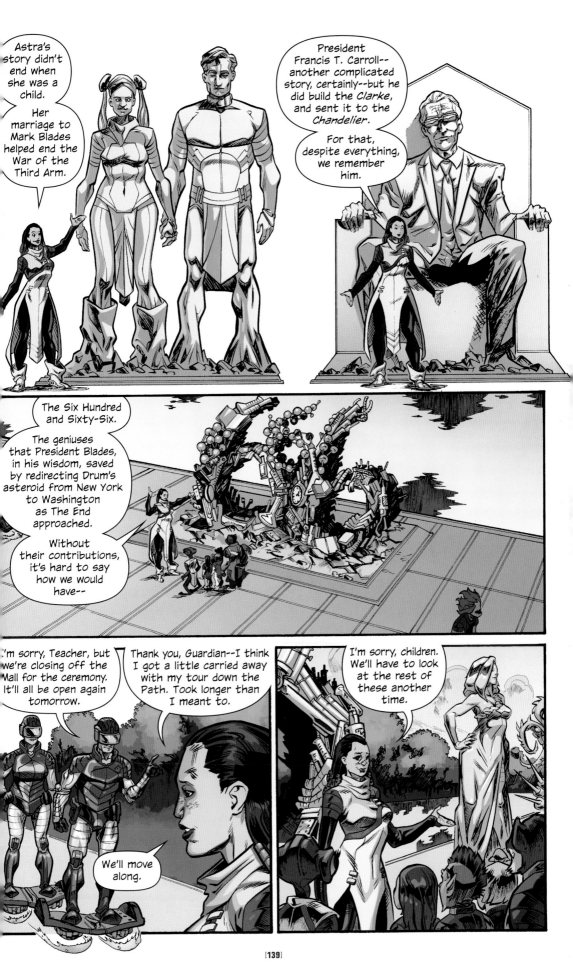

Astra's story didn't end when she was a child.

Her marriage to Mark Blades helped end the War of the Third Arm.

President Francis T. Carroll--another complicated story, certainly--but he did build the *Clarke*, and sent it to the *Chandelier*.

For that, despite everything, we remember him.

The Six Hundred and Sixty-Six.

The geniuses that President Blades, in his wisdom, saved by redirecting Drum's asteroid from New York to Washington as The End approached.

Without their contributions, it's hard to say how we would have--

I'm sorry, Teacher, but we're closing off the Mall for the ceremony. It'll all be open again tomorrow.

Thank you, Guardian--I think I got a little carried away with my tour down the Path. Took longer than I meant to.

I'm sorry, children. We'll have to look at the rest of these another time.

We'll move along.

[139]

Why did we have to go, Teacher Maya?

Well, it's a very special day. Once, every four years, all of the humans in the refuge vote to... does anyone know what it means to vote?

It means *choosing*.

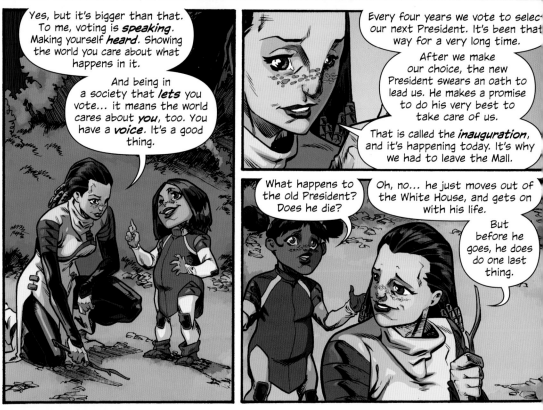

Yes, but it's bigger than that. To me, voting is *speaking*. Making yourself *heard*. Showing the world you care about what happens in it.

And being in a society that *lets* you vote... it means the world cares about *you*, too. You have a *voice*. It's a good thing.

Every four years we vote to select our next President. It's been that way for a very long time.

After we make our choice, the new President swears an oath to lead us. He makes a promise to do his very best to take care of us.

That is called the *inauguration*, and it's happening today. It's why we had to leave the Mall.

What happens to the old President? Does he die?

Oh, no... he just moves out of the White House, and gets on with his life.

But before he goes, he does do one last thing.

Children, it's the most *wonderful* tradition.

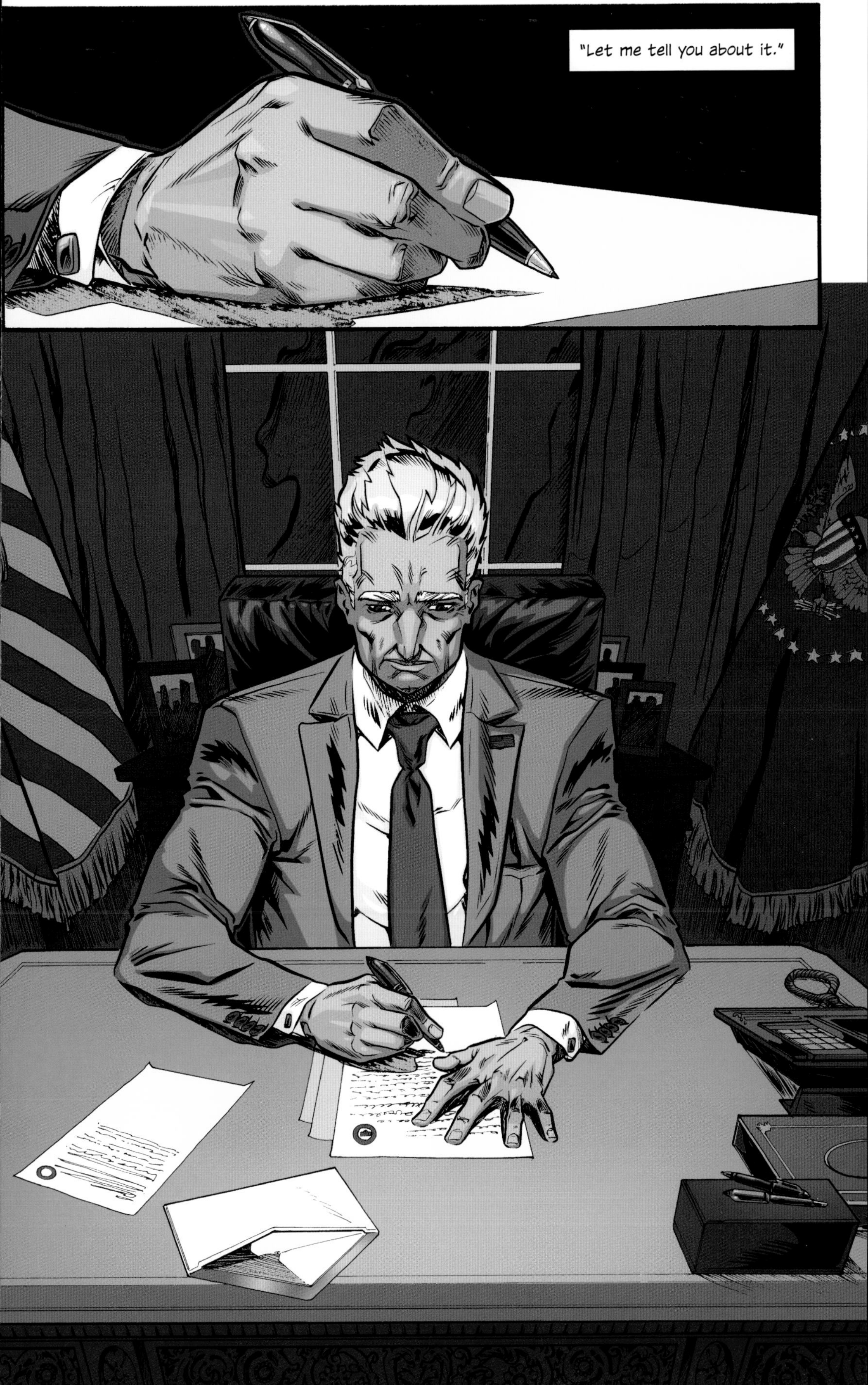
"Let me tell you about it."

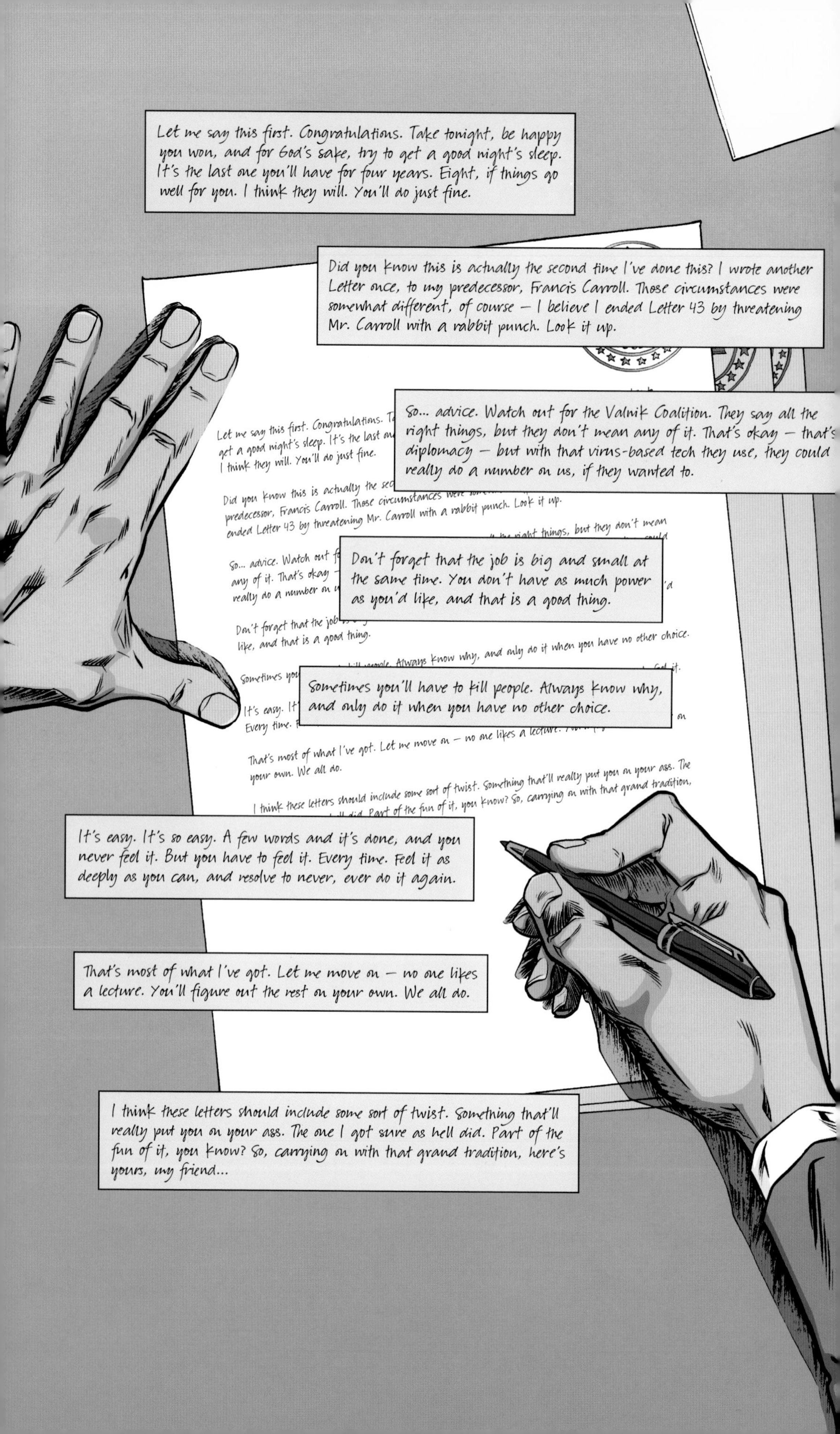
Let me say this first. Congratulations. Take tonight, be happy you won, and for God's sake, try to get a good night's sleep. It's the last one you'll have for four years. Eight, if things go well for you. I think they will. You'll do just fine.
Did you know this is actually the second time I've done this? I wrote another Letter once, to my predecessor, Francis Carroll. Those circumstances were somewhat different, of course — I believe I ended Letter 43 by threatening Mr. Carroll with a rabbit punch. Look it up.
So... advice. Watch out for the Valnik Coalition. They say all the right things, but they don't mean any of it. That's okay — that's diplomacy — but with that virus-based tech they use, they could really do a number on us, if they wanted to.
Don't forget that the job is big and small at the same time. You don't have as much power as you'd like, and that is a good thing.
Sometimes you'll have to kill people. Always know why, and only do it when you have no other choice.
It's easy. It's so easy. A few words and it's done, and you never feel it. But you have to feel it. Every time. Feel it as deeply as you can, and resolve to never, ever do it again.
That's most of what I've got. Let me move on — no one likes a lecture. You'll figure out the rest on your own. We all do.
I think these letters should include some sort of twist. Something that'll really put you on your ass. The one I got sure as hell did. Part of the fun of it, you know? So, carrying on with that grand tradition, here's yours, my friend...

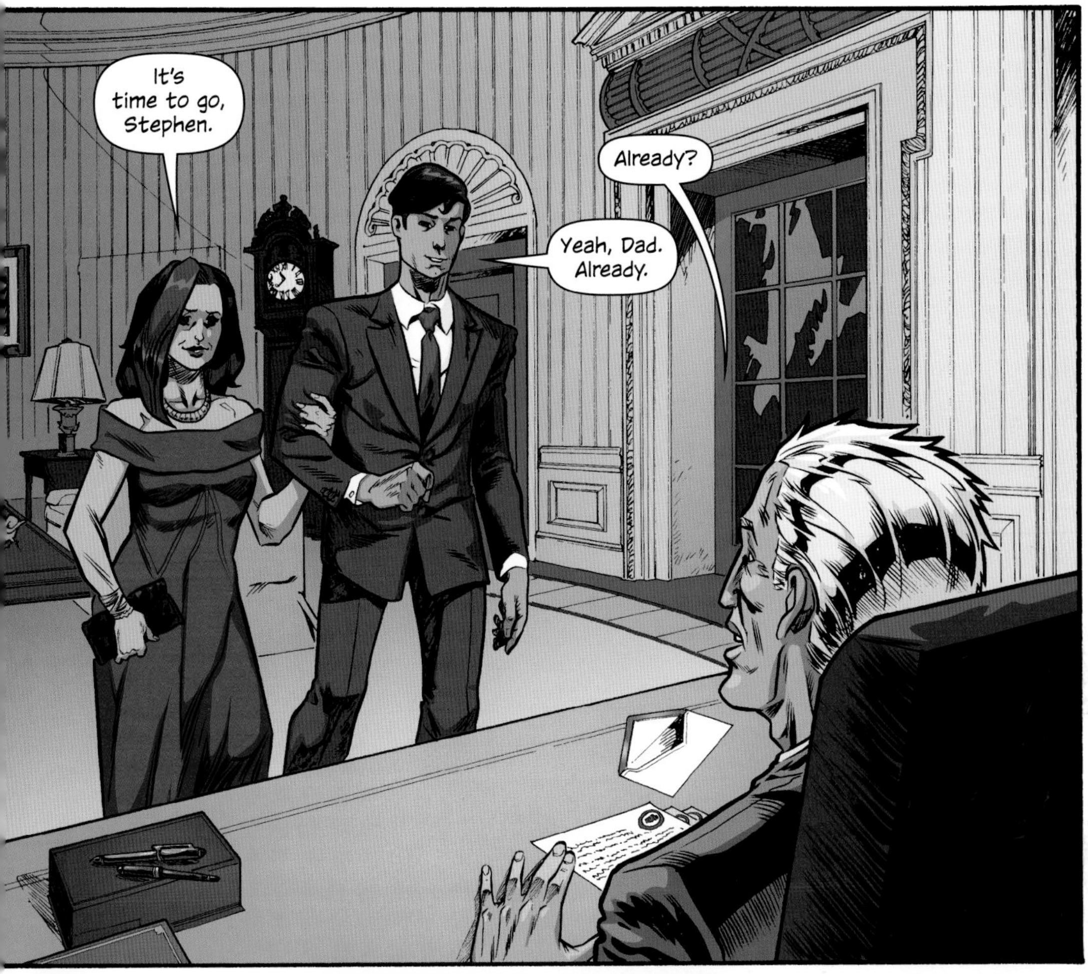
It's time to go, Stephen.
Already?
Yeah, Dad. Already.

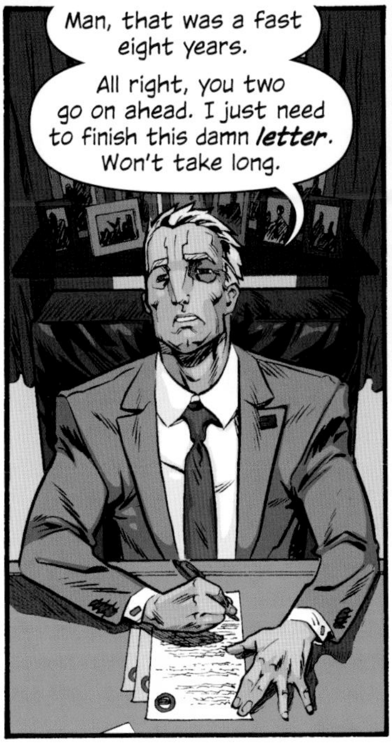
Man, that was a fast eight years.
All right, you two go on ahead. I just need to finish this damn *letter*. Won't take long.

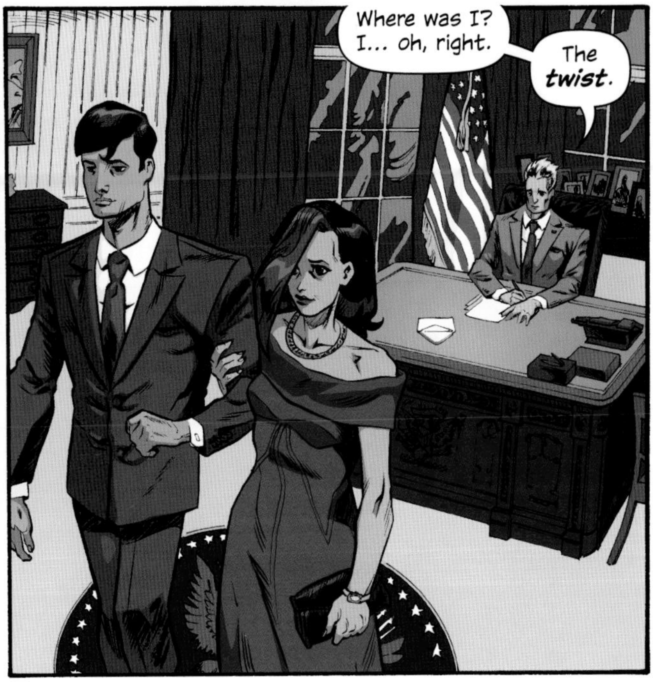
Where was I? I... oh, right.
The *twist*.

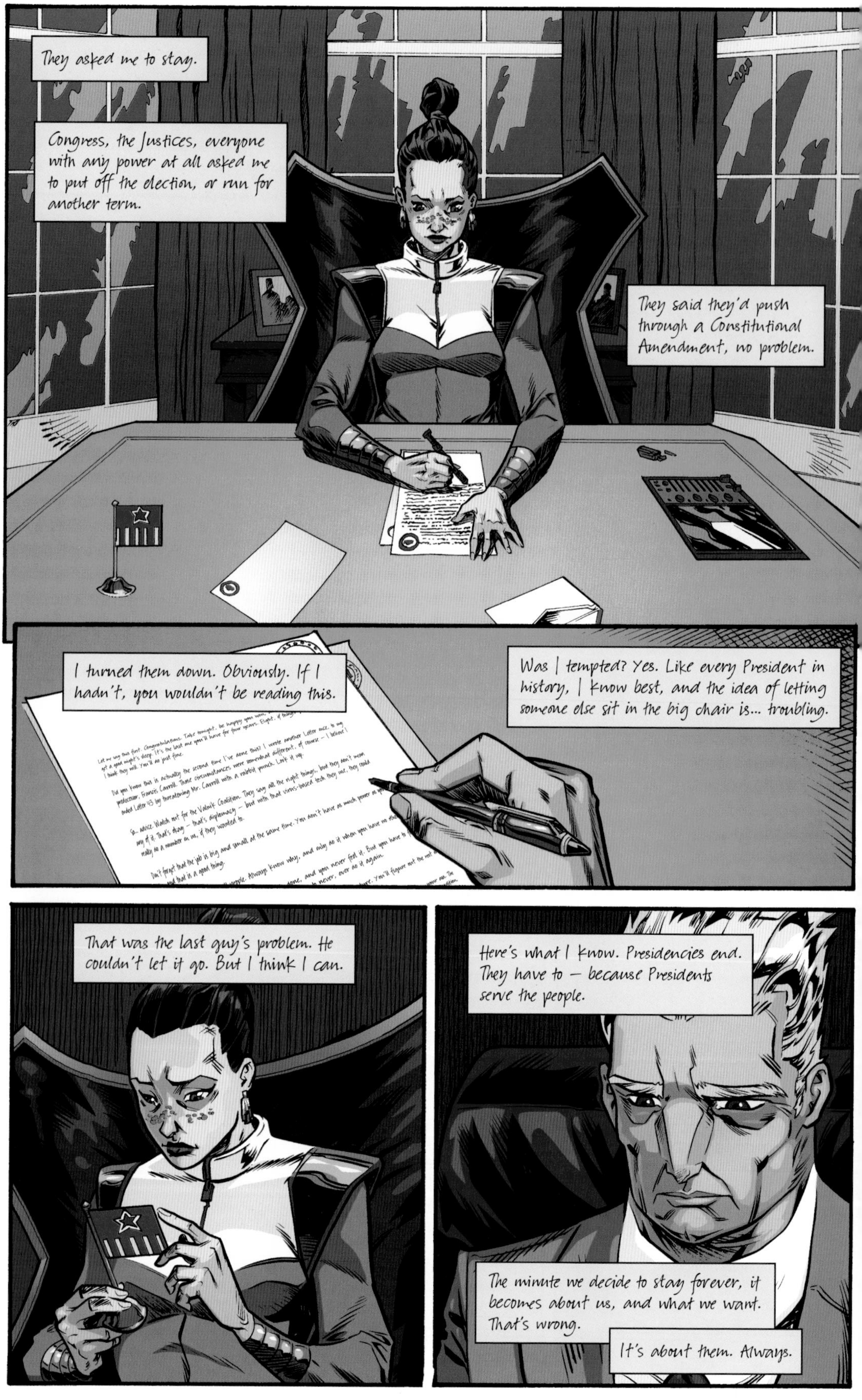
They asked me to stay.
Congress, the Justices, everyone with any power at all asked me to put off the election, or run for another term.
They said they'd push through a Constitutional Amendment, no problem.
I turned them down. Obviously. If I hadn't, you wouldn't be reading this.
Was I tempted? Yes. Like every President in history, I know best, and the idea of letting someone else sit in the big chair is... troubling.
That was the last guy's problem. He couldn't let it go. But I think I can.
Here's what I know. Presidencies end. They have to — because Presidents serve the people.
The minute we decide to stay forever, it becomes about us, and what we want. That's wrong.
It's about them. Always.

We find ourselves in a unique position out here — your Presidency won't be like any that came before it, just as mine wasn't.

But that's all right. The world changes, and so do we. You'll do fine. Just remember what I said.

...er at all asked me to...

...tional Amendment, no problem.

They have to — because Presidents serve the people.

...couldn't let it go. But I think I can.

...er, it becomes about us, and what we want. That's wrong.

...e position out here — your Presidency won't be like any that came ...'t.

...world changes, and so do we. You'll do fine. Just remember what I said.

It's always about them.

Stephen F. Blades

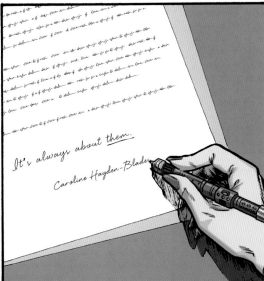

It's always about them.

Caroline Hayden-Blades

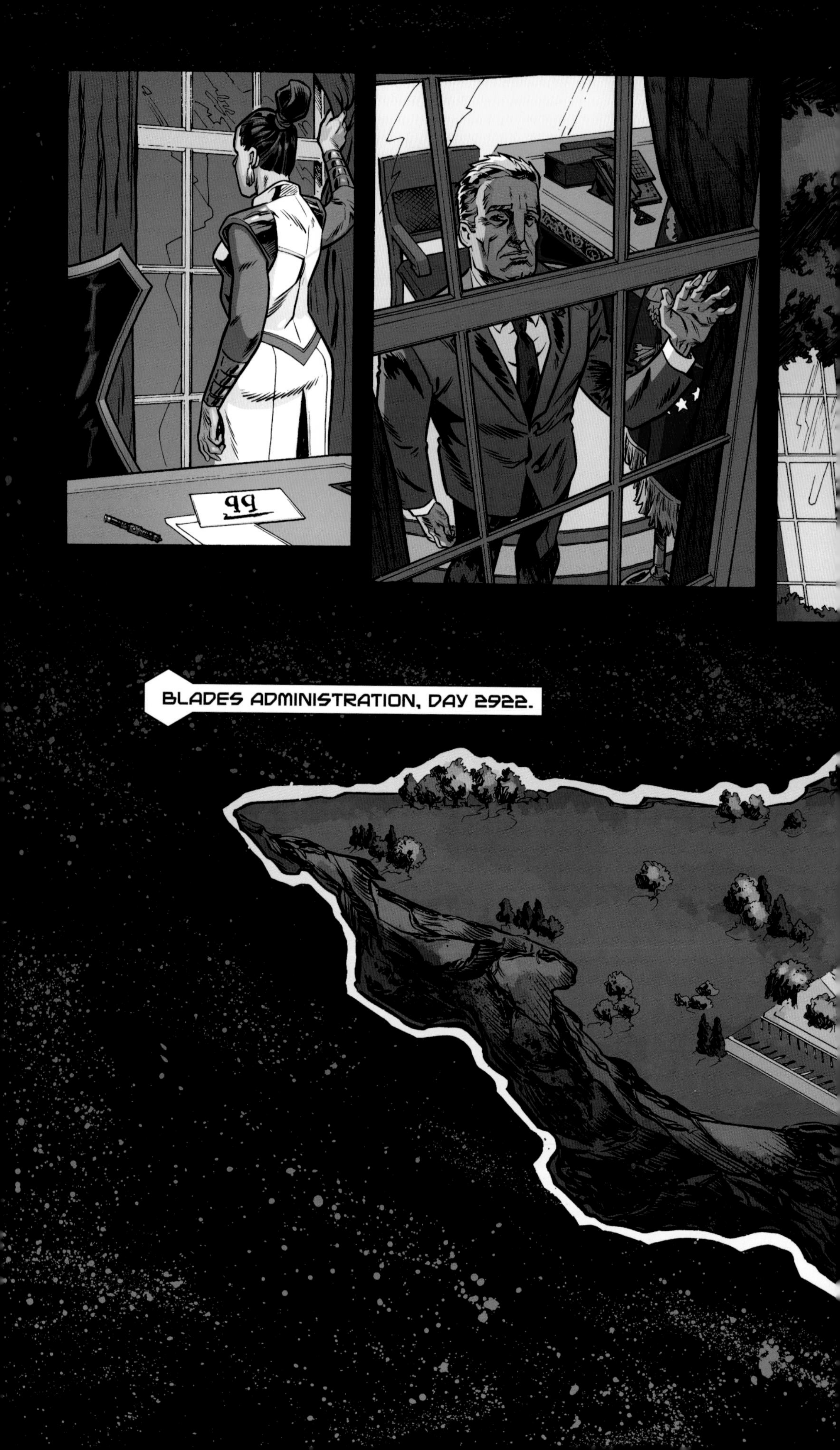
BLADES ADMINISTRATION, DAY 2922.

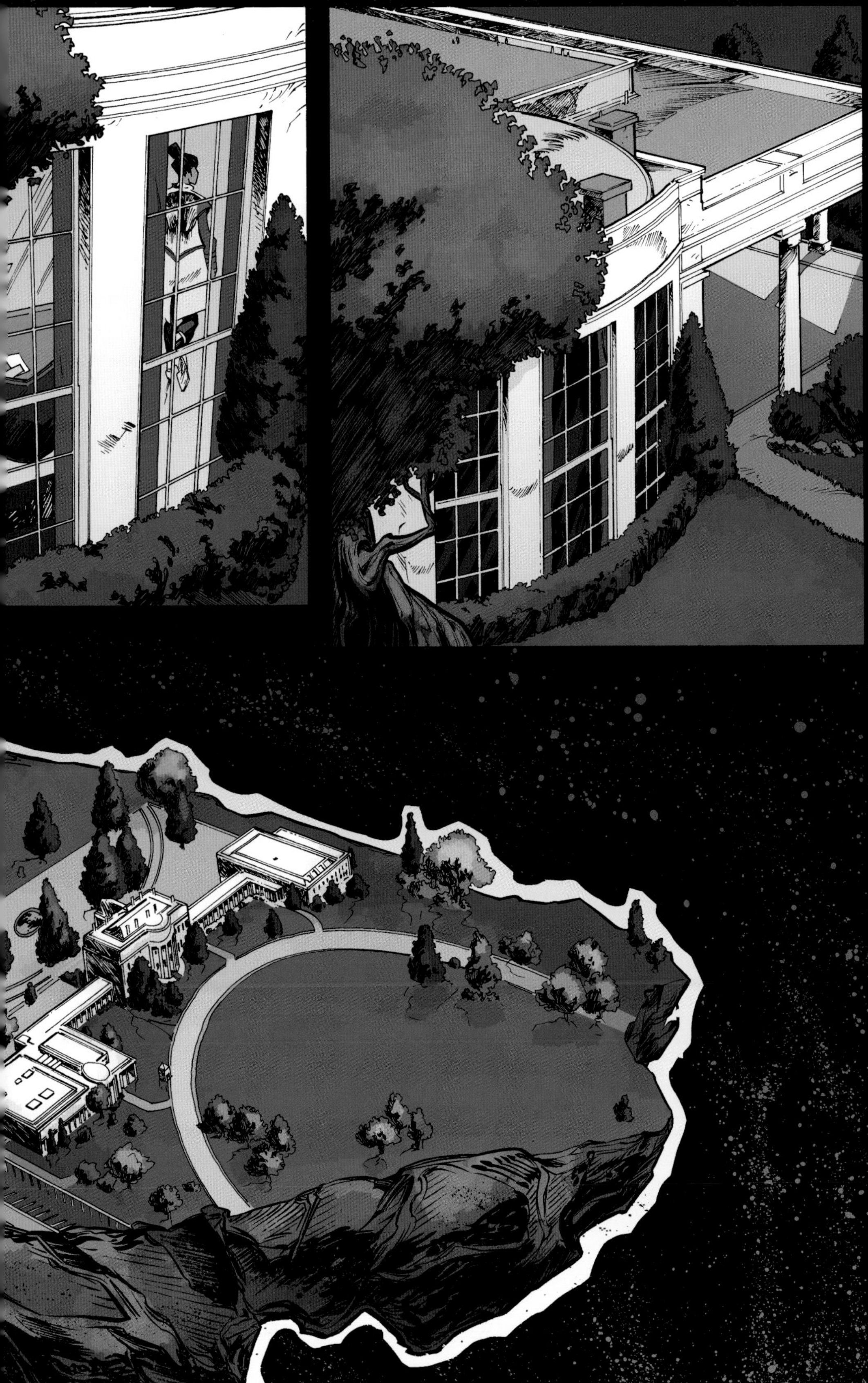

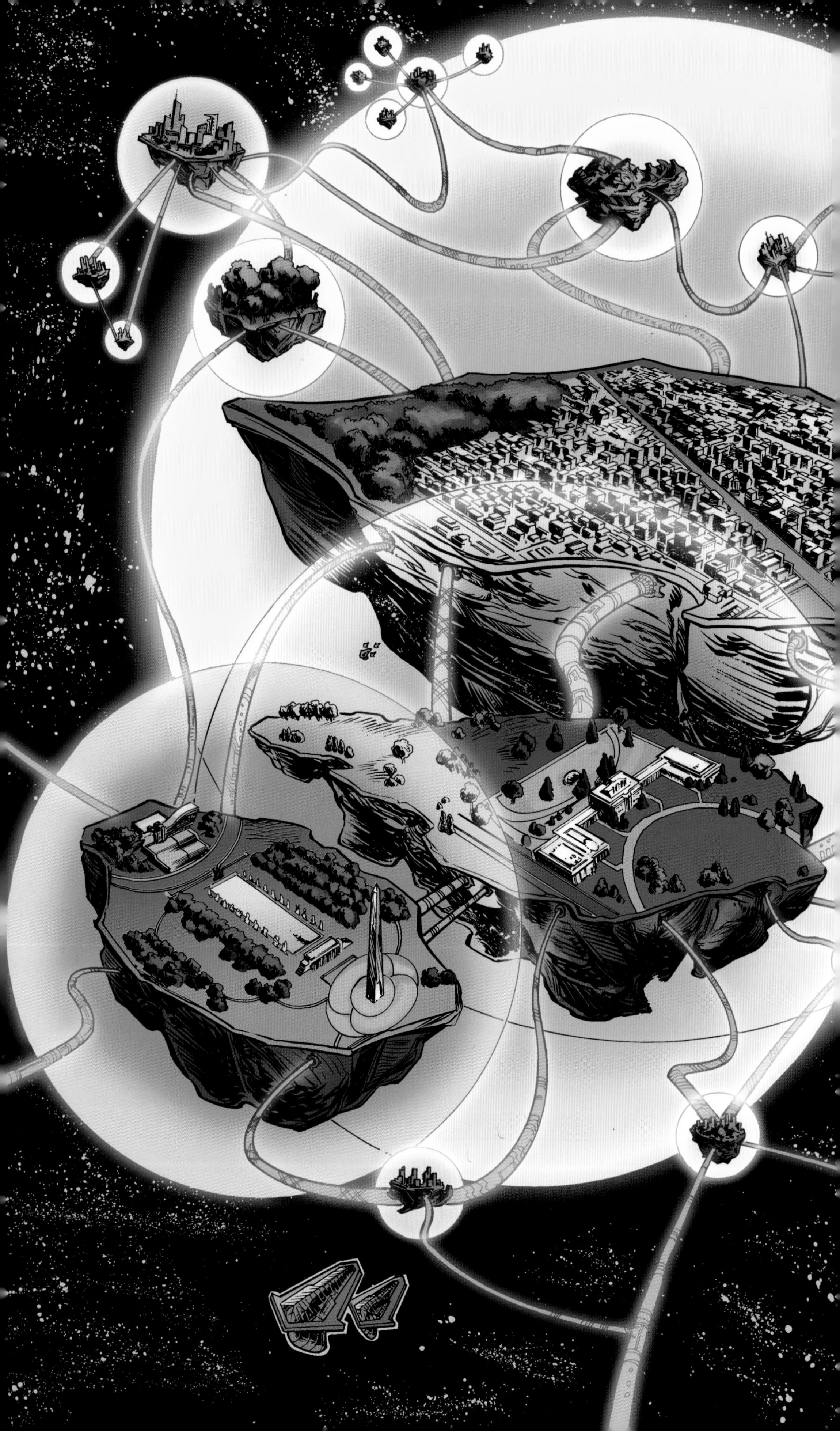

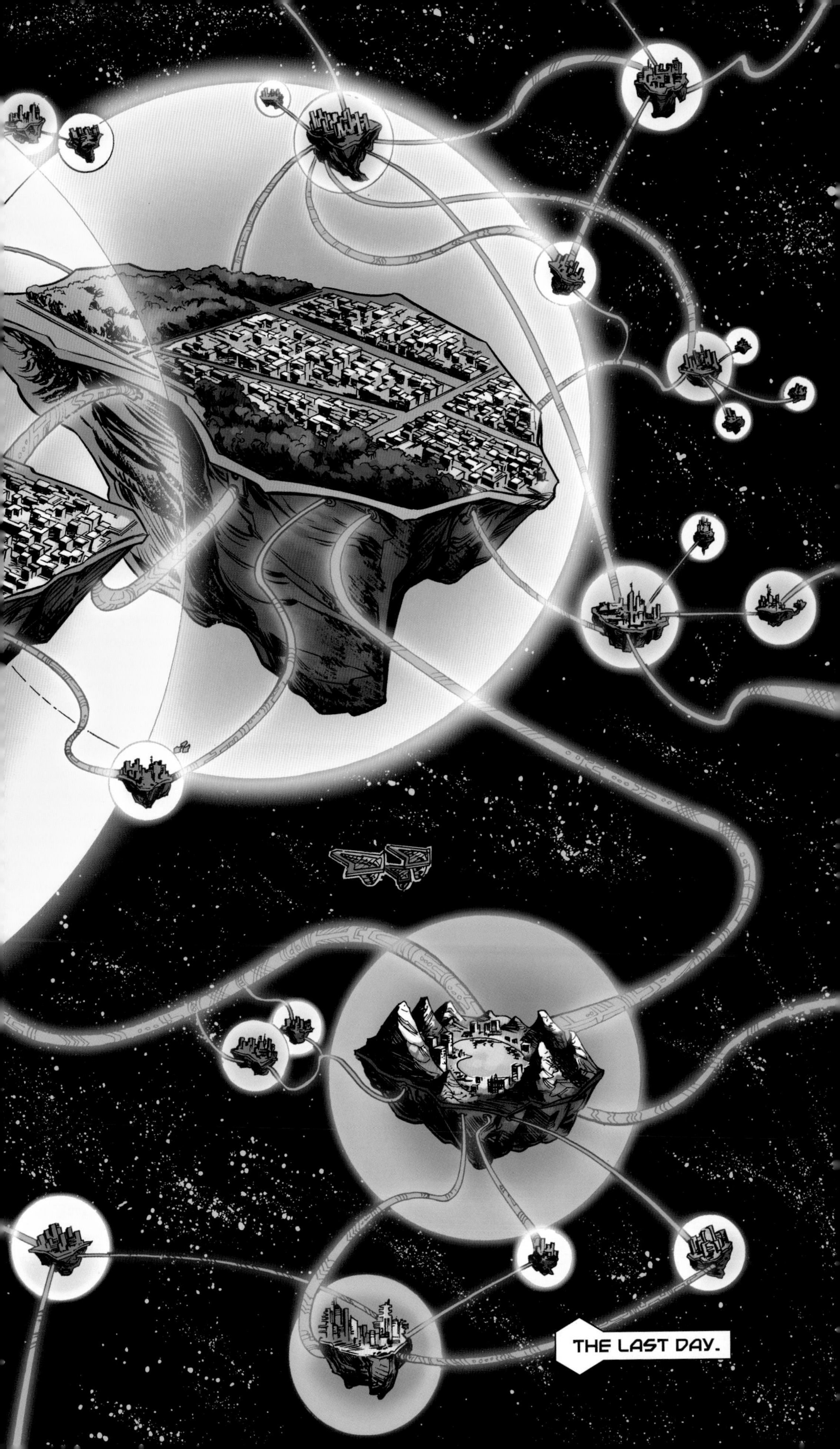
THE LAST DAY.

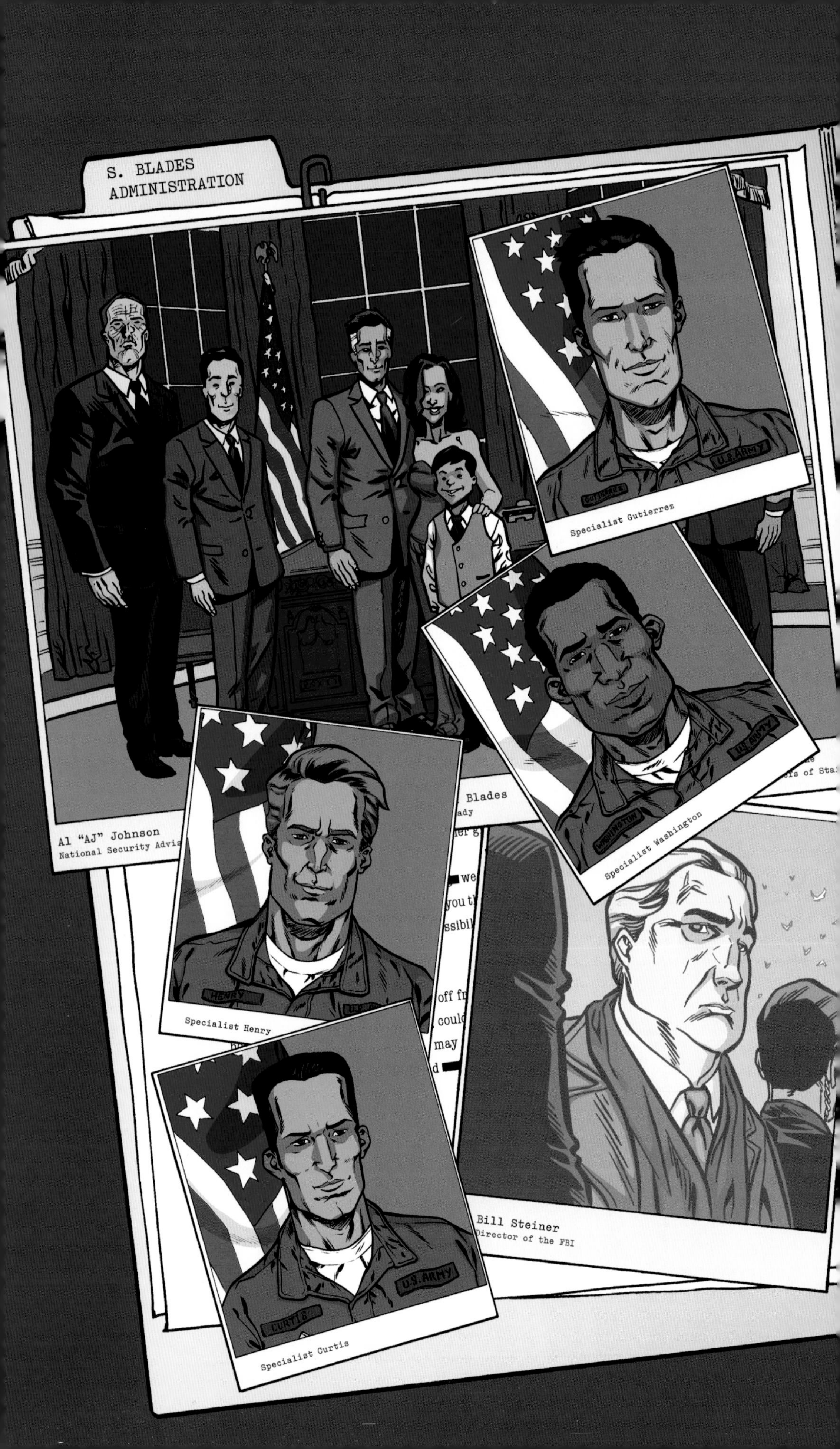
S. BLADES
ADMINISTRATION
Specialist Gutierrez
Blades
Specialist Washington
Al "AJ" Johnson
Specialist Henry
Bill Steiner
Director of the FBI
Specialist Curtis

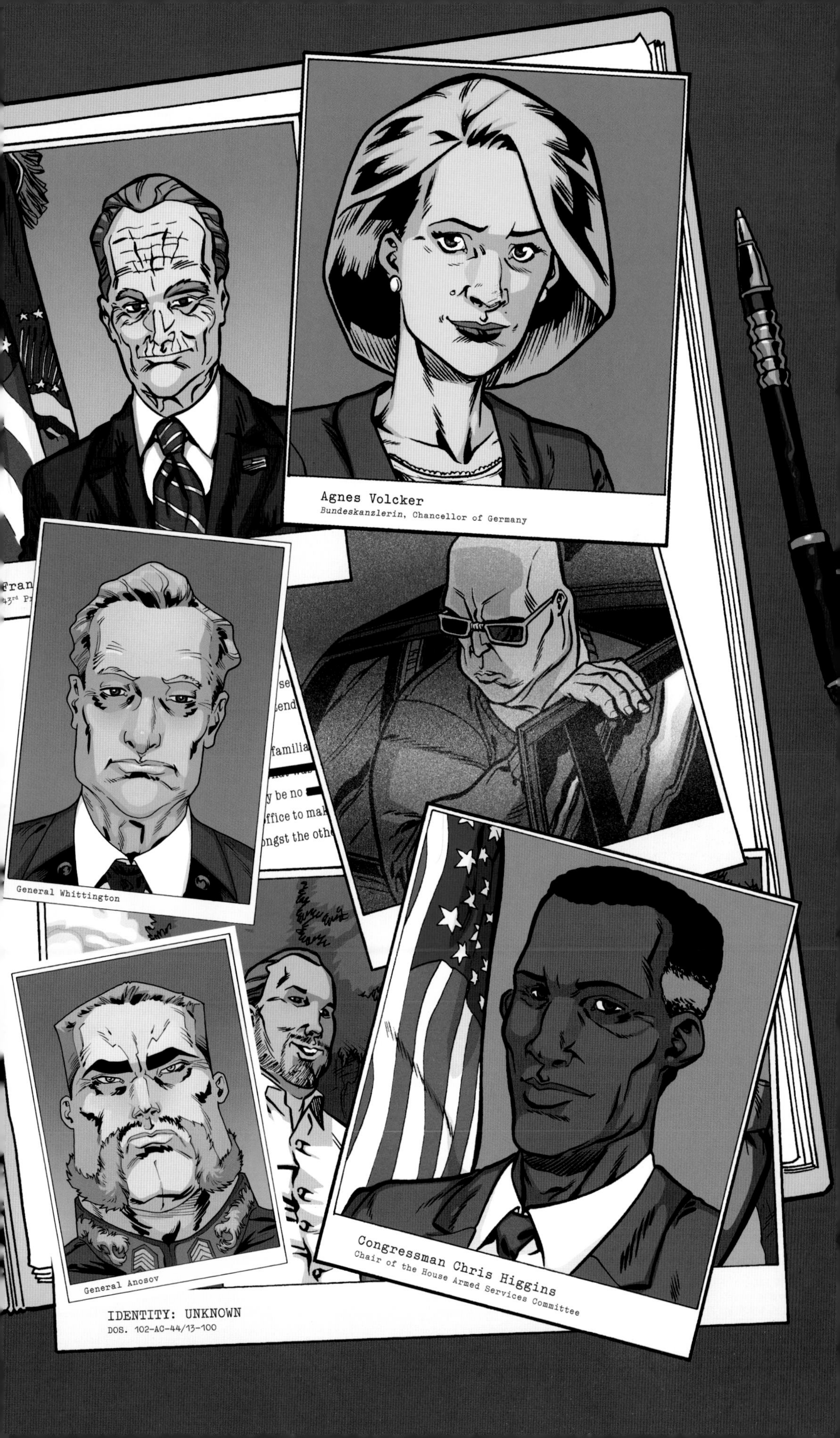
Agnes Volcker
Bundeskanzlerin, Chancellor of Germany
General Whittington
General Anosov
IDENTITY: UNKNOWN
DOS. 102-AC-44/13-100
Congressman Chris Higgins
Chair of the House Armed Services Committee

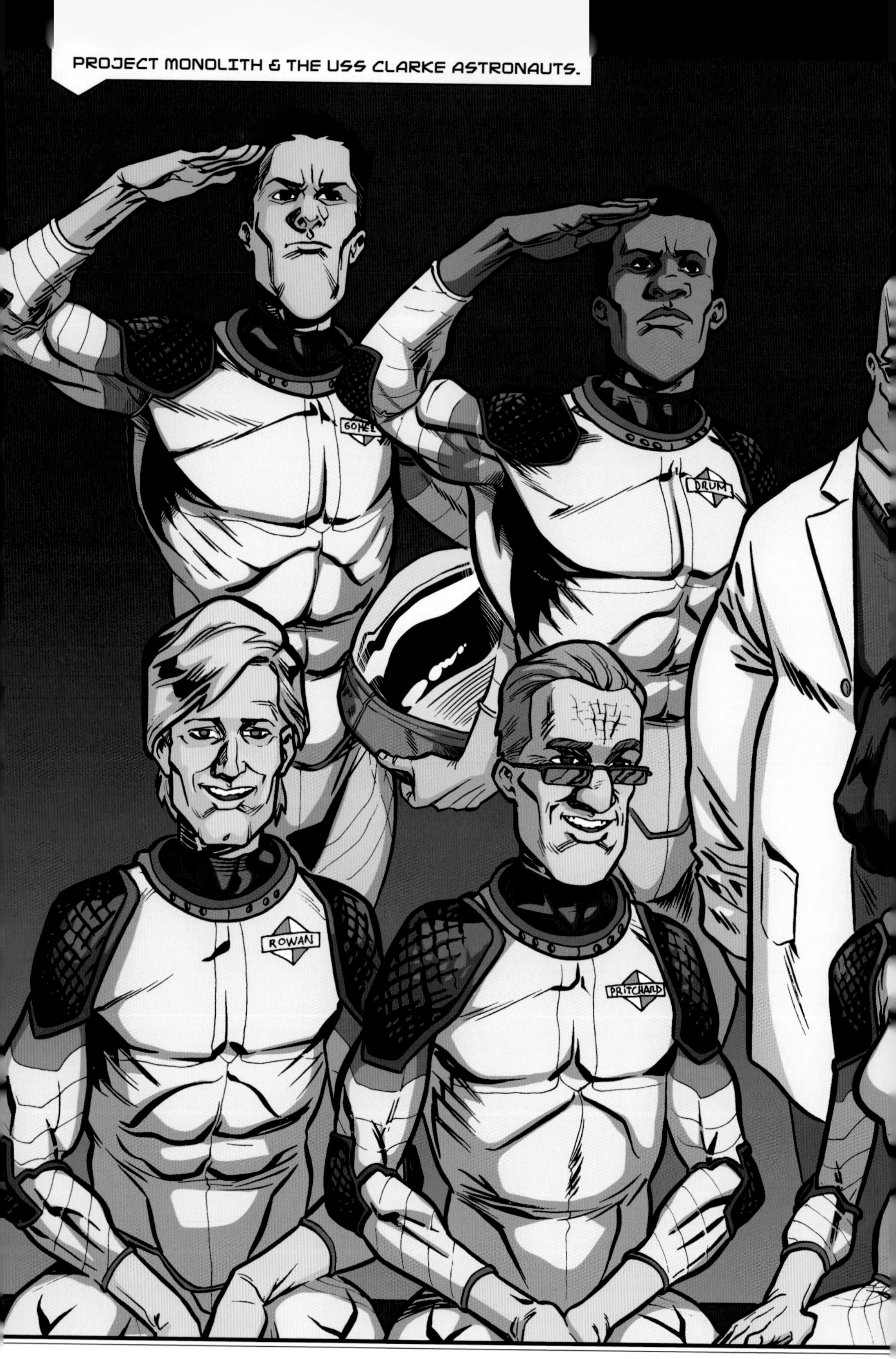
PROJECT MONOLITH & THE USS CLARKE ASTRONAUTS.
DRUM
ROWAN
PRITCHARD

TOP ROW [FROM LEFT TO RIGHT]:

LIEUTENANT ALBERTO GOMEZ, MAJOR GABRIEL DRUM, DR. PORTEK [HEAD OF PROJECT MONOLITH], **COLONEL JACK OVERHOLT, SERGEANT JOHN WILLET**

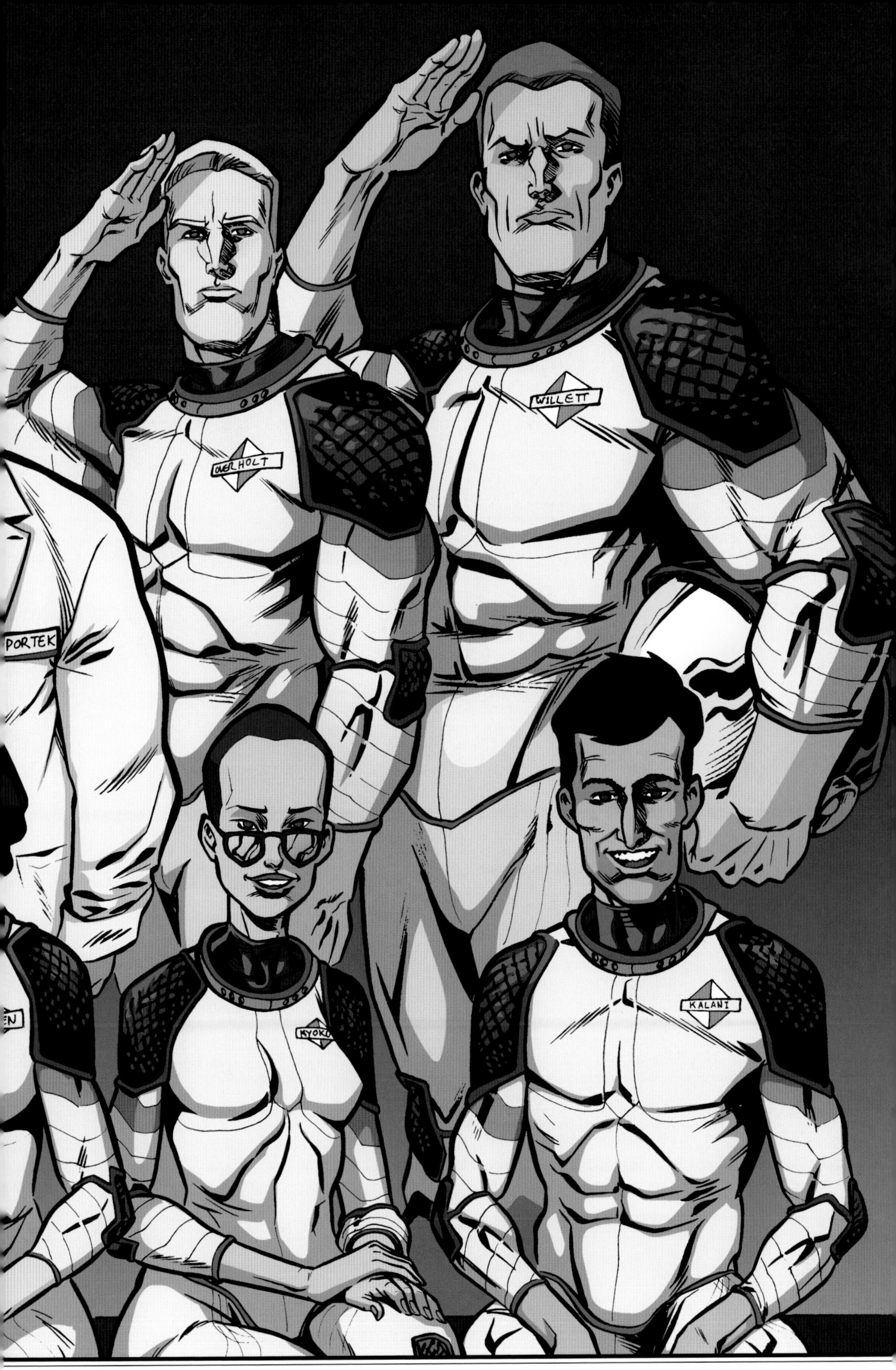

OVERHOLT
WILLETT
PORTEK
KYOKO
KALANI

OTTOM ROW [FROM LEFT TO RIGHT]:

ARY ROWAN [GEOLOGIST], **DONALD PRITCHARD** [CHIEF ASTRONOMER], **HARLOTTE HAYDEN** [SENIOR MISSION COMMANDER], **KYOKO TAKAHASHI** [DOCTOR], **ANESH KALANI** [LINGUIST AND COMPUTER SPECIALIST]

1999

Non-terrestrial construction project discovered in the asteroid belt by astronomer Andy Howlett.

2000

US President Francis T. Carroll authorizes Project Monolith, with stated mission goal to investigate alien anomaly, under Director Edward Stanton.

The United States invades Iraq.

The United States invades Afghanistan.

Edward Stanton

2001

The first members of the *Clarke* crew—Charlotte Hayden and Cary Rowan, both members of the vessel's scientific team —are recruited into Project Monolith.

Colonel Jack Overholt enters into discussions to lead the *Clarke*'s military team.

NOVEMBER— President Carroll wins re-election to a second term.

2002

Sergeant John Willett recruited to join *Clarke* crew, conditional on agreement of Overholt to lead military team.

Clarke orbital assembly launches commence.

CLASSIFIED.

2003

Edward Stanton replaced as head of Project Monolith by Dr. Radislav Portek. Portek urges Carroll to take a more militaristic approach to the alien anomaly.

DECEMBER 17— The *Clarke* departs Earth orbit.

2004

Senator Stephen H. Blades announces that he will attempt to secure the nomination as the Democratic candidate for President in the 2006 election.

Cindy Reed (NSA), Brian Michter (Secretary of Defense), Francis Carroll (P.O.T.U.S.), Brid
Carroll (First Lady), George Cohen (Chief of Staff), Chairman of the Joint Chiefs

2005

OCTOBER—
President Carroll recruits Elijah Green into Project Monolith.

NOVEMBER—
Stephen Blades is elected President with 54% of the popular vote.

2006

JANUARY 6—
Blades receives a letter from his predecessor informing him of the existence of an alien presence in our solar system and the measures that have been taken to deal with it: Project Monolith.

SUMMER—
Ex-President Carroll enters into a secret alliance with Germany, providing them with information about the alien presence in our solar system.

OCTOBER—
US Forward Operating Base Hurricane (Afghanistan) is destroyed in a nuclear attack perpetrated by German operative – the initial military action of World War Three.

2007

NOVEMBER—
In retaliation for the destruction of FOB Hurricane, President Blades uses orbital defense platform LEOPRD to destroy the headquarters of the First Panzer Division outside Hanover, Germany, while simultaneously revealing the existence of the aliens in the asteroid belt to the world.

NOVEMBER-DECEMBER—
World War III. US forces, along with primary allies France and the People's Republic of China, battle Die Allianz der Freien Erde (the Free Earth Alliance, which includes Germany, Russia and Great Britain, among other nations, and is secretly led by ex-President Carroll).

2008

JANUARY-MARCH—
War.

APRIL—
Manila destroyed.

MAY-SEPTEMBER—
War. Escalating losses on both sides.

OCTOBER—
President Blades authorizes Operation Endtime, a ground invasion of the North German coast using all remaining US military assets, intended to capture A.F.E. leadership and end the war.

NOVEMBER 28—
A deal is struck with Russian leadership to betray the A.F.E. and force them to accept the cease fire.

NOVEMBER 29—
★ Ex-President Carroll secretly takes control of the LEOPRD, cau sing it to fire on Moscow, erasing it from the map. The weapon subsequently explodes in orbit.

★ Hours later, the world-ending asteroid slows, changes direction and lands on the National Mall in Washington, D.C.

★ *Clarke* astronaut Gabriel Drum emerges and requests a meeting with President Blades.

NOVEMBER—
Operation Endtime fails. With no remaining options, President Blades prepares to surrender.

NOVEMBER 27—
Thanksgiving Day— Blades learns that a large asteroid will impact the planet within a matter of days, and forms a plan to use the LEOPRD to destroy it in exchange for a no-fault cease fire.

Charles Soule
Writer-In-Chief

Alberto J. Alburquerque
Executive Artist

Dan Jackson
Executive Colorist

Crank!
Chief of Letters

THE
WHITE HOUSE
1600 PENNSYLVANIA AVE NW, WASHINGTON, DC 20500

FROM THE DESK OF THE 44TH PRESIDENT, STEPHEN HENRY BLADES

NAME:

Charles Soule

LOCATION:

Brooklyn, NY, United States of America

BIO:

Charles Soule was born in the Midwest but often wishes he had been born in space. He lives in Brooklyn, and has written a wide variety of titles for a variety of publishers, including others' characters (*Swamp Thing, Superman/Wonder Woman, Red Lanterns* (DC); *Thunderbolts, She-Hulk, Inhuman* (Marvel); and his own: *27, Curse Words* (Image); *Strongman* (SLG) and *Strange Attractors* (Archaia). When not writing—which is rare—he runs a law practice and works, writes and performs as a musician.

One of his biggest regrets is never personally witnessing a Space Shuttle launch.

Charles Soule
Writer-In-Chief

Alberto J. Alburquerque
Executive Artist

Dan Jackson
Executive Colorist

Crank!
Chief of Letters

THE
WHITE HOUSE
1600 PENNSYLVANIA AVE NW, WASHINGTON, DC 20500

FROM THE DESK OF THE 44TH PRESIDENT, STEPHEN HENRY BLADES

NAME:

Alberto Jiménez Alburquerque

LOCATION:

Madrid, Spain

BIO:

Alberto Jiménez Alburquerque (AJA) is an artist born, raised and currently living in Madrid, Spain. He has put lines in French comic-books (BD's) for almost a decade now, working for Paquet Ed. and Soleil Ed. Some of his titles are: *Fugitifs de l'Ombre* (Paquet), *Le Dieu des Cendres* (Soleil), and *Elle* (Soleil). He has also drawn some short stories for the American comics *Skull Kickers* (Image) and *Pathfinder's Goblins* (Dynamite), and *Robert E. Howard's Savage Sword* (Dark Horse). He's currently the regular artist in the new series *Letter 44* (Oni Press) with writer Charles Soule and is starting a new project for the French market with Glénat Ed.

N. L-44Z-ØN1.1Ø.A

Charles Soule
Writer-In-Chief

Alberto J. Alburquerque
Executive Artist

Dan Jackson
Executive Colorist

Crank!
Chief of Letters

THE
WHITE HOUSE
1600 PENNSYLVANIA AVE NW, WASHINGTON, DC 20500

FROM THE DESK OF THE 44TH PRESIDENT, STEPHEN HENRY BLADES

NAME:

Dan Jackson

LOCATION:

Portland, Oregon, United States of America

BIO:

What is the most unfair thing you can think of? Got it in your head? Okay, forget that because there's a worse one: There's this guy who gets paid money for coloring comic books. Right. Dan Jackson has been gainfully employed to one degree or another with the coloring of comic books for the better part of 17 years. He's done other Great Big Projects with the fine folks at Oni Press, and he's done a bunch of covers and short projects with them as well. He's a pretty versatile guy. Even writes his own bios.

Mr. Jackson lives in the beautiful Pacific Northwest with his scorching hot wife (see? UN-FAIR!), and two hilarious kids.

Charles Soule
Writer-In-Chief

lberto J. Alburquerque
Executive Artist

Dan Jackson
Executive Colorist

Crank!
Chief of Letters

THE WHITE HOUSE

1600 PENNSYLVANIA AVE NW, WASHINGTON, DC 20500

FROM THE DESK OF THE 44TH PRESIDENT, STEPHEN HENRY BLADES

NAME:

Sarah Stern

LOCATION:

Mt. Vernon, NY, United States of America

BIO:

Sarah Stern is a normal regular human from planet Earth and nowhere else. An artist and colorist from New York, she does Earth activities like riding bicycles and breathing nitrogen-rich air. She uses her normal amount of arms to be the artist of *Cindersong* (Hiveworks), and the colorist for *Goldie Vance* (Boom!) and *Mighty Morphin' Power Rangers: Pink* (Boom!).

SER-471337.C /// DOS. 102-AC-44/13-100 /// AUTH. JMB*JS

CLASSIFIED

N. L-442-0N1.10.A

MORE BOOKS FROM ONI PRESS

LETTER 44: VOLUME 1
ESCAPE VELOCITY

CHARLES SOULE, ALBERTO JIMÉNEZ ALBURQUERQUE, GUY MAJOR, AND DAN JACKSON

160 PAGES /// SOFTCOVER /// COLOR INTERIORS

ISBN 978-1-62010-388-3

LETTER 44: VOLUME 2
REDSHIFT

CHARLES SOULE, ALBERTO JIMÉNEZ ALBURQUERQUE, AND DAN JACKSON

160 PAGES /// SOFTCOVER /// COLOR INTERIORS

ISBN 978-1-62010-206-0

LETTER 44: VOLUME 3
DARK MATTER

CHARLES SOULE, ALBERTO JIMÉNEZ ALBURQUERQUE, AND DAN JACKSON

160 PAGES /// SOFTCOVER /// COLOR INTERIORS

ISBN 978-1-62010-272-5

LETTER 44: VOLUME 4
SAVIORS

CHARLES SOULE, ALBERTO JIMÉNEZ ALBURQUERQUE, DAN JACKSON, AND SARAH STERN

160 PAGES /// SOFTCOVER /// COLOR INTERIORS

ISBN 978-1-62010-355-5

LETTER 44: VOLUME 5
BLUESHIFT

CHARLES SOULE, JOËLLE JONES, DAN JACKSON, AND MORE

136 PAGES /// SOFTCOVER /// COLOR INTERIORS

ISBN 978-1-62010-446-0

www.onipress.com

FOR MORE INFORMATION ON THESE AND OTHER FINE ONI PRESS COMIC BOOKS AND GRAPHIC NOVELS, VISIT WWW.ONIPRESS. COM. TO FIND A COMIC SPECIALTY STORE IN YOUR AREA, CALL 1-888-COMICBOOK OR VISIT WWW.COMICSHOPS.US.